# NEUTRALIZING MEMORY

# NEUTRALIZING MEMORY

## The Jew in Contemporary Poland

**Iwona Irwin-Zarecka**

Transaction Publishers

New Brunswick (U.S.A.) and London (U.K.)

First paperback reprint 1990
Copyright © 1989 by Transaction Publishers, New Brunswick, New Jersey
08903.

Library of Congress Catalog Number: 88-12234
ISBN: 0-88738-227-4 (cloth); 0-88738-840-X (paper)
Printed in the United States of America

Irwin-Zarecka, Iwona.
    Neutralizing memory: the Jew in contemporary Poland/Iwona Irwin-
Zarecka.
    p.  cm.
    Bibliography: p.
    Includes index.
    ISBN 0-88738-227-4
    1. Jews—Poland—History—20th century.  2. Holocaust survi-
vors—Poland. 3. Children  of  Holocaust  survivors—Poland.  4. Poland—
Ethnic relations.  I. Title.
DS135.P6178   1988                                   88-12234
943.8'004924-dc19                                    CIP

FOR JOSHI

# Contents

# Acknowledgments

The work on this book spans nearly six years and four countries: Canada, the United States, France and Poland. Throughout, I have been very fortunate to receive assistance from a great many people who were willing to share with me their experiences, their insights and their time. I warmly thank all of them. I can only mention some; I know the others would concede it is better that way.

For most of the time, I was a doctoral student at the University of California in San Diego, with the earlier report on my research becoming my dissertation. It was thanks to Bennett M. Berger, my thesis supervisor, that my study left the drawing board. I greatly appreciate his trust, patience and critical probing. H. Stuart Hughes, through his encouragement and suggestions, made my venture into the historians' territory both possible and rewarding. I am grateful to Michael S. Schudson for introducing me to new ways of thinking about culture, ideology and memory, and to Bennetta Jules-Rosette for her continuous support. It was Richard D. Madsen who finally convinced me this study could be done. Alain Cohen helped me to find the ways to do it.

At the early stages of my research, I profited a great deal from discussions with the other faculty members as well: Timothy McDaniel, Joseph Gusfield, Chuck Nathanson in Sociology, and Robert Edelman in History. Being able to participate in some of the seminars of the "Laboratory of Human Cognition" group, with Aaron Cicourel, Hugh Mehan and Michael Cole in particular, has added a lot to my understanding of understanding. For my exposure to so much intellectual excellence, I am very grateful to the late César Graña, who had, in effect, made me decide to come to UCSD. His contribution to this work was substantial in analytical terms as well; I deeply regret he cannot offer me his critique.

Working on a dissertation while a few thousand miles from one's

ix

university is not without problems. Thanks to Wendy Tenuta, these problems did not include the stresses of dealing with innumerable rules and regulations. I thank the University of California, San Diego itself, and especially the Department of Sociology for their financial assistance which lessened my monetary concerns.

The research was assisted by a grant from the Joint Committee on Western Europe of the Social Science Research Council and the American Council of Learned Societies with funds provided by the Ford Foundation and the National Endowment for the Humanities, together with Doctoral Fellowships from the Social Sciences and Humanities Research Council of Canada and the Memorial Foundation for Jewish Culture. I greatly appreciate the support of all these organizations.

Kurt Jonassohn, at Concordia University in Montreal, has been looking out for me for a long time now; his extensive help on this project is very much appreciated.

H. David Kirk, who was my teacher at the University of Waterloo back in 1975, reminded me of the continuity in my concerns. His critical comments on the first draft of this manuscript and his aid in connecting me with some of the people who share these concerns have been most valuable.

I received equally valued support from other people who made comments and suggestions regarding the work in progress: Phyllis Albert Cohen, Leo Chall, Frank Chalk, Tadeusz Szafar and Gabrielle Tyrnauer. During the writing up of this study, I was assisted by the different readings of its first draft offered by Michael Marrus, Zofia Oryńska-Bakuniak, Robin Ostow, Arnold Rockman, Harold Troper, and Lawrence Weschler. I drew special encouragement from the expert opinion of Jan Tomasz Gross. All of the critical voices made this study a better one; responsibility for its shortcomings is entirely mine.

Many of my ideas were first formed and formulated while in Europe in 1983/1984.

First, in Paris: my understanding of both Polish- and French-Jewish relations are greatly enhanced by many a discussion with Alain Finkielkraut and Michel Wieviorka. Thanks to the expert advice of Sarah Halperin at the *Centre de documentation juive contemporaine*, I could learn much faster and much more. Thanks to the advice by experts—the late Michał Borwicz, Paweł Korzec, Robert Paxton, Léon Poliakov—I could be a much better reader of the historians' work. But it is thanks to Maria Elster, a historian and a Warsaw Ghetto survivor, that I could begin to understand history. Her continuous encouragement, her reflections and her very practical help in obtaining much of the material I needed, made the difference.

Then, in Warsaw: this study would have lost half of its texture without the welcome from Monika and Stanisław Krajewski. Making sense of what I could observe became a great deal easier with the guidance of Paweł Śpiewak and Alina Cała.

The final formulation of my ideas has been greatly enhanced by the critical guidance of a writer, Judi Jewinski. Nancy Stade, in addition to her expert typing skills, offered a much appreciated layman's reading of the text. The practical help and editorial suggestions from Ethel Fahidy were most valuable as well.

My colleagues at Wilfrid Laurier University, especially Harriet and Andrew Lyons, made the transition from dissertation to book a great deal easier. That transition would have been impossible, of course, without the caring response from Irving Louis Horowitz and the people at Transaction.

The person whose contribution is hardest to put into words is my husband, Hugh Smyth. He has given much more than support to this project. He has made me understand that I have a home, and that my own past is a part of it. Our son Joshua, I trust, will one day pick up on this memory note; he has already made all my efforts worthwhile.

# Note on Polish Names

As a general rule, Polish names appear in this presentation in their original spelling. Original, though, when applied to names of authors whose works were published in English or French, refers to the way their names appeared in those publications. (In a few cases, this does result in using both the Polish and the English version of a name, depending on the materials cited.)

The Polish alphabet does not depart very far from the English one, except for letters which are in effect created by the addition of small signs such as a dot, a slash or a comma. In the text itself, these are of no great consequence for the reader unfamiliar with Polish. However, they do affect the order of the list of references. The sequences with which we are concerned are: ą follows a, ć follows c, ę follows e, ł follows l, ń follows n, ó follows o, ś follows s, and ż follows ź which follows z.

In the text itself, I used "Warsaw," "Cracow," "Solidarity" rather than their Polish equivalents. However, when citing publications which appeared in Poland, I retained their original spelling in full ("Warsaw" becomes "Warszawa," etc.). In the case of Polish sources published in the West, there were some inconsistencies in references to the place of publication; I opted for standard English usage of London, Paris or Berlin.

# Introduction

It is the day of Simhat Torah, the celebration of the Torah, closing the fall season of Jewish holidays. September 29, 1983. Warsaw, Poland. The service has already begun in a small, newly restored synagogue situated on the grounds of what once was the Warsaw Ghetto. Conducted by a cantor rather than a rabbi, it is attended by some one hundred and fifty men and a few women, most in their sixties and seventies, with the exception of one much younger man, sitting to the side. There are no special places designated for women here, yet all of them stay on the outermost seats. During the reading of the Torah, many of the men circulate and chat, some in Yiddish, others in Polish.

The doors open and a blonde, modestly-dressed woman, probably in her forties, comes in, takes a few steps and kneels down, crossing herself. By the time she sits down in the back, an old Jewish woman, sitting close to her, turns and starts making rather angry remarks about the inappropriateness of such Catholic gestures in a synagogue. I, too, am sitting quite close, and though I cannot hear the details of the exchange, I am able to pick up the gist of it. The two women talk for nearly half an hour; it seems that the Catholic lady has managed to explain her actions by pleading ignorance and interest and has been "granted pardon." Towards the end, the two women appear to be making arrangements to meet here again, now at a regular Saturday service, so that they can continue this impromptu class on Judaism; the Catholic woman quietly leaves.

More people begin arriving. It is now a few minutes before the Yizkor (special memorial) service is to commence; again, there are mainly older men, but also a few women and another younger man. The atmosphere suddenly changes: there is no more chatting, only silence. During the Yizkor prayers, many participants weep openly. Just as the prayers are coming to a close, the doors open and in come two teachers leading about

1

forty schoolchildren, between ten and twelve years old.[1] All of the boys have their heads covered with handkerchiefs. The attention of everyone is drawn to this small crowd gathering at the back. Teachers begin the tour by pointing to a mounted plaque which expresses gratitude to the Polish state for the restoration of the synagogue and commemorates its official opening in April 1983. With the Yizkor service now over, a number of participants leave, allowing the visitors to move closer to the center, the quiet lecture continuing. I leave too and find myself on a busy Warsaw street. Most of the buildings around me are about thirty years old. . . .

Just as the opening few notes in a piece of music often set the tone and the mood for the whole composition, this little scene in Warsaw's only synagogue is more than a vignette. It is important for two reasons. First, because I happened to observe it on my first day back in Warsaw after a ten-year absence—it was my very first live encounter with my subject matter, so to speak, and as such it has become imprinted in my memory perhaps more than any other piece of "Warsaw data." Secondly, because this scene happens to bring together and bring forth most of the major themes of the present study, while calling for a layer-by-layer interpretive approach—an approach which was to become my main method of dealing with the material.

What we see here is a celebration of the Torah, this core of the Jewish heritage, by the remnants of the Jewish community in Poland, witnessed with a good deal of curiosity by a middle-aged Catholic woman and a group of Polish schoolchildren. This human encounter takes place in a building only very recently restored with the help of the Polish government, as the large plaque at the entrance attests, a plaque which, interestingly enough, makes no mention of assistance from Jewish organizations abroad. Finally, we can readily observe the utter ignorance of Jewish ritual on the part of Catholic visitors, an ignorance colored by both respect and interest.

What one does not see, but can easily find out by asking a few questions and by reading a few press articles, is the background of both the participants and the setting. There are here a few Orthodox Jews. But, for the most part, people here belong to a sizeable group of old-Communists-now-disillusioned-returnees-to-Judaism; two of the young people, on the other hand, represent the religious core of a small group of their children, in generational if not real terms, who have been re-discovering their Jewish roots. The official opening of this synagogue took place as a part of the ceremonies commemorating the 40th anniversary of the Warsaw Ghetto Uprising only a few months earlier, ceremonies organized on a grand scale and bringing to Warsaw over a thousand Jewish visitors from abroad, including many from Israel, invited despite the still broken diplomatic relations between Poland and that country.

To appreciate more fully the meaning of this 1983 scene, one has to move back in time. Not so long ago, the whole situation would have been impossible. There was no synagogue in Warsaw, and the few meeting halls where Jews would pray remained rather empty for many, many years. Some Jews were not interested; others were afraid. These were not good times for celebrating one's Judaism. The silence of the older generation meant that many young Jews were growing up with very little knowledge of their heritage, and in extreme (yet not so rare) cases they would not even know that one or both of their parents had been Jewish. That a Catholic woman who was probably born just before or during World War II crossed herself upon entering a synagogue may seem peculiar; it is not, not when we consider the other kind of silence, the silence about the Jews which had prevailed in post-war Poland. For a group of Polish schoolchildren to tour a synagogue might have been disruptive to the participants in the service, but it is also indicative of a gradual change taking place in Poland, of the efforts to retrieve the lost traces of Jewish presence and to make them into permanent elements of Polish collective memory.[2]

Just what, exactly, these children are likely to learn from their teachers, their parents and the media is another question; in fact, it is *the* question as far as this study is concerned. Putting aside, for the moment, the ambivalence that many Jews might feel upon hearing about efforts ultimately to incorporate the experience of Polish Jews into the memory of Poles, the key issue is not whether it should be done, but rather what happens when it *is* being done. What happens when the previously prevailing silence is gradually broken? What is likely to replace ignorance? What fills in the blanks suddenly perceived to be there? What is the role assigned to the Jew, now that he has been invited into Poland's "memory household"? Is the effort to retrieve Poland's Jewish heritage also a beginning of a full confrontation with the moral challenges of the past? In short, what does it *mean* to remember the Jews, in Poland, today?

To answer these questions was to inquire into both the past and the present of Polish Jewish experience. Ideally, such an inquiry should have meant drawing together several researchers—historians, economists, political scientists, literary critics, anthropologists, psychologists and sociologists—each offering a different perspective. In practice, I could only approximate such a multidisciplinary "forum" with sources from a variety of fields, questions from a variety of angles and interpretive tools from a host of disciplines.

The belief that the best research results come from a broad, open exchange of ideas on a given *problem* is one I share with an increasing

number of cultural analysts. Where my study may depart from the preferred intellectual paths is in its insistence that my own experience *not* be
screened out of the analytical process. I am, after all, no outsider to
questions about Polish-Jewish relations. Having grown up in Warsaw, in a
family where the Polish Catholic traditions of my mother blended with the
secular Jewishness and the Leftist outlook of my father, I would draw
from my memories many of the questions which informed this inquiry.
(For a number of Polish Jews of my generation, questioning the past
involves a difficult confrontation with their parents' ominous role in the
Stalinist oppression. My case is different, in that my father had never
aspired to a position of power within the Party, and, during the Stalinist
period, acted as a defense attorney.) Indeed, at one point, I looked at my
own "story" as if it were just another piece of data on the texture of
Polish-Jewish experience. At another point, while bringing to the fore
certain key assumptions guiding the contemporary discussions of the
"Jewish question," I again turned to my own past for some help; because
I had shared these assumptions, I could better interpret them.

Overall, I decided to use my knowledge of an insider as a valuable
heuristic aid, well beyond the obvious advantages of familiarity with the
language. Yet precisely because I was an insider, I also needed to work
with the larger-than-usual awareness of my own commitments. I dare not
pretend neutrality on the subject. Polish-Jewish history is not a subject
one can be morally neutral about. What I can promise is that I have
maintained a critical stance towards *all* the available sources, exactly
because I tend to view that past from a Jewish perspective.

Translated into analytical practice, the increased caution about possible
biases resulted in my repeatedly searching and re-searching for material
which could contradict my hunches. It also meant a continuous effort to
broaden the analytical field itself to avoid interpreting Polish-Jewish history solely from within. In particular, my search led to the recent literature
re-assessing the French-Jewish experience, literature which together with
my own research on the Jewish experience in contemporary France
provided the much needed comparative background to my interpretations
of the developments in Poland.[3]

Realizing that the current memory disputes, both in Poland and abroad,
center on Polish-Jewish relations during the Holocaust confirmed the need
for a more comparative approach. In turn, this meant drawing on the by-
now rather extensive literature on the position of different countries and
different people towards the "Final Solution."

More generally, my concern with not derailing the inquiry with a set of
ready answers determined the framework of this study. To make sense of
the quite sudden upsurge of interest in things Jewish required first that this

phenomenon be given a name. Making sense, I believe, was best served by avoiding categories and terms which have come to mean too much and too little. For this reason, the word "anti-Semitism" appears rather sparingly on the following pages; the focus is on describing ideas, attitudes and actions instead.

Following considerable research, research which revealed the complex motivations behind the individual and social actors' involvement in bringing the Jew into the public arena, I decided to focus on the *results* of their efforts. Calling these various efforts a "Jewish memory project" was to draw attention to the fact that whatever reasons Poles might have for inviting the Jew, the ultimate effect of granting him so much public visibility is one of *constructing* memory. If we think of collective memory as a "storehouse" of symbolic resources for thinking about the past, then all the books, articles, exhibitions, films, seminars and public discussions devoted to Jewish themes, together with the physical restoration of cemeteries or places of worship, all become new additions to be stored. How are these memory pieces constructed, what kind of memory work is being done, who are the memory workers, what are the institutional supports available to them and what are the obstacles they face—these were my questions of the "Jewish memory project."

The present manuscript is a result of well over five years of intensive research. Not meaning to discourage the future student in this area, I must emphasize that a project of this kind takes time—time to read, time to listen, time to reflect. There are no short-cuts. In that sense, there is no method, no way to narrow one's questions and still come up with reasonable answers.

One example will illustrate the difficulty. Drawing on the *published* discourse on Jewish themes in Poland between 1983 and 1987 should be a straight-forward proposition. It is not. Polish culture is not confined within Polish borders. There are Polish writers publishing abroad while living in Poland; there are Polish writers publishing in Poland while living abroad. On what basis can one exclude some voices and include others? Clearly, if the focus were to be on the Poles' relations with the Russians, émigré publications could not be ignored. But what about the Jews? This question cannot be answered without at least some analysis of the way in which Polish émigrés have talked—and not talked—about things Jewish. In other words, it is only *after* an extensive reading of émigré sources that one may decide, as I did, to use them mainly as interpretive aids rather than as primary data. And then again, the question is only partly resolved. When the émigré journal *Aneks,* appearing in London, published a series of articles under the heading "Jews as a Polish Problem" in 1986, articles which were a major contribution to the discussion of Polish-Jewish relations, I simply had to wait. By mid-1987, these were still not subject to any public debate *in* Poland, or, for that matter, in the émigré press.[4] They could thus safely become secondary sources.

Then, there was the question of the analytical status of many studies which formed part of the "Jewish memory project." Considering the scarcity of research done on assimilation or on the Jewish community today, can one afford not to consider findings reported in Poland, only because one is also analyzing how they came to be in the first place? I decided I could not, but again, only after my own research provided me with enough of the basis to judge the research done by others.

The problem here was not, however, restricted to sources from Poland. I needed to cover a great deal of territory to decide which historians to trust and which to approach from a purely sociological position. At times, the choices were relatively clear: Ringelblum's work on Polish-Jewish relations during the Holocaust, for example, while written at the time, has since been corroborated by the work of many others and now serves as a basic source. At other times, it proved much more difficult to decide which *part* of a whole could be a safe secondary account and which part of the same whole should not: Korbonski's account of the Polish underground (of which he was an important member), while widely quoted as reliable, included some rather obviously self-congratulating statements on Polish aid to the Jews, statements which could become only "memory data."

At issue here was much more than methodology, of course. For as I sifted through the various history books, I was gaining two equally important pictures. One was the picture of what actually happened—in 1943 or in 1946 or in 1968. The other was the picture of how the story of what happened has been told—and *not* told—in Poland. To gain some sense of these two pictures, it was not enough to piece them together, though. They had to acquire a background.

Much of this essential background came, as I have said, from materials on the French-Jewish experience, especially during the early stages of my project.[5] To illustrate: in 1983, Halimi published a detailed study of denunciations which took place during the Second World War. To read about literally millions of letters from ordinary Frenchmen denouncing Jews, Communists, resistance fighters—including more than a few family members—was to gain quite a different perspective on the blackmail of Jews in Poland. Yet to *read* about it, in a widely available book and without hearing an outcry of protest, was also to gain some perspective on the ways in which this topic has been silenced in Poland.

In some studies, "gaining a perspective" on the subject is not a big issue: theory and results of previously done research set the questions and help in arriving at answers. In this study, to gain a perspective was a research task in and of itself, especially once it became a study of the current public discourse about the Jew. There is no such thing as *the* meaning of texts, especially in a society as politically divided as Poland. And there is no plausible way to detach today's words about the past from either that past or the words spoken yesterday. What all this implies in terms of research practice is a need to contextualize every bit of the memory work one is analyzing. It also calls for a great deal of "translation" once the task of analysis is complete.[6] Indeed, the very structure of this presentation can be seen as a set of context blocks used to illuminate the discussion of discourse neutralizing memory, contained in chapter 6.

Each of these blocks was constructed differently, each construction calling for different methods. The "Polish memory" block, which comprises chapter 1—the discussion of the significance accorded the past in current politics—was built on a combination of direct observation with data and insights provided by others. The "Jewish memory" block, presented in chapter 2—the analysis of the place of the Jew in Poland's memory, was built by piecing together historical accounts, available analyses of Polish-Jewish relations, insights from eye-witnesses and historians and, finally, my own interpretation of it all.

In the investigation of the "Jewish memory project" itself, an investigation reported here in chapters 3, 4 & 5, I relied on primary data. Most of the published materials are fairly easily available; the underground sources can be obtained with the help of people close to the opposition as well as through émigré channels (though in that instance, there are problems of pre-selection). To observe and to participate in discussions among the "core initiative" group takes no more than one contact person. The project is not a covert operation, and the group of people most actively involved is small indeed; it also welcomes interesting and interested foreigners. My fieldwork in Warsaw was not all that different from any other sociologist's. I knew the language, in the very concrete and in a more metaphorical sense of the term. Most of the time, rather than conduct formal interviews, which might have appeared artificial I shared in the discussions I was a part of; on at least one occasion, it was my own project that came under much critical scrutiny. All in all, I was treated as both a fellow investigator and a friend.

Memory workers are themselves engaged in often complex projects on Polish-Jewish history. To them, I was not an outsider, but someone equally concerned with Poland's Jewish heritage. Not only was I told about what has been happening over the last few years, but I was given a great many analytical hints, if not fully developed interpretations. For a while, and as a friend, I began indeed to see the world through their eyes. The advantages of coming so close to the subject began to be displaced by the drawbacks of "conversion." It has taken me a long time to be able to step back again. But I have no regrets; understanding the issues as they were understood by insiders provided a big interpretive edge.

The one regret I do have is that my two visits in Warsaw could not possibly supply me with enough material on memory work done through television and film. What somewhat compensates for this absence of audio-visual content to my discourse data is the still predominant role of the printed word in competition over collective memory. But I do not doubt that my analysis could be vastly improved by data I did not have. The two films which I did include in my analysis—the Polish-made *Austeria* and Lanzmann's *Shoah*—were in fact more important for understanding the ways of memory work than a host of publications. In both cases, though, the lessons on memory work were *not* drawn from the films themselves. It should be re-emphasized that the sociological analysis I propose here is about the *process of memory construction*. It is not the works but the work behind them and with them which one aims to illuminate. Or in practical terms, whatever categories and heuristic devices might prove useful in specific cases, all these interpretive tools should help us to understand *how* memory is constructed rather than perceive the end product alone.

Although all this may appear rather obvious, it is not, as I learned the hard way. I did, at the beginning, treat all the different bits and pieces of discourse and imagery about the Jew which had appeared on the public scene as one would a body of texts. I was looking for patterns and for the ideological antecedents, for some shared assumptions and for tensions between the different positions, in short, for a coherent structure. And I felt I was close to the end when I realized that my analysis had excluded, almost by definition, a huge part of the "Jewish memory project," that is, all of the "imported" Jewish material. I was also reminded by people who well knew Poland's cultural politics that it was altogether misleading to draw ideological parallels without, at the same time, drawing out the differences between often identical positions; an official statement and a Church homily do, after all, carry very different weight.

It was in an effort to avoid a "textual bias" that I turned my attention to the *forms* of memory work itself. Considering how the overall aim of the "Jewish memory project" has been to make room for the Jew within Poland's memory, it made sense to look first at the different approaches taken. The categories which I ultimately adopted—those of the nostalgic, instrumental and critical modeling of memory—are formal categories. Knowing which mode is involved in any given instance tells us nothing about the ideological bent of the contents; it indicates only the relationship between the host memory and the Jew.

The main advantage of using these categories is their ability to illuminate the most immediate context of any memory text, namely the one of production.

An additional advantage of approaching the "Jewish memory project" in just such a way is that it made perfect sense on the inside. In fact, Paweł Śpiewak, a sociologist at the University of Warsaw and a very active contributor to the current discussions, spoke in exactly the same terms when we compared notes in 1984.

At that early stage of my analysis, it was especially encouraging to find out that the interpretive grid I was adopting was not distorting the meanings at hand. (This is not to say that the *results* of my analysis would necessarily be approved by the memory workers, only that they would make sense to them.) I was, after all, working from the ground up.

"Working from the ground up" did not, however, always mean making sense of the efforts to reconstruct the memory of the Jew. Indeed, back in early 1982, when I began this study, all of it was to be devoted to the dynamics of silence and forgetting.[7] At the time, I thought, reflecting on Polish-Jewish experience after the Holocaust could not but focus on the Jew's disappearance from history books and from Auschwitz, as well as on the Jews' own efforts at becoming invisible.[8] The explosion of "noise" around things Jewish in 1983 made it impossible to "listen to silence" for long. Yet if my immediate attention had to shift to account for the new public developments, the questions about silence remained. They remained in the heuristic background, as it were, for I was consistently as concerned with what was *not* said as I was with the words on record. They also remained in the foreground of the second chapter's analysis of the "memory void" which once surrounded the Jew. Finally, it was the questions about silence of "Auschwitz without Jews" which provided the key to my understanding of the neutralization of memory.

I should stress that neither my preoccupation with silence, nor my ultimately focusing on the ways of neutralizing memory grew out of intellectual concerns.[9] Indeed, this whole study began—and continued—because of my commitment to the memory of Polish Jews. In its course, I had to, more than once, confront my own heritage. That such a confrontation would prove difficult was inevitable. But I also learned that critical reflection, however intellectually and emotionally demanding, *can* bring one closer to understanding problems at first defying explanation.

That the dark chapters in a country's history are neutralized is a concern of moral order. That such neutralization of memory affects wide areas of the past, in many parts of the world, poses an intellectual challenge as well. I do hope that the analysis presented here moves us closer towards meeting that challenge.

## Notes

1. Group excursions are a very common and very important feature of education in Poland. Starting in the early grades, children visit museums and historical sites as well as factories and farms, often by travelling across the country.

2. "Silence," as it is used here, designates *both* the phenomenon of not talking about certain subjects at all and that of not saying something while saying something else (when the un-said can be treated as more meaningful than the said).

   "Collective memory," in departure from the classic formulation by Halbwachs (1968), includes both what he called "historical memory"—remembrance of things past as passed on from the previous generations—*and* what he called "collective memory," i.e., things literally remembered by a given collectivity at a given time.

3. My focusing on France was dictated by a number of analytic as well as pragmatic considerations: the troubled French-Jewish history, the impact of French ideals on the Polish democratic thought, the presence of a large Polish emigre community in Paris, and my familiarity with the language.

4. In June 1987, I consulted with Jan Tomasz Gross, the author of one of the articles in that issue of *Aneks,* an article which I thought was most likely to provoke a debate. He told me that the only response to his essay on the Holocaust was in the form of warm letters from readers who liked it. He also suggested that a potential for discussion was greatly reduced by the appearance of the article by Błoński *in* Poland, an article I discuss in chapter 6.

5. Later on, I was to include a host of studies dealing with other countries as well, always with the same objectives in mind. [I should add that apart from reading, I was also seizing every opportunity to talk to historians. In Paris, I was able to consult with Paweł Korzec and Michał Borwicz (on the Polish Jewish side) and with Léon Poliakov, Robert Paxton and a number of younger French researchers working at the "Centre de documentation juive contemporaine." In Canada, Harold Troper, the co-author of the first extensive account of Canadian policies vis-à-vis the Jews, *None Is Too Many,* (1983) shared with me his research experience and the story of how this book became a national bestseller.]

6. It was this need to "translate" the context of words which made me decide against using more direct quotations from the texts I studied.

   I also know that to assess my particular intepretation of a given text, that text must be read in the original, as even the best translation takes away the whole important layer of connotations.

7. If I had been *in* Poland at the time, my perspective would likely have been quite different. Among young opposition intellectuals (as I was to discover later), discussions on Jewish topics began in 1977/1978. The "Jewish memory project," however, did not acquire high public visibility until early 1983.

8. As one of the first steps, I forced myself to sit down and read nothing but Holocaust literature for over three months. I was essentially testing myself and my ability to research a topic which would inevitably bring emotional pain. But I was also testing the very notion of silence through this inquiry into the ways of talking about the Holocaust, for at that point, I was still uncertain whether much, if not all, of the post-Holocaust silence in Poland could not have been a result of the very human and quite universal difficulty of communicating a tragedy of such monstrous proportions.

9. Both ideas, though, *became* intellectual concerns as this study progressed. The notion of "silence" in particular is now generating considerable interest among students of communication (see: Tannen and Saville-Troike, eds., 1985). It is being recognized that silence not only structures speech, but communicates in and by itself, especially in the context of ritual. What is not being recognized is that silence does not need to be silent. In this respect, my analysis of the many instances where silence is not absolute, but rather comes all dressed up in words, brings the study of silence closer to the center of current inquiries on ideological discourse.

# 1

# Poland: Past in the Present Tense

September 1983. The mood in Warsaw is grim. Martial Law, officially lifted back in July, seems to have permanently imprinted people's hopes. Indeed, the very fact of its having been lifted means an obvious delay for any real change. Apart from the more external and the more annoying aspects of state control over its citizens, the core of the repressive legislation is still firmly in place. A person can now be prosecuted solely for being unemployed, or, in the regime's language, for acting as a "social parasite." Though explicitly aimed at the varieties of "hooligans," this particular law is of special concern to many opposition activists, often faced with, at best, uncertain prospects of steady employment in a country where the state ultimately employs everybody.[1] Some opposition leaders are in jail awaiting trial, on charges which could bring life sentences. Others are in hiding. Lech Wałęsa, this "ex-leader of ex-Solidarity" as the government spokesman put it, is back at work in Gdańsk, every one of his moves monitored by the security forces. About the only visible signs of defiance which one can see in Warsaw are flowers, flowers on the graves, flowers at the monuments, flowers forming a cross in front of a church where Polish Primate, Cardinal Wyszyński, was laid to rest two years earlier.[2] Even the awarding of the Nobel Peace Prize to Wałęsa does not make people speak out openly.

It is a beautiful autumn, sunny, warm, very pleasant. And yet, even the main streets of the capital become practically deserted after dark. There are no more lines at the bus stops. Few cars pass by. I am told that this too is a legacy of Martial Law, with all its curfew regulations. But there must be more to this, so pronounced, a retreat into private lives. More children have been born in Poland during the past year, proportionately, than in most other developed countries. It is as if the family were all that was left, the only sphere where people could still exercise some control over their lives.[3] In fact, when I ask one of my old friends about her decision to have a child at perhaps the lowest point in her and her husband's lives, she explains it to me in very simple terms. Faced with the real possibility that he would be spending a few years in prison, they had to hurry. . . . But what about all the problems, beginning with the absolutely abominable conditions at maternity wards, right through the lack of even the most basic amenities?[4] What about this grand central store for children which has a lovely designed display in its windows with signs saying "we *buy?*" And what about food, vitamins, candies, all in such short supply or available at exorbitant prices at the "dollar shops"?[5]

Another old friend of mine, a mother of four small children, reassures me: "No, we are not all crazy". Her children are indeed very well dressed and very well fed, now possibly better than before. Being on the state "hit list" has some advantages, it seems. Aid from the West, distributed as it is throughout the country, is both more permanent and more extensive in the case of opposition activists.

Foreign aid, even just a few dollars from a distant cousin in America, must be what makes most Poles survive. One trip to a grocery store would be enough to convince anybody. A bag of basic supplies, not including any meat or sweets (still rationed) costs the equivalent of two days' average wage. The relation between prices and salaries, with people spending much more than they earned, had always been a puzzle. Now, however, proportions make it a veritable mystery.[6] I ask my friends how they manage, being, as they are, very much underpaid intellectuals. Each case is different and yet each is the same. They manage on less and less, and the situation is likely to get worse. Yet when I ask them how could concerned people in the West best help them, the answer is inevitably "send us books." For as harassed as they are by this ever more difficult everyday struggle to make ends meet and to find toothpaste which had just disappeared from all the stores, they feel truly concerned about the looming "intellectual starvation". University libraries, because of the lack of funds, are no longer subscribing to even the most basic Western academic journals, let alone acquiring new books. Also, throughout Martial Law, no one under the retirement age could leave the country,[7] cutting off the usual private sources of supply. In a word, they fear being isolated from Europe.

I also ask my friends about these empty Warsaw streets. Could it be that this once so vibrant cultural center has now become a huge dormitory? To this, they reply with caution. Yes, they say, people are tired, disillusioned, needing time to recover after the shock (or the "war", as many refer to Martial Law). One needs time to regain interest in public life. But, they say, remember that what you see is only what is visible out there, while we, well, we live on a different plane. This they do indeed. Even in homes of previously devoted bureaucrats, I can now hear about the most recent revelations about Stalin, published by the underground. Some people do not even bother reading the regime's press, acquiring all their news from underground journals and Western radio broadcasts instead. The very fact that the circulation of the main Party daily *Trybuna Ludu* has been cut in half, still only to leave many unsold copies, speaks for itself.

The only officially published press which does enjoy wide readership is not too official after all. The lay Catholic weekly *Tygodnik Powszechny* as well as the monthlies *Znak* and *Więź* all consistently print cuts excised by the censor; in the middle of a sentence, there is suddenly this bracket, citing the appropriate legislation, and then, the text resumes. This is in itself an important legacy of Solidarity which had fought hard at least to make censorship visible.

As for books, there seems to be much less of an outright rejection of official sponsorship. Books have indeed become subject to intense speculation, with private sellers jumping their prices as much as ten times at many semi-tolerated book fairs.[8] A totally separate market, where speculation is discouraged both in principle and through pricing policies, is the underground one. The sheer amount of clandestine publishing houses is astonishing, as is the scope and variety. Though completely illegal in all stages of operation, the underground publishing appears to have no problems securing the necessary staff. There is now even a fair amount of competition for translation assignments, jobs which, by Polish standards, pay rather well. In fact, as I am told, it is now perfectly possible, though not altogether easy, to operate as an "underground intellectual," with only the most rudimentary connection to officialdom. For in addition to an extensive network of underground journals—where there is still a great deal of room for the more academically oriented articles—there also exists an underground educational network. Discussion clubs, seminars, lectures—this veritable clandestine university modeled after the system developed during the nineteenth century partition (and taking on the same name of the "Flying University") reaches people in larger and smaller centers. This too is a legacy of Solidarity, or rather of what had made Solidarity possible—the many years of intensive educational work by the opposition.

As much as the restrictions on public gatherings under Martial Law has made these seminars very difficult, they have also become more important. It is there, as well as in the underground journals, that people speak openly about their concerns, about the present and the future. It is there that they would so passionately debate their past.

The underground is constantly publishing. The substantially largest proportion of its output consists of historical accounts, be they in the form of popular history or source materials, including many biographies (with an understandable emphasis on areas which are officially taboo, such as Soviet-Polish relations). Among the underground activities, most seem to focus on the past, with a great many memorials and commemorative gestures in general. I say "seem," for at a closer look, this veritable explosion of collective memory (see: Baczko, 1984:185–239), begun in the 1970s, then marking the times of Solidarity, and continuing today, may not be about the past at all. As one observer put it "in Poland, commemoration is rehearsal" (Weschler, 1984). In Poland, commemoration is also a statement, a statement about one's loyalties, one's tradition, one's vision of the future. Ultimately, it is a statement about one's identity.

To many Western observers, the very intensity of the Poles' devotion to their past is one that borders on obsession. Especially during 1980–1981, when so much seemed to be at stake, when so much *was* at stake, the sheer time and energy spent on "memory work" became a major challenge to those interpreting Polish developments in perfectly logical social science categories (see: Krzemiński, 1986). Why would anyone, in a country rapidly moving towards an economic collapse, prefer to celebrate events which happened decades ago instead of pulling in all the available resources to deal with the immediate problems? Why would a monument be more important than repairing a near disaster in the health care system, for example? In short, why are the Poles so hopelessly attached to *symbols*?

To someone thinking in purely rational, or, more specifically, purely pragmatic terms, the spectacle of endless anniversaries—to take but one example—packed into Solidarity's "quiet revolution" simply could not make much sense.[9] And yet, I would argue, there is absolutely nothing irrational about this "obsession" with symbols and symbolic gestures in the midst of contemporary Poland's worst crisis. There is also nothing strange or peculiar about the fact that it is the past, not the future, which predominates in the present public discourse. What *is* strange, at least in terms of the well-established categories of political systems, is the strength of *competition* in the public sphere. For in a country often labelled, from within and from without, as "totalitarian,"[10] collective memory, if nothing else, no longer belongs to the authorities in power.

"He who controls the past controls the future"—the famous observation cum prediction made by George Orwell in *1984* could not fit better. Except that Orwell, in his portrait of Big Brother, provided him with all the strength and resources, leaving nothing beyond the sheer will to survive for other members of the "totalitarian paradise." For Orwell, *everyone* may in the end be crushed and forced to obey, even worse, to say "I love Big Brother". In the end, a society with no memory offers no resistance.

People in Poland do not need to read Orwell to appreciate his vision. But, at least in the year 1984, the reality of the book *1984* was something they feared for the future, not something they lived in the present. To many Poles, especially as they look to the east—at times with contempt, at times with despair—it is clear that *they* have not given in. The possibility that they might is always there, though. Polish intellectuals today talk about "sovietization" as *the* greatest danger to the people. It is something they feel must be fought at all costs (costs primarily to themselves, we should add). Sovietization *could* happen. Indeed, sovietization—this destruction of the fabric of social solidarity and, ultimately, of the moral fibre—is already happening. Force, inertia, complacency—all the very human needs for a minimum of material comfort can and do make many Poles today act as if they were powerless, isolated and normless individuals. "Anything goes" as the ethics of everyday life is what one can already observe in many segments of society. And the fact that such demoralization is a *product* of the system renders it all the more frightening. For there is now little hope that the system will change, not in this generation and not in the next.

What is it about this system which engenders demoralization? One could, of course, discuss the question in broad theoretical terms. In this case, though, it might be more useful to draw on the answers supplied by social practice, or to look closely at some of the aims and means of Solidarity, this most recent and most massive effort to de-demoralize Polish society.

Solidarity, as a movement, a union, an idea, was many things. In fact, it seemed so confused and confusing at times, especially to its supporters in the West, that to attach any one label to it would most likely render the analysis meaningless. Socialist ideals, religious symbols, patriotic rhetoric, millions of people from all walks of life—all this cannot be neatly categorized, as many students of Solidarity are quick to point out. Most would agree, however, with a somewhat philosophical assessment offered from within, the notion that Solidarity was ultimately about making people, and society, into subjects again not objects.[11] If there is any one quality which could characterize the system which Solidarity set out to change, it is precisely the capacity to render people into objects, to take away the possibility of independent thought and action, ultimately to take away the responsibility for one's thought and action.

Solidarity itself was, of course, living proof that the system had failed, or, more modestly, that there must have been enough cracks in it to allow independent thinking to emerge. But what the people of Solidarity tried to accomplish then—and what some are still trying to today—is to create a space where individuals would be responsible for what they say and what they do.

One of the rather striking aspects of Solidarity was the seriousness with which it viewed *language*. For the first time in "People's Poland," people, en masse, literally refused to speak the language of the rulers. "Nowomowa" (new speech)[12] when applied to their reality ultimately spelled a lie which they refused to accept. Quite suddenly and quite radically, language was to be stripped of all the euphemisms and empty rhetoric covering up for the very real and very visible problems. It was as if common sense, held at bay for so many years by the regime propaganda, could no longer be contained. To call things what they were was one of the first and most important demands of the workers. They asked for truth from their own advisers as well, and many intellectuals who had served as "experts" actually abandoned their social science jargon for the clarity of "spoken Polish". With time, they even managed to bring the regime's apparatchiks (the bureaucrats) into the new—or very old—territory. It is enough to compare the style used in the Party weekly *Polityka*, for example, in the summer of 1980 and in the summer of 1981 to appreciate the extent of this "purification" of communications.

There were some casualties, of course. No injection of meaning could resuscitate such terms as "socialism" or "working class," terms completely discredited by their propaganda usage.[13] There was some confusion, too, as the term "us Poles" came to be appropriated by the regime, together with a whole set of patriotic symbols. The regime learned rather quickly that if it wished to be convincing at all, it too had to speak a different language. Especially as the economic situation worsened and Poland's very political existence came in doubt, it was the government which appealed to common sense, a common sense of duty to Poland.[14]

To what extent General Jaruzelski's feelings were genuine, only history can tell. What was genuine, though, was an all-out effort to recover at least some of the losses. Solidarity was not only making people speak a different language, but also making them talk about things which had earlier been taboo. It was as if a dam had opened, as if a wall of silence had come down—during those sixteen months Poles could *publicly* discuss their real concerns and their real past.

The list of subjects to discuss was a long one indeed, precepts of Marxist dogma having been applied so thoroughly to the teaching of history and to the understanding of the present. Solidarity, among its original twenty-one demands, included an end to censorship. This did not happen, but what did was extraordinary by Eastern European standards: a full scale public debate on the new laws to govern censorship. What also happened was that not only the independent press but the official media began to bring to light events, people, ideas long declared "dangerous." For example, Czesław Miłosz, probably the best living poet of the Polish language and a Nobel Prize winner, the author of *The Captive Mind* and an émigré since he "chose freedom" in 1951 (and whose works had been banned in Poland ever since) was—in October 1981—very officially visiting Poland. A collection of his poems was now very officially published, with huge line-ups at the bookstores testifying to his symbolic appeal if not to the love of his poetry. At the same time, a fragment of his poem became engraved on perhaps the most significant of Solidarity's memory works—the monument to workers killed during the December 1970 riots in Gdańsk. Many Poles who had not even heard his name before now saw him as a symbol of *their* cause. The regime, on the other hand, worked very hard to present the invitation to Miłosz as something of *its* own doing.

A battle for memory was fought on many fronts. Just as Solidarity was preparing to commemorate the August 1st anniversary of the Warsaw Uprising—an event scarcely present on the official agenda because of its dangerously direct anti-Soviet implications[15]—the state media began to devote new attention to it. The autumn of 1981 also saw an unprecedented spectacle of a Communist regime paying homage to one of the key figures in the "reactionary" London government, General Sikorski, the same general whose death is widely suspected to have been engineered by Stalin.[16] Suddenly, too, there was a great deal of discussion, some of high academic calibre and some not, of the ideas and politics of the National Democratic party, a party until then destined to oblivion under the category of "nationalistic Right." In this instance, the official media were again picking up on an interest which had first emerged within the opposition.

In all of these, the regime's task was an unenviable one indeed. It had to directly contradict its own long-established version of the past without losing credibility. And the stakes were high. It was quite obvious that without some degree of popular support, or some degree of *legitimacy,* the regime would be in no position to conduct the country's affairs at the most essential of levels—economic production. To put it differently, with Solidarity exploding the myth of the Party's representing Poland's working people, the Party needed a new myth capable of convincing the workers that they should follow its directives, no mean undertaking, especially at a time when the steadily worsening economic situation was depriving the regime of one of the most efficient tools, economic motivation. In the 1970s, with a huge input of foreign capital, it was possible to count on the people's desire for a "small stabilization." In the 1980s, with a huge foreign debt, severely damaged infrastructure and fallen productivity, the regime had hardly anything to offer in exchange for compliance. For the young people in particular—and Poland's population is young—who know that they will have to wait for their own place to live for some twenty years, who know that their children might not fare all that much better, there is little incentive other than the sheer need to survive. Yet it is with those young people and their efforts to increase productivity that any hope for a decent future lies today. These young people, though, the Solidarity generation, can no longer be treated as objects. Coercion, in and of itself, cannot and does not solve the problems, not even in the short run.

Jaruzelski's government appears to understand the issues quite well. Even during its show of force, that is after the imposition of Martial Law, it had consistently made appeals to Polish *patriotism* both to justify the extreme measures being taken and to project an image of a future "normalization." Having learned its lesson, it first removed the Party itself from center stage, replacing it with the military, a force traditionally respected and revered. It did not even attempt to recapture the pre-August 1980 situation with respect to cultural affairs. Haphazard at times, the state cultural policy—as evidenced by what was published and shown, for one—has been a persistent challenge to critics of totalitarianism. Accustomed to the more rigid definitions of acceptable public discourse in place during the 1960s, I too had great trouble making sense of what I could see and learn about in 1983 and 1984. The list of subjects under study within official structures alone was a puzzle: Arendt's philosophy, failures of socialist economy, dynamics of socialist rhetoric, émigré literature. . . .[17] A glance at the offerings in Warsaw's theaters and movie houses was only to render this puzzle more puzzling—for example, some very openly defiant plays, first staged during Solidarity's "opening," were still drawing huge crowds in the autumn of 1983. It was in the official press that one would find some of the most insightful and damaging critiques of the economic reform then in progress.

Could it be that the regime had given up on propaganda altogether, or was it in the realm of culture that society was given its "carrots" to make the "sticks" of repression and economic deprivation more palatable? Was all this liberalization of public discourse merely a smokescreen obscuring the essentially unchanged structure of the whole system? Or was it, together with the changes within the economic sphere, a harbinger of a significantly different social contract?

At the time, opinions on the subject varied enormously, both within Poland's intellectual elite and among observers in the émigré community. Three years and several important developments later, they still vary, now assuming more and more pragmatic connotations. Today, any debate as to what can and cannot change in Poland's sociopolitical system is also a debate about the morally acceptable ways of participating in public life. In that sense, Jaruzelski has already won a good part of the battle, for he has been able to convince many, if not most of the opposition practitioners that without society's *united* effort at economic reconstruction, the country is doomed. What in 1982 would be widely preceived as "collaboration" with the enemy is gradually becoming a standard and necessary position. More and more of Poland's intellectual leadership can be seen as willing to engage in some form of a dialogue with the authorities, following the leadership of the Catholic Church. The struggle is by no means over, but, at least for now, there begins to emerge a semblance of truce on the major fronts.

Of those, the conflict between the regime and the Church has been by far the most important, both in historical terms and in terms of its significance for today's Poland. In a country where over 80 percent of the population professes Catholic faith and where the Church has long represented both the traditional national unity and the continuity of "independent Poland,"[18] no amount of Communist social engineering appears to have the strength to render religion irrelevant. It is not so much that Poles are particularly devout and observant Catholics, though. As the Church's own publications lament and the official surveys reveal with a certain degree of satisfaction, the Poles' overwhelming attachment to their faith does not translate into a faithful following of religious precepts. In matters such as divorce, pre-marital sex or abortion, Poles do not behave too differently from people in more secular societies.[19] In knowledge of the basic religious dogmas, theirs is not exceptional either. What is exceptional about the Church in Poland is its role in the building and maintenance of *national identity*.

As many observers—and participants—have pointed out, it was the election of the Polish Pope in 1978 and his subsequent visit to Poland a year later which made Solidarity possible. Not only was there suddenly a great sense of national pride, but there emerged also a sense of unity and selfhood. For a great many people, including some practicing atheists, being together with millions of other Poles to greet "their" Pope had been the first and the strongest experience of being a *subject* again. For a number of people today, their participation in Church-organized activities—religious and cultural—still carries the same sense of independence.[20]

To some members of the Church hierarchy, the Polish Primate most notably among them, such a "politization" of their Church is not particularly welcome. There were numerous occasions when the official voice of the Church would speak in favor of social calm and compromise, clashing with the opinions of the lower, more radicalized clergy. Yet while the Church might be avoiding any direct confrontation with the regime, or trying not to side with Poland's opposition in any unequivocal manner, it has profited a great deal from its renewed prominence as a political arbiter. To take the construction of new churches as one indication, the sheer physical growth of the Catholic "infrastructure" has been astounding during recent years. Here again, Jaruzelski appears to have learned his lesson, for in contrast to his predecessors, he is resolved not to create any more rallying points for the Catholics' protest, especially not to follow the way that denied building permits had constituted such rallying points in the past.

Yet, where the Church's presence might be most significant today is within the realm of culture. In the aftermath of the imposition of Martial Law, many of the country's leading artists and intellectuals chose to boycott the official media in protest. Also, the prevailing tragic mood proved especially conducive to sincere "conversions," or to a return to Catholic philosophy and reflection. For some, it was undoubtedly a question of principles. For others, pragmatic considerations might have been more important. The net result is what counts—the immense growth of Church patronage in cultural affairs. From plays to exhibitions to poetry readings, there exists today a whole network of semi-official cultural expression tolerated by the state. The older established journals have gained as well. Lay Catholic publications such as the weekly *Tygodnik Powszechny* and the monthlies *Znak* and *Więź*, together with a host of new ones, now offer a home to the country's best intellectuals. And again, it is not—with some exceptions—that Poland's elite had suddenly become profoundly Catholic. Rather, these lay Catholic journals and discussion clubs are often the only viable and available forum for independent thought, unless, that is, one were willing to move underground.

During the last ten years, many of Poland's prominent intellectuals have taken that step. For some, it has meant a perpetual harassment and ultimately "blacklisting"; for others, it has meant an uneasy co-existence with officialdom. Recently, there have been signs that the regime is becoming more willing to accept the "black sheep"—and vice versa—as some new works of dissident writers appear in bookstores again.

Whatever the future, the past represents real success. The clandestine publishing network, modeled largely on the one developed during the Nazi occupation, together with the underground educational structures, is the most tangible and permanent of accomplishments of the Polish opposition. The wide distribution of information bulletins, weeklies, journals, brochures, fiction and non-fiction, all produced in increasing quantity as well as quality, poses a real challenge to the official channels. It is not only that the ideas and facts they convey forge a view of reality very different from the official one. It is their very presence which bespeaks the continuing strength of the opposition. Today in particular, when the status of the opposition (both Solidarity and other groups formed since 1982) is in question, it might well be that the "clandestine culture," this "second network" as it is referred to in Polish, would become all that remains of the truly independent structures. Here again, much depends on Jaruzelski's power of persuasion, or on how much credibility he can gain by negotiating with—rather than imprisoning—the opposition.

That the current regime invests so much energy and hope in a dialogue with its opponents may have much more to do with Poland's dire economic circumstances than it has with any benevolence. Whatever its underlying premise, the result is still that there is now a fair amount of room for public discourse outside the government's direct control. Whether by choice or by necessity, the regime has essentially acquiesced to the public existence of independent thought.

Where Poland's cultural production was for decades ruled almost exclusively by the directives of an official "cultural politics," it is today subject to politics *tout court*. While we may be talking here about theater and art, literature and poetry, what is at issue is not culture alone but rather the basics of ideological domination in all spheres of life. People who, for years, had only their faith, common sense and private memories to fall back on when encircled by the official version of their past, present and future, can now draw on a host of alternative ways of seeing their world. Intellectuals and artists who, for years, supported and were supported by the system today face a choice. This choice, though, is only minimally one of cultural style. It is, rather, a choice of political affiliation.

In part to reflect this politization of culture, the term "zones" seems best to describe the present situation. For the division lines as they exist today between the official, the semi-official (Church sponsored) and the unofficial (opposition) culture are not cultural at all. More precisely, they are not formal, in a sense that one might talk about "modernist" or "classicist" trends. At most, one could talk here about differences in emphasis, with the Church quite clearly sponsoring more theologically and spiritually oriented productions and the underground focusing on subjects of a more immediate political interest. It should be remembered, though, and the point is not lost on the regime's propagandists, that however otherworldly religious concerns might appear, their very public presence is automatically a serious challenge to the atheist ethos advocated by the Communists. In that sense, *both* the Church and the underground channels work in opposition to the regime. They both aim to represent "society" versus "power";[21] indeed, for them, this dichotomy is a basic premise for their activities. Where they differ, or how they see themselves to differ, is in the area of primary goals. The Catholic Church, while it aids cultural and scientific developments, is ultimately interested in strengthening its own position as the people's spiritual guide. And while the political implications of such spiritual guidance might be obvious to everyone concerned, it is still with the opposition proper that the task of practical guidance rests. In a word, it is not the Church that offers political programs; it is the underground.

Though grudgingly at times, opposition leaders do accept that the Church is there to stay "no matter what," or that its own long-term goals might contradict those of the regime's political opponents. The Church needs and relies on compromise solutions in its continuing struggle with the state authorities. At times, the compromise might work in favor of the opposition; at other times, it might not.[22] The Church, in fact, has only recently accepted the "secular opposition" as its ally, and this acceptance is still not unconditional or uniformly shared (more on this *rapprochement* later). Thus, by its own design as well as due to the social perception of its role, the Church remains a separate force in Poland's cultural politics, however closely it may associate itself with people and groups opposing the regime.

At the level of the cultural infrastructure, the Church enjoys a status very different from that of the political opposition. Its lay publications, while suffering severe paper shortages and special attention from the censors, are legal, and so are the meetings its organizes as a part of country-wide "weeks of Christian culture," for example. Its more strictly religious journals and brochures enjoy an even greater independence, focused as they are on religious issues. The "Clubs of Catholic Intelligentsia," especially those in Warsaw and Cracow, serve as legally sanctioned forums for lectures and public discussions on themes well beyond the realm of theology. Thus, while subject to periodic harassment by the authorities, this semi-official zone remains in full public view, as it were.

Opposition structures, in contrast, are both illegal and invisible. Apart from some exceptional cases—such as the campaign for boycotting the elections—information from the underground is not readily available to people outside its established distribution network, that is, those who are not themselves involved, however nominally, in the opposition. In this unofficial zone, both the production and the possession of cultural materials carry risks of arrest and prosecution.

And while many of the intellectuals involved there are well-known to the authorities—the practice of full disclosure having been initiated by KOR in 1976—many others work under the protection of anonymity. (Anonymity need not be related to self-protection, though. Michnik, who wrote extensively while in prison, signed some of his most important statements (e.g., on emigration) with another name, quite likely to render them more effective as the voice of a "common oppositionist.")

Finally, it is this unofficial zone, rather than the Church, which draws on Western support and Western exposure. Clandestine presses must be smuggled in from abroad, together with a host of necessary materials and tools. Funding, while in part generated by profits, comes in a large part from émigrés. Many of the key publications are promptly reprinted in London or Paris; such key émigré journals as Paris' *Kultura* or London's *Aneks* are continuously brought into Poland.[23] In short, it is through the underground that the main links with a vital part of Polish culture—that which is produced abroad—are being maintained. More precisely, it is there that literature and information flows conquer geopolitical divisions.

Yet what is true of the written word, namely its growing independence from officialdom, does not apply easily to other forms of cultural production. Important mass media—radio and television—are still totally under state control, the presence of foreign radio broadcasts notwithstanding. Filmmakers, while they might be enjoying a fair amount of creative freedom, are still working fully within the official system (the recent emergence of video equipment may spell the end to this monopoly). Drama productions, apart from a small amount of little theater, still need the support of the official stage. Art exhibits, with the exception of those organized in small private or Church-run galleries, are still officially mounted. Musical productions, again with some important exceptions, are still in the official province as well. In short, despite the many encroachments on the official territory, it still dominates the realm of popular entertainment as well as what we might call "high culture," both visual and literary.

Considering my previous remarks about the success of alternative channels of publication, this last statement may seem a contradiction. Yet we must realize that the foremost quality sought in the written word issuing from the semi-official and underground zones is neither aesthetic superiority nor entertainment value, but *truth*. In a country where ideological acrobatics have long been in charge of what is said and how, in a country where both the past and the present are subject to constant manipulation and alignment with smaller and larger points of doctrine, the alternative is seen as nothing less than truth.

People who turn to lay Catholic journals or to lectures organized by the underground "Flying University" are not after a different kind of culture, but after a different kind of knowledge. They might, at the very same time and without any problems of conscience, enjoy a movie or a play or a concert offered in the official zone, but grow suspicious when listening to a T.V. journalist describing the country's economic ills.

They are also after a different kind of language. If years of censorship mean that creators and audiences alike have grown accustomed to locate meaning "between the lines," today's offerings outside the official zone provide some very welcome training in saying things directly. For that matter, to win some badly needed credence, today's offerings within the official zone have begun to imitate that very directness of language. And it is only at this level that one can indeed talk at all about *competition* on the cultural front. At stake here are not prizes and honors, or even popular acclaim, but rather "property rights" to Polish culture—the question of who can be seen to represent society's real concerns and real values, in a word, who can be seen to stand for the "real Poland".

But how does one define this "real Poland"? What may constitute the basis for the "ownership claims"? Or what makes it possible to discredit one's opponent as *not* speaking for the Poles?

It is precisely at this point that the battle for memory enters with force. For in order to stake claims on the present and the future, in order to argue—plausibly—that one has a right to represent the "real Poland," it is essential first to establish a connection with the past. Societies, much more than individuals perhaps, rely on the past to define themselves. They may at times engage in a more or less thorough re-definition exercise, they may even "invent traditions", (Hobsbawn and Ranger, eds., 1984) but they cannot, so it appears, discard the past completely. Even when an attempt is made to break with the immediate past—as was the case when the Polish People's Republic was established in 1944—one cannot afford to break all ties. To do that or to forge a completely new identity might be possible theoretically, but it does not work in social practice.

That Poland's Communist regime understood this rather late may account in part for its present difficulties as well as for the zeal with which it seems to be "catching up." After decades of at best ignoring and at worst denying huge chunks of collective experience, the authorities find themselves today in desperate need of links with the past. Their experiment in social engineering did not succeed; with nearly all socialization resources at their disposal, they still could not create a "new Pole." What they had created in fact, was a generation prepared and equipped to fight them, since education, no matter how tightly controlled, ultimately made people more intelligent and capable of independent judgment.

As I have said, the current regime appears to have a fairly good grasp of the nature of the problem. Instead of evoking "socialist values," it is calling upon patriotism. Instead of persisting in silencing national heroes of the wrong "bourgeois" kind, it is seeking to appropriate them. Instead of appealing to some bright future, it is "re-discovering" some bright past and some not all that bright. To establish its own "natural" connection with the national heritage, it is not enough to claim credit for strengthening the national virtues. It is perhaps even more necessary to pin the national faults on one's opponents.

The definition of what constitutes a virtue and a fault is, however, relative, at least in as much as broad categories of civic behavior are concerned. It is especially relative in a country which has known only one twenty-year span (1918–1939) of full sovereignty in the last two hundred years. To secure national survival, Poles have learned to resist foreign oppression. Their training in self-government, cut short as it was by the outbreak of World War II, did not reverse this generally adversarial relationship to state authority, followed, as it was, by the imposition of the Communist rule. Today's situation, while it has no exact parallels in history, invokes for many Poles the memory of their long, long struggle for independence. It is not direct memory, of course, but it is no less powerful. Resemblances can indeed be striking.

In the early 19th century, after years of despair and then a failed insurrection against Russia (1831), Polish poets gave the nation a vision to keep it alive. Romanticism not only extolled the virtues of armed struggle, a struggle against all odds, a struggle where one measured one's means by one's goals—but also exalted failures in that struggle into national martyrdom. A strong messianic undercurrent of Romanticism gave Poles some hope and some solace: Poland, this "Christ of the nations," may have been destined to suffer but it would also experience resurrection. In the meantime, Poles were not to remain passive. They were to safeguard their precious heritage and to resist their oppressors at every opportunity without much regard for the human cost.

When the next insurrection failed in 1863 the costs proved too high. Finally it was recognized that no national effort could succeed unless it involved the whole nation, mostly made up of illiterate peasants. Romanticism, so appealing to both the nobility and the newly emerging intelligentsia, now came in for some sharp criticism. If Polish culture was to survive, if Poland was to be ready for independence, argued a new generation of Polish writers and intellectuals, Poles had to concentrate on the "organic work" to bring society into modernity. "Positivists"—as members of this movement came to be called—did not deny the value of independence, but they opposed the all too heroic efforts to achieve it. Theirs was not so much a struggle against oppression as it was a struggle for strengthening the social fabric, with the emphasis on educating the masses and furthering economic development. Working for the good of the nation was now to replace the Romantic notion of dying for it.[24]

In the actual practices of actual people, the romantic and positivistic ideals often co-existed. Under different historical circumstances—and

Poland in the 20th century was to experience both the joy of renewal and the terror of occupation—the very meaning of heroism and work for the good of the country would see many a transformation. During World War II in particular, resisting the Nazis meant both the armed struggle and the continuous effort to preserve social institutions, especially that of education (see: Gross, 1979). And, today, as we have seen, one of the central tenets of the opposition, so often accused of being hopelessly romantic, is a very positivistic notion that society, to survive, must have its own "independent structures."

The word "accused," though, should cue us to what is at stake in the current debates. For while neither romanticism nor positivism gave birth to well-defined political doctrines—more precisely, both were variously used and manipulated by various political forces—they did, over the years, become part of a very political conflict. It is not a conflict betwen Left and Right, though each side might, at times, speak in deceptively familiar terms. It is rather a conflict between what some analysts call "ideal" and "real" politics, a conflict between the moral and the pragmatic approach to public life.[25] It is a conflict of special poignancy in Poland today, both for the regime and for the opposition.

Having given up on the visions of the bright future, the regime now portrays itself as the only force capable of conducting Polish affairs in a "realistic" fashion. To those who might wish to oppose it, it cites the hard facts of Poland's geo-political position. Under the circumstances, it argues, any romantic idealism is not just naive but dangerous (one need look no further than Solidarity). The way to act patriotically lies in working together—"national unity" is a favorite expression in the current propaganda lexicon—to solve Poland's economic, social and ecological problems. Justifiably proud of their long tradition of fighting for freedom, Poles should nevertheless abandon their heroic dreamland and get on with the tasks at hand. Instead of revering their martyrs, they should follow the constructive examples of statebuilders.

The alternatives proposed from within the opposition vary. They vary as to the degree of coherence and in the parameters of the political programs, from an outright rejection of the present system in the name of a future free Poland, through a struggle for society's autonomy within the system, to an uneasy accommodation with the authorities. The opposition, then, far from being naively romantic, offers a whole range of more and less "realistic" propositions. Yet what it appears to share, together with the Catholic Church, is a pronouncedly *moral* perspective on social and political life. For both, the present system is not merely something one does not like or something which does not work—it is evil, corrupt and corrupting to the core, immoral and demoralizing.

When, in 1976, a group of prominent intellectuals and opposition activists formed the Committee for Workers' Defense (KOR), ending years of separation between the "ideologues" and the workers, and thus paving the way for Solidarity, they defined their objectives in strictly moral terms. KOR members and sympathizers included people of every conceivable political persuasion, Catholics and non-believers, people with very different, at times antagonistic, backgrounds. What they all shared was a deep moral outrage at social injustice, a deep sense of moral duty to help those in need (see: Lipski, 1983c). Solidarity itself, at its grassroots level in particular, provided a platform for voicing many a moral objection to the corruption of the system. The very language of "truth" and "justice" was not mere rhetoric but an expression of genuine moral concerns.

Ethical considerations do not easily translate into political programs. They nevertheless act as guidelines for one's approach to civic life, guidelines which all too often preclude the purely pragmatic orientation advocated by the officialdom. Yet to talk meaningfully about ethics, about duties and responsibilities, about truth and justice, it is not enough to use mere words. One needs examples to propagate ideals, especially when they are couched in the very language of one's opponent. Some of these examples come directly from the lives of today's oppositionists.[26] Their refusal to give in, to abandon their principles, is perhaps the best lesson on moral politics. Other examples come from the past. Historical figures seem to testify that Poles have long known the value of freedom and justice. Once again, collective memory becomes a crucial resource. Once again, the point is not lost on the regime's propagandists.

Just as the opposition is now so often being accused of incurable romanticism, its corollary, martyrology, also comes under a heavy attack. Of all the memory terrains, this one is perhaps the most explosive. On the one hand, nobody, including the regime, can claim patriotism without showing reverence for the national heroes who suffered and died for the country. On the other hand, the Poles' attachment to martyrology—so much a part of the prevailing image of Poland as a *victim* of oppression— is dangerously close to celebrating today's active opposition. (At times, these links are very direct. The 1940 Katyń massacre, where thousands of Polish officers were killed by the Soviets, could not be a more direct reminder of the source and the nature of Poland's suffering.)

With so much of recent Polish history being so closely associated with the Russian and then the Soviet domination, commemoration indeed becomes a rehearsal. And while it is possible for the regime to appropriate those heroes who fought against Russia, it finds it difficult, even today, to mention those who died under the Soviet occupation.[27] In short, it becomes a delicate balancing act to be able to appear patriotic without reigniting anti-Soviet sentiments. One part of this act is played today with the help of history books; those earlier politicians who did not consider Russia their mortal enemy are promptly being rediscovered. Another part relies heavily on the present, with a continuous outcry against the "revanchist tendencies" in West Germany, for example, an outcry fortified by constant reminders of Poland's suffering under the Nazis. Finally, there has also been a gradual and subtle shift away from the "victimological" discourse to one emphasizing the identification between the nation and the state.

It is, of course, difficult to predict the rate of return on this new strategy. The previously open ideological domination did not succeed. Even Poles with nothing more than common sense could see right through the lies. Today's situation appears much more complex, especially with respect to the battles on the memory terrain. If statements on prosperity and happiness could not possibly resonate with the Poles' own experience, appeals to tradition can. At the same time, with the memory of Martial Law so fresh, the Poles' sense of defeat and suffering can only re-energize all the symbolism of martyrdom, and thus pose a definite challenge to all the work-oriented and state-oriented appeals to patriotic duty.

It is against this backdrop of the past, occupying so much of the center stage in debates about Poland's present and future, that one must view any "memory project" on the public agenda today. Resurrecting the ideas and the heroes of Polish nationalism, to take but one example, is not an exercise in historiographic adjustment. Bringing them back into the public arena, after decades of officially-imposed silence, not only corrects an altogether one-dimensional vision of Poland's past, but also, most importantly, re-defines nationalism as a now legitimate component of collective memory, as an acceptable and appropriate source of new ideas and new programs.[28] The whole undertaking may indeed appear very symbolic, but it is also directly relevant to today's politics.

Yet could the recent interest in things Jewish have similar relevance? How could the memory of a people that have all but disappeared carry any practical significance? If the concern is of a moral order, how can it not?

## Notes

1. The state in Poland does not own all the means of production. Agriculture is mainly in private hands; there are also small sectors of services left to private initiative. Both, though, are tightly controlled via legislation and taxes.

   The law against "social parasites" is still in effect in 1987. Even the official side acknowledges the need to re-define it (Podemski, *Polityka,* Feb. 28, 1987). In practical terms, thousands of Solidarity activists, released from internment in 1982–83, were given a special status as "subversive elements" (*wilczy bilet* in Polish), making them unemployable in the main areas of the economy. The situation of intellectuals was somewhat better; many did return to their research posts. All those I talked to in Warsaw in 1983 and 1984, though, expressed fears of being fired.

2. Originally, the cross was prominent on one of the central squares in Warsaw. The regime, apparently growing tired of being forced to remove it daily, opted for a simple solution: the whole area was fenced off for "structural improvements." The cross was then moved, with its being on the Church property offering some guarantees of permanence.

3. In 1982, Poland's birth rate at 19.4 was surpassed only by Ireland (20.3). By comparison, West Germany's was 10.1, the United States'—16.0 (*Information Please Almanac*, 1987:135).

4. Conditions in the hospitals in general and in the maternity wards in particular have steadily deteriorated over recent years. "Deteriorated," means that the only way to prevent a newborn from communicating diseases is to take him home as soon as possible.

5. The network of shops where one uses hard currency (or an equivalent in special coupons, now traded openly) has existed for many years. It is only in the 1980s, though, that these shops operate not as suppliers of certain luxury items, but of basics as well (in Poland, that also means alcohol). Several items, from toothpaste through chocolate to building materials can be obtained only there.

6. That mystery is only partially solved when one allows for the fact that a great many people earn additional income through working in their spare time or by engaging in all kinds of mostly illegal trade operations, in other words, for a growing sphere of "second economy". [For a good discussion, see: Weschler, 1984.]

   According to very official reports (Kwiatkowski, *Polityka,* March 21, 1987), it is only thanks to the "privatization" in the economic sphere, including perfectly legal ventures into entrepreneurship on a small scale, that the standard of living can be maintained for the "middle majority" of the population.

7. Compared to other Eastern European countries, let alone the Soviet Union, Polish regulations on travel have been fairly relaxed. During the 1970s in particular, it was common for many Poles to spend at least a few months abroad, substantially augmenting their income and, in the case of intellectuals, their libraries. In this respect—as in others—Martial Law was a severe blow to the (relative) freedom of movement.

8. Even today, after several increases, officially set book prices are relatively low when compared to such items as food or clothing. It has been one of the major components of government's cultural policy to make books as widely accessible as possible. The drawbacks of centralized and state-controlled publishing are many, though: poor quality, extremely long "production cycles," editorial policies unresponsive to the readership preferences. In a state of economic chaos and inflation, books became a temporary investment for some a source of additional income for others.

9. Weschler (1984) offers a good "translation" of Poland's memory celebrations for the North American reader.

10. It is perhaps only natural that the designation "totalitarian" prevails, especially in the émigré discourse. The present system in Poland is very difficult to name,

and it *is* characterized by the state's attempts to exercise total control over the citizens. The problem begins when adopting the term "totalitarian" leads to equating the situation in Poland with that of the Soviet Union and to obscuring the very basic differences in the degree of repression in the two countries.

11. "Solidarity as an expression of 'subjectivity' of Polish society" was a view put forward by Bortnowska, a Catholic intellectual, in early 1981 (quoted in Weschler, 1984:112).

12. "Nowomowa" (new speech) has many of the characteristics of the Orwellian "Newspeak". Poland's political system, for example, is described as "popular democracy"; subjugation to the Soviet Union becomes "friendship and cooperation"; a strike turns into a "work stoppage".

13. It is characteristic, for example, that even when the workers' demands were perfectly compatible with socialist principles, the term itself would be avoided at all costs (see: Touraine et al., 1982).

14. The very names of various institutional bodies established under (and after) Martial Law speak a patriotic language of "national salvation", "national unity", "national reconciliation".

15. The Warsaw Uprising, which began on August 1, 1944, and lasted for nearly two months, claimed 200,000 lives and resulted in the destruction of much of Warsaw. Initiated by the Home Army, it was an attempt to establish an independent Polish government in Warsaw, largely in response to the Soviet domination of the eastern part of Poland. Soviet Army, in fact, was at the time on the right bank of Vistula, and it did not move to help in the fight against the Germans. While there are many conflicting views on the wisdom of the decision to stage that battle, there is also a prevailing sense among Poles of having been left to die by the Soviets.

16. For a good discussion of the memory battles of 1981, see: Baczko (1984:185–239), Weschler (1984:120–125).

17. Analyses by Polish sociologists which form part of a comparative Canadian/Polish collection on "dependent societies" (Breton et al., eds., 1986) are another example of such defiance in the area of scholarship. For an overview of the situation in the sphere of historical research, see: Kridl Valkenier (1985).

18. The 80% figure is often cited in the official media; Catholic sources place the proportion of Catholics in Poland at 96% (the difference is possibly due to the differences between "registered" Catholics and those identifying with the Catholic religion).

19. In a review of recent studies on the subject, one finds, for example, that over 80% of Polish young people engage in sex before marriage; what is more, most of them do not perceive this as a conflict with their religious beliefs (Wróblewska, *Polityka,* Oct. 25, 1986).

20. As but one example, the Church of St. Stanisław Kostka in Warsaw, located in the northern part of the city, close to homes of many opposition intellectuals, became the focal point for independent-minded Poles with its monthly mass "in the intention of the fatherland". (This was the parish of Father Popiełuszko, who was murdered a year later by the Security Forces.) The interior of the church was an "island of independence", with plaques commemorating Solidarity as well as Poles who were killed by the Soviets during World War II. Patriotic celebration was not universally praised, though; among the regular parishioners, there were voices of sharp criticism in relation to using the church for non-religious purposes.

21. The opposition between "society" and "power" (the Polish term *władza* covers both power and authority) is not new; it dates back to the period of partitions. What gives it so much strength today is the recent past; with Martial Law, the dividing lines became crystal clear. One should keep in mind, though, that this dichotomy is more of an ideological construct than a reflection of Poland's complex realities. Do teachers, for example, who are all civil servants, belong to the side of "power"?

22. In 1983, for example, the Pope's visit to Poland—while Martial Law was still in effect—received an almost equally divided sum of positive and negative reactions, both within the opposition and in society-at-large (Ł.J., 1983).

23. This is not to say that the practice is legal; it is not. Yet while in the 1960s, those bringing *Kultura* across the border had a show trial, today, repression now assumes more mild forms (recently, the punishment is frequently through large fines). Seizure of material supplies remains a major problem for underground publishers.

24. The most popular writer of the time, though, Henryk Sienkiewicz, whose novels are said to have formed much of the Poles' historical consciousness, wrote mainly about the glorious past, fully in keeping with—and perpetuating—the vision of a noble, besieged nation.

25. Bromke applied this dichotomy most extensively in his study of Poland (1967). While I find the distinction itself useful, I disagree with Bromke's assessment whereby the "real" approach emerges as necessarily better.

   It is difficult to formulate political programs on moral considerations alone. Yet the developments in Poland show that while it takes a great deal of time and effort to build "real" policies on an "ideal" base, it is definitely not impossible.

26. Michnik's writings from prison (1985) exemplify his own sense that this is so.

   Bielecki's "letters to my son" (1986), also written while in prison, are another direct expression of the educational value of experience. On a less positive note, keeping a constant watch on the actions of the elite figures in general may have a paralyzing effect on social initiatives; Michnik, in his polemics with Wierzbicki (1985:169–199) warns against the dangers of self-righteousness.

27. Of the 3 million Poles who lost their lives during World War II, possibly as many as one-half perished in the Soviet Union (see: Gross & Grudzińska-Gross, 1983).

28. This is not to say that Polish nationalism now receives unanimous praise. It says only that while historical studies of it are being published officially and the nationalist ideals figure prominently in the unofficial discourse, this whole tradition acquires a certain legitimacy.

# 2

# Poland's Jews—A Memory Void

The current abundance of public discourse about things Jewish in Poland should not make us forget that only a few years back the picture looked quite different. Indeed, it would be difficult, if not impossible, to appreciate the recent work on this "Jewish memory project" unless one appreciates the extent of the void it aims to replace.

The numerous "firsts" of recent years are one valuable indication of just how bare was the symbolic space once accorded to the Jew. In 1983 alone, there came the first general introduction to Polish Jewish history as well as the first reprint of a by-now classic history book by M. Bałaban; the first exhibitions of Jewish artifacts in national museums; the first popular introductions to recent Jewish history, politics and culture, both in Poland and abroad, included as review articles and translated materials in special issues of the Catholic monthlies *Znak* and *Więź* as well as *Literatura na świecie,* a cultural journal; the first translation of a work by I. B. Singer; the first generally available editions of two basic sourcebooks on the Warsaw Ghetto; and the first collection of poetry translated from Yiddish (a collection prepared in the late sixties by Salomon tastik, whose other book, dealing with the Jewish Enlightenment, and published in two thousand copies in 1961, had been for years the only available source of information on the history of Polish Jews . . .).[1]

Along with the deluge of introductory texts and original materials on the history and culture of Polish Jewry came frequent calls to open a discussion of Polish-Jewish relations, a subject formerly perceived taboo. There seemed universal agreement that "the time had come" to break the silence,[2] without delving too deeply into the reasons for such a very cautious—to say the very least—treatment of the topic by Polish media. By the fall of 1985, Polish television would show a selection of episodes from *Shoah,* a nine-hour film on the Holocaust produced in France by C.

Lanzmann. The Polish government, which had first officially protested against the portrayal of Poles in this film, was later to make an uncut version of *Shoah* available in local cinemas. The result? An extensive discussion on T.V. and in the press, another first.

The last few years have also seen the first Polish appeals to preserve and restore at least some of the more important physical traces of Jewish heritage. A volunteer committee, in itself a rarity in Poland, was formed to "preserve Jewish historical monuments," calling for aid from both the state and individual supporters as well as from Polish Jews now living abroad.[3] While the committee's main concern lies with the care of Jewish cemeteries, especially those with tombstones of high historical or artistic value, another appeal, launched in 1985 by Jerzy Tomaszewski, one of the foremost specialists in the history of minorities, called for memorial plaques to be installed in every town and village where the Jews once lived (*Polityka,* Nov. 16, 1985). There is also now the first exhaustive documentation of Poland's Jewish cemeteries, compiled by Monika Krajewska, one of the initiators of the committee mentioned above; it is a unique testimony to their state of general decay and abandonment.[4]

As diverse as these initiatives are, both in form and in origin, they all seem to share the basic resolve to *remember* the Jew. "To remember" may mean "to learn," or to make Jewish history and culture more familiar to the Polish public; it also means "to re-assess," or to bring at least some of the issues in the area of Polish-Jewish relations into a public forum; to remember, finally, is to care physically for the memorials to Poland's Jewish heritage. Yet, ultimately, to remember is first to create a permanent space for the Jew in Poland's collective memory, a space which can then be gradually furnished with items of interest and relevance to those engaged in the reconstruction work.

Much of this study is concerned with the actual operation of this "Jewish memory project," with what is being done and by whom, as well as with the reasons for undertaking the job in the first place. Yet to be able to make sense of it all, we must begin with a moment of reflection regarding the project's *raison d'être,* or to ask what happened to the memory of Polish Jews in the country where they had lived and died? What made it possible for the Jew to be excluded from Poland's memory? In short, how can we account for the fact that such a project is at all viable?

The question "what happened to the memory of the Jews?" is both a question about the fate of Jewish survivors and a question about attitudes on the part of Poland's memory keepers. And while much of the answer here belongs to the period following the Holocaust, it is also rooted in the long history of Polish-Jewish relations, or, more specifically, in the history of collective definitions of the Jew.

During the 1920s and 1930s, Poland was home to Europe's largest Jewish community; though over three million Jews constituted only about ten percent of the country's general population, their concentration in towns and cities in a country with a still rural character meant that Jews accounted for about one-third of the urban dwellers; that proportion might reach as high as eighty and ninety percent in many places.[5] It was a community whose roots in Poland were deep indeed; it is generally estimated that their history in Poland dates back to the eleventh century, close to the beginnings of Poland itself.

For most of their history, the Jews were a community apart from the rest of Polish society; in a country where feudalism lasted longer than in the West, Jews, by virtue of both their rights and their obligations, formed a kind of separate estate, distinct from the nobility and the peasants, as well as from the Christian third estate. When combined with the differences in religion, culture and language from a predominantly Catholic society, the Jews' separatedness under law acquired many of the characteristics of a *caste* situation.[6] While Jews would come into frequent contact with their Polish neighbors, such contact was generally restricted to economic matters, leaving their social and cultural life intact and well within the limits of the Jewish community, very much in accord with the precepts of traditional Judaism, one might add. Both sides really knew very little about each other, and on both sides, there developed a whole repertoire of types and stereotypes facilitating and simplifying dealings with the other (Hertz, 1961).

If one were to judge on the basis of Polish literature in general and poetry in particular, the image of the Jew was by no means purely, or even predominantly, negative then; though there would be much disdain for the usurer, and much ridicule of the strange habits there was also a good deal of respect for the special wisdom the Jew was seen to have.[7] Yet however diverse the literary portraits of the Jew, virtually all of them would depict him outside his proper environment as if he had existed only *in relation* to the Polish society; the Jew would be judged on the basis of Polish norms and values and never on his own (Hertz, 1961). In short, while his presence might have been woven into the fabric of common proverbs, popular jokes and literary images of Polish life, the Jew as a Jew remained essentially a Stranger.

Although the Jew, in the role of an economic middleman, had been a prime target for hostility and frustration, his function was also a needed one; with the exception of a still very weak Christian urban middle class, the Jew was not in direct competition with people in other segments of society.[8] It was not a guarantee of a pleasant life, but it was a guarantee of a well-defined position within a well-defined system. His foreignness, too, was well-defined in religious terms, again, not allowing for much sympathy on the part of the Catholic majority (indeed, often the contrary) but providing for a set of rules to guide all social interaction. His dependence on the rulers of the land, with all the restrictions as to the allowed means of livelihood or areas of settlement, was cushioned by the privileges of self-jurisdiction granted to the Jewish community. His life, though affected by the outside world, was still lived very much within a community of faith, tradition and culture, a community with its own sense of time guided by the Jewish calendar, with its own language—Yiddish—and with its own history.[9] Briefly then, while the Jews were occupying an isolated place within the larger society, neither they nor others considered this position particularly problematic. There was enough social space to accommodate a Stranger.

With the breaking down of the feudal system, however, the rules of Polish-Jewish coexistence began to change, adding quite a different dimension to the figure of the Jew in public discourse. While he never really ceased to be a Stranger, his presence would come to be perceived as a problem and eventually, as a major social problem, a "Jewish question" calling for solutions.

Things changed rather rapidly during this nineteenth century, and then, on many planes simultaneously. The Jewish community had by that time lost much of its autonomy; while still predominantly traditional in outlook, it was now being swept by new trends, originating in the West, trends which meant a total re-definition of its place within the society-at-large. *Haskalah,* the Jewish Enlightenment, saw Polish Jewry, with its distinct customs, language and values, as an essentially backward community needing modernization through education on the one hand and Polonization on the other.[10] Propagated mainly by members of what we would call today the upper middle class, the ideas of progress-as-assimilation were gradually to extend their appeal to include much of the middle class as well. As Jews were entering the ranks of a newly forming intelligentsia, no longer adhering to the precepts of orthodoxy, they would aspire to an equality of status with their Polish counterparts, or to full participation in the country's affairs.

The challenge which these aspirations represented to their caste position would be coupled with challenges originating on the other side. Poles, who had traditionally held business occupations in deep disrespect, now began to enter them in growing numbers, propelled by a delayed, yet intensive, urbanization and industrialization. And the new working class emerging in the cities would now become yet another terrain where Polish and Jewish interests began to compete directly.

The Jew was no longer merely a rival of a weak stratum of Polish craftsmen and tradesmen, for he would now be present in all the main spheres of both economic and cultural endeavors.

Competition alone, even under the conditions of a rapid modernization which saw vast numbers of Poles dislodged from the tranquility of life on the land, does not explain why the very presence of Jews was defined as problematic. The shift came in seeing the Jew not just as a competitor and thus a partner of sorts, but as an *intruder* and thus a threat to national wellbeing.

Paradoxically, perhaps, the Jew came to symbolize that threat on both ends of the tradition/modernity spectrum, making it virtually impossible for him to escape such definition. For most Poles, struggling throughout the nineteenth century to maintain an identity as a nation (it should be kept in mind that the country was then partitioned among Prussia, Austria and Russia) and conceiving this identity as inseparable from the Catholic tradition,[11] the Jew was both an old enemy and a new one: Catholic teachings had long placed him in the role of a Christ killer and a corrupting agent for Catholic morality, with the very word "Talmud" possessing singularly negative connotations; now, he would join company with various free thinkers, masons and radicals, all aiming to undermine the established order with their godless attitudes and ideas. (Identifying the Jew with the forces of modernity is one of the predominant motifs of modern anti-Semitism in the West as well.) As in any mythical construction, it did not quite matter that the two figures of the Jew were worlds apart; the consistency of evil was, after all, maintained (see: Wilson, 1982).

For a very few social reformers, advocating progressive and chiefly Western ideas, the emancipation of Poland's Jews would come to mean— just as it did in the West—granting them the rights of citizenship as individuals rather than as members of a group. A Jew was seen as a potentially good citizen as long as he would abandon his centuries-old customs and rituals, stop using the "jargon," namely Yiddish, and begin to dress and behave in a civilized, namely Polish, manner. Since Polonization appealed to still a very narrow stratum of Jewish assimilationists, the task of reforming the Jews must have appeared tremendous, yet the appeal of such a "progressive" solution to the "Jewish question" bore little relation to its chances for success. Put simply, the idea that Jews as Jews could contribute something valuable to Poland's national or cultural development was totally outside the frame of reference of even the most ardent advocates of equality.[12] In effect, "equality" itself, as defined within the ethos of progress, reform and humanism, entailed a prescription that Jewishness should not matter in dealing with another human being, a subtle, yet very powerful expression of a condescending attitude, and one which would live much longer than any specific remedies devised at the time for treating the Jewish problem.

The very notion of "remedies" brings us to the key to understanding the emerging pattern of discussing things Jewish—the powerful imagery of *disease,* entering discourse in both individual and social forms. Deeply anchored in the religious myths of the Jew poisoning Christian souls—and Christian wells—an association between Jewishness and disease gained a good deal of strength in secular translations.[13] At one level, the Jewish community came to be perceived as a kind of tumor, spreading through all the healthy cells of society, suffocating the economic life and poisoning the cultural one. Weak at first, this particular metaphor was to mark the discussions of the "Jewish question" among the defenders of national purity, organized politically at the end of the century into the National Democratic Party.[14] At another level, the Jewish disease would be seen as much more contained, plaguing individual Jews rather than society-at-large; it would be thought of as curable at first, and only later assumed to leave traces impossible to efface.[15]

The difference between open anti-Semitism and calls for tolerance seems to lie in their proponent's respective assessments of both the specific dangers the disease presented and the possibility for cure. The former saw simply no way to make a Jew really "healthy," (even a conversion to Catholicism came to be suspect); the latter considered assimilation a good enough remedy, not to be put in question, at least not in public.

We can now better appreciate why the very presence of the Jews came to be seen as a major threat only when the old social order had begun to collapse, for once the caste position of the Jews was no longer regulating their interaction with and within the larger society, there were fewer and fewer "natural" barriers to prevent contamination, as it were. The process itself was not unique to Poland; the "Jewish question", in its modern form, had arisen earlier in the West of Europe, also with the fall of the feudal system (see: Arendt, 1973). In France, the first country to grant Jews equality under the law (after the French Revolution), all the efforts were focused on making Jews into good Frenchmen by "civilizing" them, which ultimately meant ridding them of the backward apanage of Jewish tradition; an integration of individuals and not one of a people was the goal. In France, too, the imagery of disease and contamination gained much currency during the second half of the nineteenth century, and this is the discourse originating on the Left as well as on the Right (Sternhell, 1983). And it was in Germany, where the Jews were fewer, more assimilated and more frequently converts to Christianity, that the notion of curing this "Jewish cancer" acquired, as we know, its most deadly significance.[16]

Yet if Poland was not unique in terms of the *forms* taken by the dispute over the "Jewish question", it was unique in terms of the *magnitude* of the dispute itself. Already high on the agenda when the country did not politically exist, the "Jewish question" became one of the main preoccupations of a newly independent Poland after 1918, at least judging by the intensity of parliamentary debates and the thrust of many press polemics of the time (see: Korzec, 1980). At times, it seemed as if most, if not all, of Poland's social and economic problems—and there were many in an under-developed country, freshly re-united after one hundred and fifty years of partition—could be ascribed to the presence of a large Jewish population and could not be fully solved until the "Jewish problem" had been solved.

There were, of course, sharp differences in both the diagnosis of the problem and the proposals for dealing with it, spread a long a wide political spectrum. At one end, the increasingly Rightist government tightened restrictions so as to stifle Jewish economic life and thereby facilitate the ultimate goal of such policies—Jewish emigration. A plan to force at least one million of Poland's Jews to leave the country had been seriously considered in both its logistical and international implications just before the outbreak of World War II (see: Friedman, 1972).

At the other end, the Communists, who together with the left wing of the Socialist Party were the only ones consistently to attack anti-Semitic policies and practices, advocated what they saw as the ultimate solution to the "Jewish problem," namely the creation of a new, thoroughly secular society in which Jews would enjoy full equality and integration, provided, of course, that they became fully assimilated. The Right saw the source of the "Jewish problem" in the very essence of the Jew; the Left, in keeping with its overall approach to historical interpretation, placed the emphasis on the economic and social condition of the Jews as it had developed over the centuries of feudalism, as it existed under capitalism and as it was to change under socialism.

Positions emerging in between these two extremes would variously combine elements of both approaches and offer different schemes for dividing Jews into potentially good and potentially bad candidates for integration. But while I do not wish to minimize the often deep divisions existing between the different views on the "Jewish question," they all had one main thing in common: the basic premise that there was indeed a question.[17] Thus, however diverse the positions on this subject might have been, we should realize that they all operated within the same frame of reference, one where it was tacitly assumed that the Jew constituted a *problem*.

Within such a frame of reference, the qualities intrinsic to Jewish history and Jewish culture would not disappear, but they would be taken outside their proper context and become relevant only in terms of the overall "Jewish question." For example, the keeping of Shabbat, the mainstay of traditional Jewish family and community life, would be seen as—always within the "problem approach"—one of the major obstacles to overcome if Jews were to be integrated within Polish society where they would have to follow rules established by the Christian majority.[18]

The pervasiveness of the "Jewish question" on the public arena did little to bring Jewish culture into the popular vocabulary, generally speaking;[19] if anything, the reverse was the case. The preformulated stereotypes and mythical constructions were both necessary and sufficient to perpetuate the essential definition of the Jew as a problem. Even those Poles who would take the side of the Jews in heated debate appealed to the Polish tradition of tolerance or to universal ethics rather than devote much effort to informing the public about the actual developments within the Jewish community.

Polish literature of the nineteenth and early twentieth centuries, with a few notable exceptions, still looked at the Jew from a singularly Polish perspective; again, the Jew was now a familiar figure of many popular novels and stories, without the readers' becoming any more familiar with his way of life and experience as a Jew (see: Grynberg, 1984a). And, reflecting the tensions in the real world, Jews were now likely to be portrayed in conflict with the Polish environment. Again, the literary portraits were by no means purely negative; indeed, much literature of the times stood clearly apart from journalistic writing in its benevolence towards the Jews, or at least in conveying an optimistic view of solutions to the "Jewish problem" within a generally optimistic view of social progress through education.[20] The premise still was that there indeed was a problem.

In short, while the discussions of things Jewish preoccupied public discourse of the times, the "problem approach" left little room, if any, for the Jews' views of themselves. Jewish culture, then flourishing in Poland in literature, drama, poetry, prose, held little meaning or interest for most Poles. The Jewish community, by then sharply divided along religious, political, social and cultural lines, was a problematic presence; Poles saw little to be gained by knowing more about its members, their lives, their concerns, their ideas.[21] Indeed, as is often remarked in present day discussions of the inter-war period, although Jews and Poles might have lived in the same country, politically and geographically, the gap between their respective experience was so tremendous that they might as well have lived in two different worlds.

This general picture of the "Jewish problem" displacing the notion of natural human contact does not alter much even where the two cultures actually came together. For although the ranks of Polonized Jews were growing rapidly during the first decades of the twentieth century, and many such Jews came to contribute actively to Polish arts and letters, their potential as ambassadors of Jewish culture was never fully actualized.[22] Often, they would know very little about the life of their people, coming as many did from families assimilated for two or more generations, families priding themselves on being Polish patriots. More importantly, the very process of Polonization often meant taking on the values of the majority as one's own, or, in this case, looking at the Jew through the filter of the "Jewish question."[23] Jewishness itself came to represent a stigma, something one was best advised to ignore, to pretend was not there[24] (very much in keeping with the views of that segment of the Polish intelligentsia which had become home for most of these Polonized Jews). In an effort to belong truly, a Jew had first to disassociate himself from the Jewish masses, their concerns, their lives. It was, psychologically, a rather high price to pay for social acceptance, and one which was quickly to become much too high a price in terms of individual dignity. As the climate in Poland became increasingly anti-Semitic, such Jews would see their right to Polishness increasingly being denied; many began to establish links with other Jews (see: Hertz, 1979). By that time, though, it was too late; with the war approaching, an opportunity to create a better understanding of the Jewish world was no longer there.

Under the Nazi occupation (1939–1945), the exclusion of the Jew from a common universe of discourse and experience became a physical reality as well, with the Jews forced into ghettos, sealed off from the outside world. The idea "Jew equals problem," translated by the Nazis into a whole variety of terms from "typhoid" to "cause of all wars," ultimately came to signify death. The degrees of assimilation were now to acquire an immediate survival value, as Polonized Jews had at least a chance at "passing" on the "Aryan" side.[25] For most of Poland's Jews, though, there was no escape from the death sentence pronounced by the "Final Solution": of the three hundred thousand or so survivors—about ten percent of the pre-war population—only about fifty thousand survived in Poland itself; the rest were Jews who either found themselves on Soviet territory after the September 1939 invasion of eastern Poland by the Soviet Union or subsequently fled there from the Germans.[26]

For a brief time after the German invasion of Poland on September 1, 1939, there appears to have been a chance for Poles and Jews to unite against the shared enemy. Poles and Jews did in fact fight together then; numerous reports, especially from Warsaw, convey a sense of camaraderie in the struggle and one of sharing in the despair of defeat. A short time later, though, other reports, carried by Poles who managed to cross the border from the East back into the Nazi-occupied territory, began to raise doubts about the Jews' loyalty to Poland. For if Poles generally were traumatized by the Soviet invasion, Jews—at least in the popular perception—were all too happy to greet the new rulers and to join their ranks in what amounted to another occupation.[27]

The idea that Jews as Jews had much more to fear from the Nazis than from the Soviet regime did not reduce the prevalent sense of betrayal. Under the circumstances, such a response was understandable: the main thrust of the Nazi oppression during the first few months of the occupation was directed against Poles in general and the Polish intelligentsia in particular. The very fact that some Poles who felt especially vulnerable would equip themselves with the "Jewish badges" for *protection*—in 1940—is one of the better indications of how the situation was defined in those early stages (Gross, 1979: 185-6). While Nazis quickly declared the Jews subject to special treatment—including forced labor and lowest food rations—it was the Poles, those in the country's elite, who were targeted for deportations and executions.

Even the establishment of the ghettos which, in Warsaw, meant the forced relocation of tens of thousands of both Jews and Poles, did not spark any wide protest. After many months of the Nazis' giving free reign to and actually provoking attacks on the Jews by Polish "hooligans," ghetto walls appeared to some as a form of protection (see, e.g. Ringelblum, 1974: 37–57). It was not until late 1941 that it became increasingly clear to the Jews just what kind of "protection" they were being offered. Hunger, disease, terror turned the Warsaw ghetto, with its nearly one-half million inhabitants, into a virtual concentration camp (see: Gutman, 1982). With no "deportations to the East" yet, the ghetto was destined to die. On the other side of the walls, life—by comparison—seemed normal, normal, that is, for a city under occupation.[28]

Not only was the situation of Jews in Warsaw especially difficult, but it was also of special significance for the Polish attitudes and actions. The center of the growing resistance to the Nazis, Warsaw was the center of an "underground state," with its political divisions and debates as well as the extensive network of clandestine press (see: Gross, 1979). And it is primarily on studies of Warsaw and Poland's leadership's positions that the historians today base their claims regarding the Poles' attitudes and behavior vis-à-vis the Holocaust.

At the center of many controversies surrounding this subject is Warsaw as well, more specifically, the events on both sides of the wall before and during the April 1943 uprising in the ghetto. At issue is not simply the degree of moral and material support extended to the Jewish fighters, but rather the very meaning of that struggle to the Poles, leaders as well as the people in the street. While few serious Polish historians would deny that the actual aid to the Jews, in the form of arms or resistance actions, was minimal, very few would admit that more could have been done had the Jew been perceived as equally as a member of Polish society.[29]

In terms of human lives, the fate of the ghetto fighters represents a tiny fraction in the overall tragedy of Polish Jewry. The fact that they fought alone, often to the amazement of Poles who were frankly surprised to see them fight at all[30] brings into focus, however, one of the key questions in the whole dispute about Poland and the Holocaust—the question of *solidarity*.

We may never know the exact number of Jews who survived thanks to Polish aid; we may never know the exact number of Poles who were killed for helping Jews—Poland was the only country under the Nazi occupation where even the smallest acts of aid were punishable by death—and we may never know how significant that aid was in relation to the aid that never came, the aid from the Allies.[31] Numbers, though, are not the only thing that matters. If so many of Polish Jewish survivors hold Poles in such contempt today, it is not because of numbers, it is because of words,[32] words they heard and remember, words of satisfaction at Hitler's solution to Poland's "Jewish question", words of sudden praise for Jews who decided to die fighting, words of total indifference. The Jews also remember fear, fear not directly of the Germans, but of any Pole approaching them on the street or in the forests, fear they could not contain from their eyes, fear that so often betrayed them. And those are the memories of those who *survived*.

Even looking at records by the very people who had helped them survive—many of which were first published in Poland—does not alter this bleak picture. First, they too were afraid, afraid of their neighbors, their relatives, their friends. Most of all, it often required great courage to define the Jew as a human being worth saving.[33] The risks, we should remember, were extremely high. But we also should not forget that the same high risks, the same death penalty, were attached to many a "normal" activity[34], and most particularly, to all activities related to resistance. And Poland's record of resistance is indeed exemplary, in terms of both the armed struggle and the preservation of social institutions and of the social fabric itself (see: Gross, 1979).

The question of the record of Polish resistance in respect to the Jews is much less clear. On the one hand, it was thanks to the efforts of the Polish underground (AK) that the world was first and then again and again informed about the atrocities committed against the Jews (appeals for help which went largely unanswered) (see: Laqueur, 1980). It was also thanks to a unique *organized* effort by a host of underground groups that many Jews, including many children were able to survive on the "Aryan" side.[35] That effort, though, came in *September 1942*, that is *after* the great majority of Polish Jews had already been murdered. Yet by its own leadership's estimates, the Home Army—the largest of the underground forces—was doing *too much* for the Jewish cause, too much, that is, from the point of view of popular support (Engel, 1983, 1987; Gutman, 1986). As for the rank-and-file, there are records of cooperating with the Jewish partisans as well as records of the killing of Jews who were hiding in the forests.[36] The extreme right wing of the underground had in fact openly advocated—and engaged in—fighting the Jews as well as Communists. And the not-so-extreme groups within the Poland's far reaching "underground state" had openly debated the future solutions to Poland's "Jewish problem" (Gross, 1986; Smolar, 1986), just as hundreds of thousands of Jews were being shipped to the gas chambers. Most important, perhaps, is the fact that Jews were *excluded* from this "underground state," that with the war came a re-definition of the civic society from a multi-national body to one reserved for the Poles only. [The Polish government-in-exile did have Jewish members but its underground representation in Poland itself did not.]

What all this means is that the war itself had not altered—to any significant degree, at least—the Poles' definition of the Jew, it had not made the Jew any less of a problem, so to speak. The war also had a profoundly and generally demoralizing effect on society, an effect rarely discussed, for it was not in line with the heroic vision shared by the Poles of their own resistance to the Nazis. Taking over Jewish property, even before the owners were known to be dead, was only a small part in the overall picture. And so was becoming accustomed to the fact that the Jews were dead.[37]

Within a few months of the Liberation came the realization of how pervasive was the destruction. As the survivors searched for other survivors, first in their home towns and then, in larger centers where Jewish aid organizations would be established very early on, they often found themselves alone. It was not just the other members of their families that they would search for in vain; their whole world had disappeared. Time after time, of a community a few thousand strong, only one, two, three persons had remained alive. Jewish places of worship were destroyed or abandoned; Jewish homes all had new Polish tenants, some having moved in within days after the Jews' departure, others having had to wait for the Germans to leave the choice locations they had occupied; Jewish shops all now belonged to new owners, as did most of the property left behind.

There was hardly a trace that the Jews once lived there. Warsaw's Jewish quarter had been razed as the Nazis methodically completed their task of ridding that city of its nearly four hundred thousand Jews. And, with most of the victims killed in the extermination camps, there were also no cemeteries, no individual graves, no memorials to their death. It was more than the three million Polish Jews who died—it was a people, their way of life, their culture, even their memory.

Yet, few of the survivors were willing to accept such a sentence. Those who did left Poland very shortly after the war ended, feeling the wounds were too deep to heal at this one huge mass graveyard, and hoping to rebuild their lives far away. But many resolved to stay, and when later joined by some one hundred and fifty thousand Jews returning from the Soviet Union, they tried to reconstruct not only their individual lives but their community life as well (see: DobroSzycki, 1973; Hillel, 1985; Borwicz, 1986).

The challenge was enormous, yet it did not appear insurmountable; for the first time in Poland's history, Jews were now considered fully equal citizens under the law and, more importantly, were guaranteed not only freedom of religious expression but open access to *all* occupations and professions.[38] Granted an opportunity for real integration, and seeing how, also for the first time, the new government was taking a very definite stand against anti-Semitism, many Jews who would not otherwise have been happy with Communist rule saw it as a chance to begin anew, on an equal footing with the others, a chance to belong. Small shopkeepers and artisans would now form Jewish cooperatives, working hard for a market ravaged by the war. Educated Jews were pouring into the ranks of the new administration, filling posts they could never have occupied before, now not only open to them, but calling for their skills at a time of great shortage; the Polish intelligentsia, the prime target of the Nazis, was both severely depleted and not trusted (often justifiably so) by the new authorities.[39]

What developed then was rather paradoxical: with so many fewer Jews than ever before, their relative power within the larger society was greater than ever before. For one, the country was now ruled by a Communist minority, a minority which had traditionally included a disproportionately high number of Jews and which had been generally less affected by the war losses, since many of the Jews with Leftist leanings were more likely than other Jews to have escaped early to the East and thus also more likely to have survived.[40] Secondly, adding to the Jews within the strict governing elites were those many who supported the new system as the source of hope for a better, more just society and a fair deal for the Jews (see: Nowakowska, 1950/1983).[41] They would also believe that the horror of the

Holocaust would in itself constitute a form of guarantee that there would be no return to pre-war hostility and discrimination.

With time, they were to be proven wrong on all counts. To begin with, it soon became clear that Jewish survivors were not exactly welcome. More often than not, upon returning to his home town, a Jew would be greeted with the neighbors' surprised look, mixed with a certain disappointment rather than joy; there was a sense that he should have been dead. Numerous witness accounts report the phrases heard by returning survivors, phrases essentially giving Hitler credit for "solving our Jewish problem," and the feeling that just when it had seemed that the problem was solved, Jews were coming back, coming back, it would be feared, not only to reclaim their property but to take revenge (see: Hillel, 1985; Gilbert, 1985: 811–831). The fact that they were often coming back armed with the power of the new state's authority did not help matters. For with or without basis, the Jew would now become identified with the Communist, thus doubling not only the fear, but also the hatred.[42]

In a country in the grip of a veritable civil war, in which the regime was fighting both widespread popular opposition and organized military resistance, a Jew would become an ideal target. An estimated number of Jews killed during the first year after the war, some by underground units, others quite spontaneously by ordinary members of local populations, reaches several hundred (see, esp. Polonsky, ed., 1980). Yet if attacks on individual Jews were commonplace, they would frequently remain unknown beyond the borders of a given locale. There would be rumors, of course; there were also some escapees, telling their stories, but there were not enough rumors and stories to result in any widespread reaction other than a gradual movement towards larger centers, where larger numbers provided some degree of protection against the unexpected popular wrath.[43] And while many Jews were leaving the country, many more were still arriving from the East, making it that much less evident that something was going fundamentally wrong.

In July 1946, the situation changed dramatically. News of the pogrom in Kielce, in which forty-one Jews were killed and many more seriously injured, provoked a panic. It was not the first pogrom—earlier ones had come in Cracow, Rzeszów, Chełm—but it was the first on such a scale and the first where members of the local authorities were directly involved. Ignited by the age-old tale of ritual murder, a huge crowd had gathered outside the local Jewish community house, cheering the killings going on inside and making certain few would be able to escape unharmed. Within a few hours it was all over; the wounded, fearing for their lives in a local hospital, were promptly, though not without difficulty, transported elsewhere (Hillel, 1985).

There was and still is much debate over who should be held responsible for this massive outbreak of anti-Jewish violence. While the Communist authorities would place the blame squarely on the Fascist-type underground, later and elsewhere, historians (e.g. Checinski, 1982) have speculated about the extent of Soviet involvement in what appears to have been a skillful provocation (unpublished testimonies I had access to confirm their suspicions.) Yet whatever politically motivated manipulation one envisions behind the scenes, the fact remains that the crowds in Kielce acted more than responsively to the initial spark, a fact not lost on the Jews in Poland at the time. The Jews were also keenly aware that their demands for just punishment of the murderers might have to go unanswered, for while eight of the instigators were quickly tried and executed, their trial sparked a wide popular protest (Hillel, 1985). The search for other perpetrators of Kielce crime practically stopped. And, though appreciating the voices of Polish democrats raised in their defence, the Jews knew that without strong support from the Church there would be little hope for any real change in attitude among the population at large. The Church, however, was first silent on the issue; then, when it did condemn the killings, it also made clear that the Jews should not be surprised at justifiable popular anger against their intrusion in Polish affairs—as far as the Church was concerned, the Jews were now siding with Poland's enemies, namely the Communists, and so should be prepared to bear the consequences (see: Wieviorka, 1984; Smolar, 1986).

The signals were all too clear for thousands of Jews, as they began to flee, often on foot and often illegally crossing the border. Within a few months, large communities which had been established in the western part of Poland (lands taken over from the Germans and thus much more receptive to Jewish settlers) saw their populations depleted; smaller communities, especially those in central Poland, were now disappearing altogether. All in all, some one hundred thousand Jews left the country (Gilbert, 1985), many hoping to make their way to Palestine, a destination then very much in favor with the Communist authorities. The appeal of the Zionist solution to the "Jewish question" was at its highest, even among those who had previously opposed it, both ideologically and sentimentally (Hillel, 1985).

Poland, after close to nine centuries, could no longer be considered a home.

And yet, if the Kielce pogrom and its aftermath convinced many Jews to leave, a fair number chose to stay. Among them was a group important in both size and social position—Jewish Communists, socialists and, more generally, people supporting the new regime; for them, it seems, the ideological commitment or simply the commitment to the reconstruction of Poland had priority. But there were also Jews who felt it necessary to stay in Poland precisely because they were committed to Polish Jewry, Jews who refused to break the historical continuity of Jewish presence in this country (see: Borwicz, 1986).[44] Yet if the motivations to remain in Poland were constant, the situation had changed: now, both the Jews and the Jewish community were strongly encouraged to become "invisible."[45]

Keeping in mind that the majority of Jews who resolved to stay and to participate in the rebuilding of Poland's economic and cultural life were already highly Polonized, and remembering that the official "internationalist" doctrine prohibited differentiating between Jews and non-Jews, the shift towards "invisibility" no longer appears to be a simple reaction to the anti-Semitic climate of the day.

In other words, the initiative often belonged to the Jews themselves, who were convinced that complete integration was now both possible and desirable, and strengthened in that conviction by the democratic public opinion. At the same time, the pressure to blend into the background, exerted on Jewish Party activists and members of the administration in particular was by no means purely ideological. In subtle or direct terms, a Jew would be told to change his name and to avoid any public display of his Jewishness; many of those who were not told did so out of concern for the cause. When assessed realistically, the minority position of the proponents of a socialist Poland could only be hurt by the perceived and high Jewish involvement.[46] In practice, of course, invisibility was not always possible: some Jews were already too well known for them suddenly to change colors; some had the "wrong" physical attributes; some, though speaking perfect Polish, had retained just enough of a Yiddish inflection to make them easily identifiable. Imperfections aside, however they generally came to be identified—and to identify themselves—as "Poles of Jewish origin",[47] with emphasis placed on the first term and a polite silence covering the rest. Again, individual variations notwithstanding, their Polishness was not to be questioned; their Jewishness gradually to disappear altogether.

It should not be forgotten that we are talking about the period immediately following the Nazi genocide, a time when it would have been difficult, if not impossible, neutrally to "remind" someone of his Jewish ancestry—when the memory of the deadly significance of such reminders was all too fresh. For Communists and democratic Poles alike, the very mention of someone's Jewish roots against that person's wishes constituted a racist remark; to bring the topic up in non-Jewish company was anti-Semitism by definition. Jewishness became reduced to a creation of the hostile environment.

Finally, while the Left would earlier have seen a societal transformation as a sufficient guarantee for a permanent solution to the "Jewish question," it had to accept that in the aftermath of Kielce this new social order was not by itself spelling the end to anti-Semitism. What was needed, and what was implemented, was a double-front strategy: on the one hand, Jews were to be made more "productive" and more equally distributed throughout society; on the other hand, the vestiges of old anti-Semitism, this product of the capitalist order, were to be actively fought, together with other remnants of the "bourgeois mentality", one should add. [It became illegal, for example, to make anti-Semitic pronouncements in public, and the law was enforced. It was also during this early period that a number of prominent Polish intellectuals wrote, highly critically, about anti-Semitism (see: Smolar, 1986).] A sense of modest optimism prevailed, for while no one would claim that the "Jewish question" had already become insignificant, there was also much hope that it might, given time and a proper education. Thus with concerted efforts on both sides, the Jews' complete assimilation appeared as not only a desirable goal but an attainable one.

What about those Jews who did not wish to assimilate, those Jews who were hoping to bring new life into the Jewish community, to continue as Jews? For them, time presented increasingly bad odds. The post-Kielce wave of emigration had severely depleted their ranks, while the post-Kielce atmosphere was depleting their hopes. Then, the positive attitude of the new regime began gradually to change, as the demands of ideological dogmatism grew with the tightening of Communist rule. Jewish Jews would now often be accused of a "nationalist deviation," one of the main threats to the success of the socialist revolution, during the days when Polish nationalism came under heavy attack as well. The 1948 consolidation of power, joining the Communist and Socialist parties into a "United Polish Workers' Party" under Communist control meant that the political life of the Jewish Left was over (except, of course, for the Communists themselves). A growing Cold War climate meant that contacts with as well as aid from Jewish organizations abroad would no longer be tolerated (see: Hirszowicz, 1986). And a growing pressure to transform the society into a truly secular one left little room for the worship and teachings of Judaism.

Within a few years—the process would be completed in 1949 when the Communists took control of Poland's Jewish community organizations—the life of Polish Jewry came to depend on the state.[48]

What did this imply in actual practice? To take but one example, the Jewish Historical Institute, located in Warsaw and providing some centralized facilities for the work of various historical commissions created almost immediately after the war (as the survivors felt an urgent need to record as much as possible), was eventually to become the sole arena for research on Jewish history. Now such research was first restricted to the Holocaust, and then directed in accordance with the demands of Marxist historiography as it was officially defined. The result? The Institute's task would be to demonstrate that the only good Jews during the war were the proletarians and activists of the "proper" Left, helped in their struggles by the only good Poles, namely the Communist underground (see: Wein, 1970).

It would be a serious mistake, though, to equate such dependence on the state (shared as it was with Poland's cultural life at large) with a total state control over the realm of collective memory. For as important as the official historiography is for defining and re-defining collective past, the past lives on "unofficially" as well. A continuity of popular tradition, relying on small and private acts of remembrance, is further helped by the collective mythology as captured and perpetuated through literature and art. Indeed, as we have seen in the previous chapter, the state, with all the means at its disposal, including control of education and the extensive censorship, failed and failed badly to subjugate Poland's memory. Even the distant past, let alone the past still within the experience of the older generations, proved resistant to the abuses of direct manipulation; heroes and deeds that had been denied public memorials were celebrated privately, while blanks in the historical accounts would be filled with passed-on stories. In a way, collective memory was preserved not in spite of ideological encroachments but because of them, becoming a major field of struggle for an independent national identity and culture. The very position of the state as Poland's chief memory keeper existed primarily on paper, it seems, while the actual job was being done privately with help from the Church and then, increasingly, from the alternative cultural network created by the opposition.

Yet, as we look more closely at what happened to the memory of the Jew during the subsequent decades, we should keep in mind that the state enjoyed some distinct advantages in this field, advantages which would translate its potential for controlling memory into an actual monopoly.[49] At issue here are what might be called the "property rights" to memory, or the question of *who* was to become responsible for the construction of a memorial to Poland's Jews. Also at issue is the question of what *kind* of a memorial was to emerge or of the ways in which the Jew would be remembered. Now, in terms of memory keeping, the history of Polish attitudes towards the Jew—the long history of ignoring the Stranger and the shorter one of identifying his very presence as a "problem"—would seem unlikely suddenly to produce the wide social base of knowledge needed to counteract the regime's efforts to manipulate memory. Even the shock of the Holocaust, as we observed earlier, was not enough radically to alter the problem approach to things Jewish; indeed, if anything, it gave it a new strength, witness the attempts to eliminate the problem on the one hand and the attempts to eliminate the Jews on the other. In effect, then, although the large Jewish community had all but disappeared, the "Jewish question" was still too much a part of the present for the memory of the Jew to be quietly celebrated in his home or in what had once been his home.

The early post-Holocaust years saw a massive departure of Jewish survivors, carrying with them the memories of Jewish life as it once was and the ever more painful memories of suffering. Now scattered all around the globe, they would join other Polish Jews, who had emigrated earlier, to become the prime keepers of the memory of Polish Jewry. Resolved not to forget—and not to let the world forget—torn away from the "natural habitat" of memory, from their home towns and villages as well as from the sites of the death camps, survivors embraced writing as the only possible form of commemorating their people (see: Wieviorka & Niborski, 1983). Some four hundred and forty "Memorial Books" devoted to smaller and larger Polish Jewish communities have appeared, during the last forty years, in the United States, Canada, Argentina, Israel, France. They all serve as monuments to the past, as a kind of symbolic cemetery for the exterminated millions. Composed mainly in Yiddish, these "Memorial Books" are a way of sealing collective memory, yet often of sealing it off as well, from the younger generations no longer versed in the language of their ancestors.[50]

But the memory work has taken other, more open forms as well, be it in numerous autobiographical accounts published in English or French, or in research undertaken in such centers as New York or Jerusalem. If to those very direct efforts at memory keeping one adds the work of literature and art, preserving the picture of Jewish life as well as that of the Holocaust, the reservoir of memory appears to be vast indeed. And if we were to include here the works which, while not dealing with the past, are informed by it or to consider the whole stream of creative transformation of the Eastern European Jewish tradition, the memory of Polish Jews acquires a prominent position in contemporary Jewish life, not surprisingly, considering that about one-third of the world's Jews can trace their roots to Polish lands (Sachar, 1986).

Yet if both in spite of the tremendous losses during the Holocaust and because of them, the memory of Polish Jews lives on in different corners of the world, its impact on Poland has been minimal, at least until very recently. The Jews did not simply leave the country; they also severed their connection with it in a more than understandable reaction to the circumstances of their departure.[51] Already apparent among emigrants from the 1920s and 1930s, who were fleeing injustice, discrimination and economic hardship, and ever stronger among Jews who survived the

Holocaust only to become targets of popular wrath, was a sense that
Poland—as a country and as a nation—was so unequivocally hostile that it
was best forgotten. Thus if the "Memorial Books" recreate, in often
minute detail, Poland's "Jewish topography," they speak very sparingly
about Polish neighbors and the gentile world in general; they may contain
a good deal of nostalgia for the lost homeland, with its particular beauty
and serenity, but it is a longing after the countryside and not one for the
country itself (Wieviorka & Niborski, 1983; Kugelmass & Boyarin, 1983).
Indeed, the picture of Poland preserved by these generations of Jewish
emigrants is singularly dark, where memories of anti-Semitism experienced first-hand combine with a sense of betrayal and the anguish of seeing
one's pain treated with indifference to make up an image of the "eternal"
Polish anti-Semitism.[52] What else could one expect from a society forever
united in its hatred of the Jew but the destruction of the last traces of the
Jewish presence? What could possibly be the use of talking to Poles about
the past when they so staunchly deny any responsibility for it? Why not
simply close that chapter?[53]

Once written off, as it were, Poland appears no longer to be a major
concern for Jewish memory keepers. Individual initiatives, be they to erect
a monument, to preserve a grave, to publish memoirs in Polish (abroad) or
to argue over historical truth, even when coupled with more organized
efforts to influence Jewish affairs within Poland, were never enough to
affect significantly the memory void surrounding the Jew. The most
concrete testimony to this state of affairs may be found at Jewish cemeteries around the country, but especially in Warsaw. Their absolute decay
cannot be explained by simply blaming the state. Nor was there much of
an invitation from the other side either to discuss or to contribute to the
preservation of the Jewish presence in Poland's collective memory.[54]

From the Polish perspective, such a sealed off memory was best left
abroad if the "Jewish question" were to be solved; there, after all, it was
as "invisible," as the Jews themselves were encouraged to become. The
assimilation project could only be hurt, it was believed, by granting too
much room to Jewish Jews, and, it would definitely be hurt by bringing up
in an open public forum the concerns felt and expressed by people who
saw this project as an impossible mission.[55]

But what about the Jews still in Poland? Were they somehow less
concerned with remembering the past? Or were they not allowed to
remember? The answer lies somewhere in the middle. On the one hand,
those Jews remaining in Poland were, as we said, in large majority
committed to Polishness and committed to the enormous task of rebuilding
the war-ravaged country. For them, the present and the future had priority,
not the past.[56] They were eager to and they did participate in the often

exhilarating work of creating a new society; the disillusion with Communism would come much later, just as the awareness of Stalinist excesses did not emerge until after the fact. They not only accepted, but frequently propagated the model of "silent Jewishness," keen on rendering the whole issue irrelevant, both in public and in private. At home, steeped in secular tradition, there was no room for Jewish ritual; oftentimes, there was often no room for any talk about the past (see, e.g., Blumsztain, 1985). In a way, those Jews were migrating symbolically into the world of Polish priorities, Polish concerns, Polish values.

For others, the times were not conducive to celebrating their Jewishness. Pressures on the remnants of the Jewish community made it very difficult to maintain some form of continuity of tradition.[57] And for people such as historians, writers and artists, directly involved in public memory keeping the restrictions imposed by the state were gradually to define both the field and the means of their work.[58] Finally, they themselves would restrict their efforts, or at least focus them, on the area seen as calling for most immediate attention—the Holocaust experience. The memory of Polish Jews was thus to migrate again, now inwards, away from the richness of life and into an abyss of suffering. Memory became martyrology.

The very focusing of remembrance on the years of the greatest tragedy in the history of the Jewish people was by no means unique to Poland. To this day, the Holocaust figures so prominently in the Jews' sense of their past that a number of critics have begun to fear it could overshadow all else—with the possible exception of Israel—as a force informing Jewish conduct and attitudes in the modern world (see: Neusner, 1981). What was unique to Poland was a gradual displacement of the Jewish-identity-forming function of memory by one of an almost exactly opposite nature. The evoking of Jewish martyrdom, be it by the Jews themselves or by sympathetic Polish novelists and poets, has served as a reminder of the ultimate evil of anti-Semitism; it would strengthen the rejection of discrimination and intolerance, already advocated in principle, and it would create some much needed empathy for the Jew. It would not, intentionally or otherwise, work to set him further apart. For in Poland, the lessons drawn from the Holocaust, as we observed earlier, were detrimental to any maintenance of Jewish identity; complete assimilation was the ideal to the near exclusion of all other options. For the tragedy not to repeat itself, the Jew was never to be singled out again. The very distinction between Jews and non-Jews was to disappear together with the "Jewish question," securing and secured by the Jew's "invisibility." Jewish martyrology was thus all that was to remain of the Jewish presence, a constant warning of the dangers of chauvinism and prejudice.

In time, though, Jewish martyrdom would be displaced again, so as no longer to serve exclusively Jewish causes, even within such a narrow definition. The emphasis shifted from deploring anti-Semitism to deploring Nazism *in toto*. And a continuous condemnation of Nazism, justified as it was on moral grounds, would also serve an important political function: the new regime was, after all, closely allied with the Soviet Union, the extolled liberator of Poland, and this alone was believed to offer some much needed basis for its popular support. In other words, reminding Poles of just how cruel the German occupation had been was also a way of convincing them that they should be grateful to the Communist forces for regaining their freedom.

Within such a new, universalized framework, memory of the Jew proved to be a valuable aid. The mass extermination of the Jews not only *was* evil, but was also fairly far removed from the political concerns of the moment. We need to realize that, as important as martyrology has been for the new regime, it has by no means been problem-free. With the major role in the Polish resistance played by the Home Army (AK) associated with the Polish government-in-exile in London, and with the major event being the 1944 Warsaw Uprising, organized by the AK in hopes of establishing a non-Soviet provisional government in a freed Warsaw and costing the lives of two hundred thousand people and the virtual destruction of the city, memory of the war demanded tremendous work to keep in line with the official picture of Communist bravery and bourgeois apathy. Under the conditions of a veritable civil war, to commemorate the heroism of one's present enemies was simply out of the question, just as it would be even to mention the victims of the other occupant, namely the Soviet Union.

From this point of view, one could say that, the Jews were relatively "safe"; indeed, a monument to the Warsaw Ghetto fighters was erected in 1948, at a high point of silence about the Warsaw Uprising. The early post-war years generally produced an array of works dealing with the Jews' tragic fate, ranging from survivors' accounts and witness testimonies to fictional writings and poetry.

It was as if, at least for a while, the state's broad interests coincided with the Jews concentrated efforts to secure a prominent position for the Jew as a victim in Poland's collective memory.

There was a problem, though, or rather two problems, both to become more acute as time went on. First, such a public commemoration of Jewish suffering, happening, as it did, during the years when Poles were being denied a chance to mourn so many of their own people, did not, perhaps could not, translate into a private mourning. As we observed earlier, what was most painful for many Jewish survivors in the post-Holocaust situation, was the general indifference, if not the quiet satisfaction with which the disappearance of Jews was greeted in Polish towns and villages. Could the public display of affection change that? Not when it came packaged within a massive propaganda effort, and especially not when it came to be identified with the new rulers, Jews and Communists, or Jews/Communists. To erect a monument to the Ghetto fighters, while "forgetting" about the Polish insurrectionists, could spark resentment rather than a moment of reflection.[59]

Thus if the Jew did exist publicly as a martyr, to some extent he existed only publicly. And, secondly, he came to be there alone, deprived of the company of the Jew from before the destruction. While Jewish martyrology could be and was useful in a struggle against anti-Semitism, the ultimate ideal of complete assimilation left little room for the celebration of Jewish tradition. Rightly or wrongly, it was thought that the best way to avoid re-kindling anti-Semitic sentiments was to talk as little as possible about the Jews themselves. [The kind of vocal advocacy of Jewish interests one is accustomed to in North America is a recent development, for Jews and for North America (see: Morse, 1983; Wyman, 1984; Abella & Troper, 1983; Nurenberger, 1985; Lipstadt, 1986).] The principle of invisibility, would be extended from individual Jews to Jewish affairs in general and Polish-Jewish affairs in particular. With the best of intentions, perhaps, silence became a preferred strategy for dealing with the "Jewish question."[60]

But *was* there still a "Jewish question"? Had it not ended with the deaths of over ninety percent of Poland's Jews? Were not survivors leaving the country by the thousands? And were not those remaining in Poland either already or close to becoming "Poles of Jewish origin"? In short, considering just how radically the situation had changed, could one really view the Jew as a problem?

True, the situation was radically different. And yet, as I argued earlier, the situation of the Jews in and by itself had been only partially responsible for perceiving their presence as a problem. The actual conditions of Jewish presence were more like building blocks in a construction planned and defined in *a priori* fashion. Thus we would be best advised to look for answers beyond numbers and events, and to look again at the collective definitions of the Jew. Did those change?

Yes and no. Yes, in that the figure of the Jew as a martyr was a new element in public discourse, displacing if not replacing many a traditional image. And yes, in that much of anti-Semitic discourse was now censored out of the public forum altogether. But no, in that the very silence adopted as a way to deal with the "Jewish question," the very invisibility of individual Jews, indicated forcefully, albeit implicitly, that Jewishness *was* a problem. And no, in that if the old arguments about economic competition had lost much of their base, another set of old arguments, now about the "corruption of the Polish soul" acquired new strength and relevance.

From the very beginning, that is from 1944 when the new Soviet-backed regime was established, the Jews were being identified with the Communist rulers. There would be nothing new in the warnings against the dangers of "Judeo-Commune" except that now the danger was no longer merely ideological, it had the face of the local administrator, military officer, chief of security. In other words, the Jew was no longer a potential threat—he was in power. And whether by coincidence or Soviet design (some historians would not rule out this possibility) Jews came to occupy the particularly sensitive posts within the new regime, in control of economy, cultural policy and, most important, internal security. That these Jewish Communists felt little, if any, allegiance to the Jewish people did not matter; that among those persecuted by them, those imprisoned and tortured, were many Jews, did not matter. What did matter was that a group of "foreigners" was now imposing a foreign system and foreign rule on the Polish people.

Let there be no mistakes: the new regime *was,* at least initially, a foreign one, with only minimal support among Polish society. It *was* a cruel regime, especially during its Stalinist phase, though not nearly as cruel as its Soviet mentor.[61] And the Jews *were* among the ranks of its most ruthless forces, with many more Jews supporting it in more passive ways. At issue here is not their guilt or innocence, but their "foreignness." Their deeds were not judged simply on their merit; they were judged as deeds of the Jews. Their crimes reflected less on the nature of a totalitarian regime and more on Jewishness itself. In short, the zeal with which many Jewish Communists were constructing this new society was all too real. That they did so as Jews rather than as Communists was a matter of definition.

The popularity of the image of the Jew-as-Stalinist is not surprising. It gave, after all, a chance for absolution to many a non-Jew involved in the abhorred apparatus of oppression.[62] As in other instances of using the Jew as a convenient scapegoat, there was just enough truth to make it convincing and just enough explanatory power to render other interpretations spurious. What was surprising, or indeed what later was to come as a shock to many Poles and Jews alike, was the ease with which the regime itself picked this imagery up and made it into an official credo. But we are now already in the 1960s, so that a word of explanation as to what happened in between is in order.

What happened was 1956, the "Polish October," a workers' revolt which brought Gomułka to power, with great hopes of constructing a *Polish* brand of socialism. Stalinists, both Jewish and non-Jewish were dethroned. A spirit of reform swept the Party, allowing an unprecedented openness of public debates. Indeed a full-fledged battle within the Party centered around the principles on which this new "Polish socialism" was to rest.The faction which supported Gomułka—and which included most of the Jewish activists—advocated wide ranging reforms in the direction of a more humane and a more democratic system; it would see the future as a return to the best traditions of the Left, a return to real socialism, unmarred by Stalinist abuses. On the other side were people who interpreted "Polish" quite literally, wanting first to rid the Party of "foreign influences," the often Moscow-trained, often Jewish Communists in other words.[63]

At issue here were both ideology and personnel; the Jews found themselves under attack on both counts. They were at an advantage, though, at least initially. Not only did they side with Gomułka, but they also had much of the media behind them. Subtle and not so subtle anti-Jewish undertones of settling accounts with Stalinism would be swiftly dealt with. The press was nearly unanimous in its condemnation of anti-Semitism. Jews would be reassured of protection from both the state and progressive forces in society-at-large (Checinski, 1982).

Not all Jews, of course. Those responsible for the horrors of oppression had to leave—many left the country, others withdrew from the public arena (see: Torańska, 1985). Those not directly responsible but directly exposed to popular anti-Semitism—parents with children in school, for example, where a brief re-introduction of religious instruction was causing much resentment of those children who did not attend (where any name-calling was usually anti-Semitic) reconsidered the pros and cons of emigration. With the borders reopened, many Jews simply seized the opportunity to make a better life elsewhere. With the arrival of many thousands from internment in the Soviet Union, people who needed no convincing as to the virtues of freedom, the ranks of Jewish emigrants swelled for the second time in Poland's post-war history.[64] All in all, by the early 1960s, only some thirty thousand or so Jews remained in the country, about one-tenth of the post-war total.

Those who did stay, though, believed as strongly as ever that the system, now so profoundly improved, would guarantee a decent life and a good future. They were not alone in these hopes. Most Poles put an inordinate amount of trust in Gomułka and his promises of a more fair and open society. The Jews were also not alone in their disappointment when, not long after 1956, official theories and practices would again become entrenched in dogmatism of Soviet origins.[65] But they were the first and the largest group to pay the price. The gradual change in the ideological line spelled not only a departure from the 1956 ideals, but also a parting with many of Gomułka's supporters. The nationalist faction within the Party was quickly becoming a powerful force (see: Lendvai, 1972).

The first to be let go were Jews in the military and security apparatus; next, those higher up within the Party echelons. The "purge" began as early as 1959, by the early 1960s, it would be quietly conducted in ever larger politically sensitive areas. (So quietly, in fact, that most Jews in the fields of culture and science as well as administration, though frequently Party members themselves, were not aware of any approaching threat (Anonymous, 1971; Checinski, 1982).)

The first public signs of trouble came in 1967, in the wake of Israel's Six Day War. Poland, which had previously supported Israel, in line with Soviet hopes for a socialist outpost in the Middle East, was now taking a sharp turn, again in line with Soviet policies. Israel was accused of outright aggression, and Zionism was condemned completely. Translated into practice on the domestic scene, this meant that Jews, all Jews, would become suspect, with their loyalty to Israel being treated as a given and their "Zionist connection" declared a serious threat to Poland's national interests.[66]

The charges were, of course, absurd on both counts. By that time, most if not all true Zionists had left Poland, and it would be hard to imagine what kind of danger Zionism could present there anyway.[67] The charges also resonated badly with popular sentiments. Poles, perceiving a great similarity between Israel's struggle for survival and their own history of fighting for independence, also felt a degree of pride, or more properly patronage, towards the Israeli fighters—these were, after all, mainly Polish Jews, often trained in the Polish military. There was much joy then over the victories of "our Jews" over "Soviet Arabs."

The situation was to change, though, and change radically. In March 1968, students in Warsaw and other cities went to the streets in protest against the increasing encroachments on democratic freedoms, against the stifling of Polish cultural and intellectual life. The spark to a long brewing revolt against the betrayal of "Polish October" was the censors' barring of the National Theater's production of Poland's foremost classic romantic play, *Dziady*. Rumored to be the Soviet response to the audience's display of anti-Russian feelings—the drama, written at the time of partition, does contain strong anti-Tsarist-Russia statements—this censorship was the last straw.[68] Within days, it looked as if the anger of students and intellectuals might ignite a much wider protest, somewhat akin to the developments in neighboring Czechoslovakia. Something had to be done. And something was.

Apart from sending in troops and closing universities, putting hundreds of people in jail and threatening others, the government used the ultimate in containment strategies—blame it on the Jews. Polish students were declared innocent victims, led astray by a bunch of Zionists, cosmopolitans and revisionists, working in concert with Western imperialism to undermine the social order. To make the accusations sound even better, a Stalinist past or Stalinist parents would be cited together with the original, properly Jewish sounding names (see: Lendvai, 1972; Blit, ed., 1968).

There was just enough truth in this new version of the "Jewish conspiracy theory" to make it convincing: among the students' leaders and the intellectuals who supported their cause, were disproportionately many, with a Jewish background and a long-time membership on the Left.[69]

As a containment strategy, it proved successful, and this on two fronts. First, the struggle for greater freedom of expression did not spread to include other issues and other segments of society; Poland's working class remained generally indifferent to call for a common front. And an attack on the country's elite, framed as it was within the anti-Zionist discourse, remained a matter of concern for the elite only. In essence, Jews were seen as paying a fair price for instituting the very system that now made them targets.[70] Thus, what was happening on the top would be of little concern to an ordinary Pole. Later, when the "purge" in the areas of culture and science translated into yet another massive wave of Jewish emigration, one could sense a kind of popular envy of those who *could* leave when everyone else was given no such choice.[71] And apart from voices from within the student and intellectual communities, there was not much public indignation over the revival of official anti-Semitism; with the notable exception of the Catholic parliamentary club *Znak,* the Church too remained indifferent.[72]

It is from those times that we have some statistics on the number of Jews in Poland, data subsequently used to estimate their present number. As a way of preparing for the "purge," the internal security service helped compile a list of all potential candidates, a list of some thirty thousand names (Checinski, 1982). This list helped to make processing of exit visa applications fast and efficient (though there were cases of Jews so successful at their invisibility that they would be excluded from the records altogether). It should be stressed that this list included the names of people with one Jewish grandmother, and that they too could leave the country, together with often extended families with no traces of Jewish ancestry. All in all, as arbitrary as such a list was, it had a great deal of practical significance, both in terms of targeting people for close supervision by the security service and for future attack, and in terms of defining who, from the vantage point of the state, was Jewish and thus permitted to leave (see also: Banas, 1979).

"Permitted" might be the wrong word to use here; Jews were being fired from their jobs, and professionals granted a chance to earn a minimum wage in manual occupations. They would often be confronted with the loss of housing, as it often came with a given job, as well as the loss of other privileges including such things as access to decent medical care.[73] At Party meetings in various institutions, Jewish members were promptly expelled, damaging even further their career opportunities. Jewish students were not readmitted once the universities re-opened.

Even when spared direct humiliation, as some were, Jews were not spared the dirt cast in a large scale and lasting propaganda campaign. That campaign appeared surreal at times—Jews were being charged simultaneously with dogmatism and revisionism, cosmopolitan outlook and chauvinism, Zionism and Trotskyism. And maybe most surreal of all, the Polish media were now zealously attacking anyone daring to condemn Poland for this very campaign, claiming that Poland was not and had never been an anti-Semitic country. With time, the very focus of media attention would shift away from charges against domestic ''Zionists'' and onto the anti-Polish slanders propagated by Jews in general (see: Lendvai, 1972). It all began to make perfect sense—the local Jews working together with their brothers abroad to ruin Poland's reputation.

One aspect of these double-talk exercises deserves our special attention, for to make Poland's case in the present meant the rewriting of the past. Starting in the early sixties, and growing to full force at the end of the decade, official historiography adopted a new line in dealing with the ''Jewish question.'' Whereas previously, Jewish martyrdom had figured prominently within a general picture of Poland's war tragedies, it would now be appropriated, pure and simple (see: Dawidowicz, 1981). The three million Polish Jews now all became Poles, and when added to the three million Polish victims of the Nazis, made up the total of *six million Poles*— victims of *genocide*.[74] The Holocaust was no longer a Jewish property. There was nothing unique in the situation of Jews, nothing unique to the ''Final Solution''.

The very distinction between ''concentration'' and ''extermination'' camps, a distinction which meant life or death, would now be erased from historical accounts. Editors of the Polish ''Great Encyclopedia'', who had ''overlooked'' this new interpretation in the 1967 edition, were subsequently fired, and a supplementary volume was issued to correct all the ''mistakes''.

Together with erasing the Jewishness of the victims came an effort to make the Jew disappear altogether. By 1974, when a representative edition of a ''History of Poland'' was published (also in English), only two paragraphs in over six hundred pages were devoted to Poland's Jews.[75] It would be easy to find works dealing with the history of a given city in which no mention was made at all of the large Jewish community which had once lived there (see, e.g. Wisse, 1978). In Warsaw, the city museum offered no indication that Jews were once so much a part of the community. Tourist guides carefully omitted sites related to Jewish history. And, at the most symbolic of places—Auschwitz—tablets in Yiddish and Hebrew lay alongside those in Polish, Dutch, Russian, French, Italian, with the inscription commemorating the victims omitting the very word "Jew." In short, silence surrounding the Jew had now been extended to cover his life as well as his death (see: Vinecour, 1977).[76]

It being an anti-Semitic campaign, there were no more stops put to anti-Semitic discourse. Erasing the traces of Jewish presence in Poland while—at the same time—giving an official seal and a public forum to anti-Jewish attacks almost had to produce some confusion. Confusion was particularly evident in an area of the propaganda offensive essential to its overall success: portraying the Jews as singularly ungrateful to Poland, both for its traditional tolerance and for aid extended during World War II. To make such an argument, the Jew not only had to exist, but his fate during the dark years of the Nazi occupation had to have been different from that of non-Jews. Internal coherence, however, did not seem to matter much there. Similarly, there was the evocation of the principle that no distinction should be made between Jews and non-Jews to rationalize the appropriation of their martyrdom; at the same time, the distinction was being applied to people to whom it least applied, people considering themselves Poles *tout court* (and often so considered by others) (see, esp. Karsov & Szechter, 1970).

Finally, it could be said that the overall thrust of the 1968 campaign contained an internal contradiction, as the Jew was at the same time exposed and made to disappear, and the "Jewish question" brought into the public arena while denied presence in the past.

If within this very condensed historical analysis, I have devoted so much attention to a relatively brief episode of 1968, it is because I have found that it *was* 1968 that marked the beginning of a process of reconstructing the memory of the Jew in Poland. In the next chapter, we will be hearing from and about the " '68 generation," a core force behind the efforts to secure a permanent position for the Jew in Poland's memory. Here, I would like to conclude by reflecting on the aftermath of 1968 for Poland's Jews themselves.

On one level, objectively speaking, 1968 spelled the end to the Jewish presence in Poland, the final closing of the final chapter, as it were.[77] According to most estimates, some twenty to twenty-five thousand Jews had left the country by the early 1970s, thus leaving behind a miniscule population of five to ten thousand, mostly elderly people, often too sick or too old to begin anew in strange lands.[78] Most of those who stayed have been living something like "internal emigration": they are usually no longer active professionally and definitely out of the political scene. Their lives revolve around their children—mostly living abroad—and their own private world. It seems now only a matter of time before this tiny community disappears altogether (see: Wieviorka, 1984; Eytan, 1982).

Yet, not all of those who remained behind fit this picture. While we are now talking about a group so small numerically as to seem insignificant, its role in Polish affairs has given it a presence well beyond actual numbers. More a collection of individuals than a group in any real sense of the word, these usually middle-aged Jews not only remained in Poland, but remained at the very center of both culture and politics. Interestingly enough, they would now be fairly equally distributed on both sides of the barricades, so to speak. And they have become even more prominent during the last six years or so when the political divide has deepened.

On one side, we now find what could be called the "court Jews" of contemporary Poland—journalists in the main, some working for the prime Party weekly, one chosen to be an official government spokesman (a highly sensitive and a highly visible position, maybe the most so in the country).[79] On the other side, within the leadership of the opposition, and more so within the ranks of opposition intellectuals at large, one still finds a disproportionate number of Jews, again highly visible and highly vocal. [Roughly speaking, Jewish involvement in the opposition *today* is much greater than that in the regime.] All in all, keeping the political differences in mind (they *are* important) there are today Jews in influential positions in Poland's life, at least, people who are publicly recognized as Jews.

Here we come to a key element of the post-1968 situation: a re-definition of who is a Jew. Both the list I mentioned earlier and the subsequent departure of so many people who considered themselves Poles—given exit visas on the condition that they sign away their Polish citizenship[80]— spelled an end to assimilation ideals. Yet it is wrong to think that there are no more Jews who would feel, think and act as Poles; if anything, those who chose to stay were often adamant about their right to Polishness.[81] It is also wrong to think that there are no more Poles who believe that a Jew could be "one of us", but even they had to accept that Jewishness does matter.

With all the stand-in terms and with all the subtle distinctions promoted by the media, 1968 did set people with Jewish ancestry apart as Jews.[82] To pretend otherwise, to say that in today's Poland the only Jews are those who so declare themselves, would be to close one's eyes and ears to both social and political realities. Thus, if it appears that I am badly misusing the term "Jew," applying it to people who would reject such a definition, and to people who would not fit into any traditional view of Jewish identity,

I am doing so only to bring my analysis closer to the world it aims to make some sense of.

Finally, it should be pointed out that the 1968 campaign brought a profound change to the terms of discourse about things Jewish—it made talking about the Jew a *political* act. If the state has not been fully successful at convincing everybody that Jews were indeed the sole cause of Poland's misfortunes, it has managed to re-introduce the "Jewish question" onto the public scene. And if discussing Polish-Jewish affairs was always a difficult and a delicate task, doing it after 1968 without in some ways legitimating or opposing the official stance would be next to impossible.

Let us take an example: in April 1967, there appeared a large volume of personal testimonies to the extent of Polish aid to Jews during the Holocaust. It was prepared in part by Władysław Bartoszewski, a prominent Polish historian, himself a member of an aid organization during the war. In 1969, a second enlarged edition was issued under the auspices of *Znak*, a Catholic publishing house. It might have been, and it probably was pure coincidence that this long prepared study appeared at the height of the media attack on the "ungrateful Jews," who were slandering Poland's good name. It would be hard, though, to read this book without wondering if the regime were not somehow right.

All this, however—the setting of Jews apart, the efforts to make them disappear from history and to make them appear all powerful in the present, the charging of the most innocent of remarks with political significance and the sudden transformation of one's Polish colleagues into Zionist conspirators—could not but raise a few questions, especially for people brought up to believe that Jewishness was not to matter. And this is precisely what happened. . . .

### Notes

1. *The Polish Jewry: History and Culture* (Fuks et al, 1982) was not available on the market until 1983. An earlier, much smaller edition of Ringelblum's materials (Sakowska, ed., 1980) was followed by a larger and a more extensive one in 1983. The diary of Czerniakow (Fuks, ed., 1983)—the head of *Judenrat* in Warsaw until his suicide in July 1942—was also the subject of a very moving essay by Zimand (1982).

2. By 1983, that silence *was* broken, with most of the credit due to Solidarity's general insistence on an open public discourse. As with other subjects, the official media campaign around the April 1983 anniversary of the Warsaw Ghetto Uprising was to make *their* treatment of Polish/Jewish relations appear novel and daring.

3. The *Citizens' Committee for the Protection of Jewish Cemeteries and Cultural*

*Monuments in Poland* was formed in 1981 in Warsaw; another one worked in Cracow.

4. Monika Krajewska, in addition to her book *The Time of Stone (Czas kamieni)* published an article on the symbolism of Jewish memorial art (1983) and co-authored one on the "reconstruction of memory" (Jagielski, 1983). Over the course of the past few years, she had also made a number of presentations at meetings and seminars devoted to Jewish culture.

5. Jews were more than one-third of the population in 70% of the towns and cities in Poland; in one-third of them, they constituted more than one-half. Only 31% of Jews, though, lived in large cities (100,000 and over), with most organized in communities containing 10,000–30,000 Jews (Goldscheider & Zuckerman, 1984:105).

6. The idea of "caste" as applicable to Jews in Poland was introduced by Hertz (1961) and used extensively by Heller (1980). More recently, historians prefer to speak in terms of the feudal notion of "estate" (see: Abramsky et al., eds., 1986). I find the notion of "caste" valuable for its emphasis on the *exclusion* of the Jews from the rest of society.

7. The ambivalence in literary images reflected the more general ambivalence prevailing in the relations with Jews, both among the nobility and among the peasants. The Jew was clearly perceived as different, sometimes alien, but not as an enemy.

8. Jews in Poland were not only, or even primarily engaged in trade. Many worked for the nobles as administrators of their estates and tax collectors. Many were craftsmen, again, in direct contact with the peasantry. Ethnically Polish, "third estate" was nearly non-existent before the 18th century; Jews were thus competing mainly with Germans and Scots, the two largest groups of burgers (see: Weinryb, 1973).

9. With their "Council of the Four Lands", Jews were virtually a state-within-a-state in Poland; their autonomy had no parallels anywhere in Europe (see: Poliakov, 1981:388–415);
    The "Council of the Four Lands" was dissolved in 1765, that is well before the partition of Poland. During the 19th century, Jews were governed by laws of Russia, Prussia and Austria.

10. *Haskalah,* which originated in Germany in the 18th century, had most impact on Jews in central Poland (Russian territory) and in Galicia (Austrian), and then, mainly in larger centers. Its ideas of a secular education for Jews were vehemently attacked by the Orthodox community. Its rational outlook carried little appeal—at least in the first half of the 19th century—to the Jewish masses, where Hassidism was most popular (see: Weinryb, 1973). Later, the modernizing impetus of *Haskalah* was to reach even the most traditional youth; by the late 19th century, though, the assimilationist tendencies were largely displaced by the arising Jewish national consciousness (see: Mendelsohn, 1981).

11. The strength of this identification between Polishness and Catholicism was indeed very much furthered by the fact that Poland as a state ceased to exist, as well as by the Russian Orthodoxy of its chief aggressor. The Catholic Church became the only truly *national* institution, capable of preserving traditional culture and values, exactly at the time when national consciousness was properly emerging (see: Davies, 1982:207–240; Symmons-Symonolewicz, 1983). The fact that "nation" and "state" were two very distinct categories in much of Central and Eastern Europe is essential here.

12. In France, the country which pioneered Jewish emancipation, the formula was very explicit:"Il faut tout refuser aux juifs comme nation et tout accorder aux juifs comme individus" (Philippe, 1979:13).

 The French Jewish *Consistoire* took it upon itself to educate French Jews on being good Frenchmen; the very word "juif" was being carefully avoided and replaced with the more neutral "israélite". French Jews, though, retained community institutions and concerns (Cohen Albert, 1977).

13. Again, Cała (1984) shows how the notion of "disease" entered the discourse on things Jewish even among advocates of the Jews. [Trachtenberg (1943/1983) offers the most extensive analysis of this matter (in general).]

14. The National Democratic party, led by Roman Dmowski, stood by the idea of "national egoism" and the complete identification between Polishness and Catholicism (see: Toruńczyk, 1983). Not surprisingly, it was widely supported by the Church (Davies, 1984).

15. There existed, of necessity perhaps, a strong connection between the social and the individual "contamination imagery". In the 1920's and 1930's, many an outcry against "Jewish domination" in Polish culture was directed against people who had long left the Jewish community, poets, writers, journalists, who created wholly within Polish ethos and language (see: Hertz, 1979).

16. Hilberg (1961) discusses this phenomenon at some length. Lifton (1986) adds to our understanding of the hold this imagery possessed when looking at the actions of the Nazi doctors in Auschwitz—where killing became transformed into healing in their own minds by virtue of seeing the Jews as cancer.

17. In many a discussion of the *Jewish* political scene in interwar Poland, the phrase "Jewish problem" appears with great frequency as well. The difference, though, is that for the majority of Jews, "Jewish problem" referred to the economic difficulties and discrimination experienced by the Jews, solving it— to various ways of ameliorating the situation. In other words, except for a small minority which would seek complete (individual) integration into Polish society, the question of the "problematic nature of Jewishness" did not arise.

18. The most indicative here might be the Poles' attitude towards Yiddish, commonly referred to as "żargon" or "szwargot", both terms being pejorative. Jews were themselves very divided on the language issue—for an excellent discussion, see: Mendelsohn (1981)—and those who advocated the use of Polish for all Polish Jews were taking a similar position, i.e., that Jewish culture as such is an *obstacle* to overcome.

19. I *am* speaking very generally here of general cultural trends. In the actual practices, it appears that the situation in the eastern parts of Poland *(Kresy)*, where Poles themselves often lived as a minority, together with Ukrainians, Byelorussians, Lithuanians and Jews, was quite different than that in Warsaw or Lodz. Greater ethnic *diversity*, for all the social and cultural barriers which existed between the groups, and for all the conflicts between them, made eastern Poles much more versed in Jewish culture as such (see especially, Vincenz, 1977).

20. It is highly significant that Jews, who were literate and on the average much more educated than Poles (even the nobility, let alone illiterate peasants), would be treated as "dark massess". The belief that the Jews needed to be educated was shared by Polish positivists and Jewish assimilationists.

21. Scharf (1984; quoted in Abramsky et al., eds., 1986:11) makes this point perhaps most succinctly: "Did it ever occur to a Pole that in a neighboring

town, or for that matter on the very same street something was happening that could engage his attention and deserved his interest? Not in the least. The Jewish population was commonly regarded as a "dark continent", backward and primitive, evoking feelings of aversion and repugnance."

22. It should be noted that by 1918, while the process of Polonization, especially in terms of language, was beginning to envelop large segments of the Jewish community, the *ideal* of assimilation was no longer a viable one, except for a small minority. In other words, as more and more *individuals* were adopting at least some aspects of Polish culture, the earlier programmatic effort to build bridges between Poles and Jews was largely absent (see: Mendelsohn, 1969; 1983; Lichten, 1986).

23. In the extreme cases, assimilated Jews would often become active anti-Semites. More prevalent was the attitude of disdain for the "primitive" Jew, one of the masses of traditional Polish Jewry (see, for example, Mendelsohn's study of Feldman, 1969).

    It should be added that this notion that the "modern Jew" was inherently better than the "caftan wearers" has been very much a part of the Jewish emancipation experience in the West, assuming often very complex forms, especially when Polish Jews came to migrate to Germany, Austria and France in large numbers (see: Aschheim, 1982; Marrus and Paxton 1981).

24. One of the best areas to study the questions of stigma (and its avoidance) is *names*. Most likely due to the Catholic tradition (as opposed to the Protestant one), many of the Biblical names—Sarah, Ruth, David, etc.—were closely identified with Jewishness. [They still are in Poland.] Thus the choice of the child's first name would often be a good indicator of the degree to which the parents identified with the traditional Jewish culture, while the change of name altogether (to a Polish-sounding one like Maria or Stanislaw)—of an effort to blend in, if not to "pass."

25. To successfully "pass," a Jew needed both the perfect knowledge of Polish language and Catholic customs and "good" physical appearance; because only Jews were circumcised in Poland, men were at an obvious disadvantage. Sheer luck also proved crucial (see: Borwicz, 1969).

26. Estimates of the number of survivors vary; Dawidowicz (1976) seems to offer the most reliable figures.

    Polish Jews, who spent the war years in the Soviet Union were by no means comfortable; some three hundred thousand were shipped, together with Poles, to the Far Eastern regions (see: Gross & Grudzińska-Gross, 1981:26). Hard labor, hunger and disease took many lives. Yet the Jews' chances at survival were still tremendously higher than of those who remained in Poland.

27. For an extensive treatment, see: Gross & Grudzińska-Gross (1981:9–18). In a recent article, Smolar (1986) emphasizes the importance of this perception of "Jewish betrayal" for the Poles' attitudes toward the Jews. Gross (1979:185–6) also places it as one of three key factors in explaining the prevailing hostility towards the Jews.

28. This theme of "hell" vs. "normality" emerges very clearly from the records (and poetry) written in the ghetto; see: Borwicz (1947). Karski (1944), a Home Army courier who visited the Warsaw Ghetto, conveys the difference very clearly in his war memoirs.

    For a polemical treatment of "normality" on *both* sides, see: Shahak (1986); also reprinted in *NYR*, Jan. 29, 1987.

29. Bartoszewski (1986), who was himself engaged in organized aid to the Jews, maintains, for example, that only those who died did "enough" to help Jews, effectively foreclosing any discussion on this matter.

30. Polish underground was—in the main—supportive of the Jews' fighting in their declarations (see: Gutman, 1982; Korbonski, 1978). Close reading of these also reveals just how deeply ingrained was the conviction that prior to the uprising, Jews were cowardly and let themselves be slaughtered.

31. It is, I think, precisely because exact knowledge is impossible to achieve in these matters that the "number game" can be played so successfully. In April of 1983, when the Polish press was filled with articles commemorating the Holocaust, the number of survivors quoted varied from 50 to 400 thousand, with the clear implication that the higher the number, the better is the Poles' record. Pilichowski (ed., 1979), representing the official Polish historiography, quotes 100–120 thousand survivors. Korbonski (1978) places that number at 200 thousand, according to the Home Army estimates.

32. Kazimierz Brandys, a Polish writer and a Jew, makes this point in his reflections on today's relations between Poles and Jewish survivors (1981:130).

33. These themes emerge very clearly in the collections by Bartoszewski (1969) and Smólski (1981). They are also central to the study of organized aid (Zegota), by Prekerowa (1982). Kuroń (1986), in an autobiographic account, discusses this very honestly.

    Tec (1986), in her recent analysis of the Polish rescuers, argues that it was their ability to think of Jews *not* as Jews but as suffering human beings which made the difference. A similar point about the lack of societal support for the rescue of Jews is also made by Gross (1986).

    It should be noted here that the situation did not change *after* the war: many rescuers preferred to remain anonymous, fearing social ostracism (Borwicz, 1986; Tec, 1986; Hochberg-Mariańska & Grüss, 1947).

34. Gross (1986) argues this point most eloquently. One must consider also that *all* the activities related to the production and sale of food for example were punishable by death, which did not prevent a vast black market from operating (see: Wolowski, 1977).

35. "Zegota", the Relief Council for Jews in Poland, was most active in Warsaw and Cracow; its main contribution consisted in providing Jews with safe places to hide, false papers, as well as small subsidies to live on. Jewish children were often placed in convents or with Christian families. It is impossible to estimate how many Jews were helped or how many actually survived, beyond the figure of 12,000 adults and 2,500 children who were "registered" recipients (Prekerowa, 1982).

36. Krakowski's study of Jewish resistance (1984) is a severe condemnation of the Polish underground, while adopting a pro-Communist position. Polish accounts (e.g., Korbonski, 1978) offer an exactly opposite picture. Memoirs by Zagórski (1971) and Borwicz (1980)—who was the highest ranking Jew in the Polish forces, but who was "passing" as most were—provide more balanced views; both confirm the killings of Jews by members of the underground (as do Trunk (1982) and Gilbert (1985)). The key point here, I believe, is that Jews as Jews were not incorporated into the Polish forces.

37. This was not a problem unique to Poland (see: Lendvai, 1972), but the sheer numbers of Polish Jews made it ever more acute. Smolar (1986) points out that what was unique about Poland was the persistent *legitimacy* of anti-Semitic discourse throughout the war.

38. In theory, Poland's 1921 constitution, plus the signing of the international Minorities Treaty, had offered Jews equal status as citizens. In practice, discrimination was both advocated and enacted. In particular, Jews were almost totally barred from the civil service.
39. Again, this phenomenon was not unique to Poland; in all countries within the Soviet sphere of influence, Jews made a disproportionately high segment of the new administration (see: Lendvai, 1972).
40. It must be kept in mind, though, that a number of Jewish Communists lost their lives in the Stalinist purge of 1938–39 (after the Party was dissolved), while Bundists found themselves imprisoned together with Jewish members of the Polish Socialist Party. The situation generally did not improve until the Nazis attacked the Soviet Union.
41. Jews were not alone in their hopes; recent developments in Poland often overshadow the realities of the early years, when many Poles of democratic persuasion placed their trust in a system promising equality, land reform and justice (see: Milosz, 1951/1981).
42. The identification between Jews and Communism dates back to the 1920's, especially in the pronouncements of the conservative Polish Church. It had gained much strength in 1939—when, as we saw, Jews were seen as collaborating with the Soviets in the Soviet-occupied zone.
43. Many of the Jews immediately affected by the attacks (or by news of the attacks) were steadily fleeing to the West, often ending up in the very DP camps in Germany they had left a few months before. For their personal testimonies, see: Gerschon (1969).
44. In individual cases, these two—quite different—reasons for staying in Poland could co-exist. (For an excellent source on the complexities of the situation, see: Nowakowska, 1950/1983).
45. An important part of the process consisted of from-the-top changes in the economic structure of the Jewish community. A whole department was devoted to "productivization" of Jews, namely training them for jobs in heavy industry and agriculture, thus breaking the traditional ties with commerce. The idea was not new; this time, though, it had some potential for success, considering the overall transformation of Polish society and the small numbers of Jews involved. In addition, Jews were encouraged to settle in the newly recovered Western territories, thus to become physically invisible in the central parts of Poland (see: Checinski, 1982).
46. To the best of my knowledge, there are no extensive records of this practice. It is mentioned by Checinski (1982), Smolar (1986) and—in Poland—by Sandauer (1982). Polonsky and Drukier (1980) offer documentary evidence on how Gomułka in particular was concerned about the impact of too many visible Jews in the party ranks. I have also relied on case histories gathered in the course of this research.
47. Though the term "Poles of Jewish origin" is today widely used in contrast to "Jews," one should not assume that it necessarily implies a complete disassociation from Jewish concerns. One does not have to agree with Sandauer's depiction of Polish writers of Jewish origin (1982) to appreciate the psychological problems involved in this dual identity. [For an excellent study of the "residual" Jewish identity of Italian writers of Jewish origin, see: Hughes (1983).]
48. A great number of Polish Jews, however, were not associated with the existing

community organizations. A very similar pattern developed in East Germany and with similar consequences; while the state there has been generally more supportive of the Jewish community, it too has used this support for very definite political purposes (Ostow, 1986).

49. This is not to say that the state was doing most of memory keeping; the work belonged primarily to Jewish writers and historians. It is to say that it did not encounter the kind of popular challenge as it did in the "properly Polish" areas.

50. As the historical value of the Memorial Books comes to be more appreciated (see: Wein, 1973; Ertel, 1982), they are likely to become more accessible to the general reader, with the publications mentioned here as significant first steps in that direction. (For a listing of the Memorial Books, see: Bass, 1973.)

51. An important exception here consists of the post-1968 emigrants, many of whom retain at least sentimental ties to Poland, with some very actively involved in the Polish émigré life (e.g., the journal *Aneks*).

52. K. Brandys (1983:33) reflects that the feeling that no one mourned the Jews, that they were to be forgotten, was more painful than the actual experiences of the Jews. Jewish scholars are not immune to this very emotional reaction (see: Krakowski & Kermish, notes to Ringelblum (1974); Ertel, 1982, Tec, 1986). Problems which this poses for historiography are discussed at length by Gutman (1986) and Mendelsohn (1986).

53. This is a "summary" of positions I encountered on numerous occasions, especially while discussing my own research. Compare, in this regard, Wisse's articles on Poland, written for *Commentary* in 1972 and in 1987.

54. With perhaps one significant exception—the new building, housing the Yiddish Theater, and displaying the best in advanced stage technology, was financed chiefly by "Joint" and this, *after* "Joint" was no longer allowed to legally operate in Poland in 1968. The Yiddish Theater, though, has been very much of a showcase of the regime's good will, all the laudable intentions of its director notwithstanding (see: Niezabitowska, 1986).

55. It is important to note that the one available book on Jewish history—Łastik's account of the *Haskalah* (1961)—presented views very much in accord with the assimilationist ideas.

56. In discussing the vibrant renewal of interest in Jewish culture and history taking place among French Jews over the last 15 years or so, Finkielkraut (1980, 1982) points to the same exhilaration with "progress" as the prime factor behind "forgetting" the past.

57. While in Warsaw, I went on a "guided tour" of the Jewish cemetery, with its conspicuous absence of graves marked with dates from the 1950s and early 1960s. My guide pointed to a grave of a close friend—who died in 1952—and recounted just how much courage it had taken to bury this man there in those terrible years.

58. They were, of course, not alone in this respect. After a brief period immediately after the war, when a number of books on Jewish themes appeared, Jewish memory keepers shared the fate of their Polish counterparts. It was only after the 1956 "thaw" that books on Jewish experience were published again, and this, not without restrictions (see: Grynberg, 1984 b).

59. Smolar (1986) also discusses this point. In recent memoirs of Grzegorz Lasota (*Polityka*, Dec. 20, 1986), who was a film producer during the early 1950's, there is a brief mention of how the censors objected to showing the scenes of

the ghetto fighting when there was still no film presentation of the Warsaw Uprising, clearly fearing just such popular resentment.

60. I clearly disagree here with analysts placing all the responsibility (and blame) on the Communist regime (e.g., Lendvai, 1972; Kołakowski, 1982). The universalistic principle, dictating that one makes no distinction between Jews and non-Jews was neither a Communist invention nor anti-Jewish in conception.

    In France, where it was very dominant, at least in the public sphere, Jewishness gradually became "génant" (a shameful embarrassment) for its proponents (see: Harris & Sédouy, 1979). Anti-Semitism, while strongly condemned, nearly disappeared from public discussions. In short, this silence cannot be reduced to political manipulation.

61. To put it simply, Stalinism in Poland had many victims in terms of arrests and persecution; there were also people sentenced to death (both for political and economic reasons). The *scale* of repression, though, never matched that in the Soviet Union itself. Poland was also spared the Rajk and Slansky kinds of show trials.

62. Moczar, the man behind the 1968 anti-Semitic campaign which played this theme so heavily, was himself a local chief of security during the Stalinist period.

63. The title of one of the participants' account summarizes it well: *Boors and Yids* (Jedlicki, 1962).

64. Checinski (1982) estimates the 1956 "exodus" to number 50 thousand Jews, with one-half consisting of the fresh repatriates from the Soviet Union.

65. Historians place the beginning of this reversal as early as 1957—when the most outspoken journal *Po Prostu* was shut down by the authorities. By the early 1960s, both the cultural liberalization and economic reforms advocated in 1956 were ideals of the past. see: Biénkowski (1971), Karpinski (1982).

66. Lendvai (1972), looking at the reactions to the 1967 Israeli-Arab war in Poland, Rumania, Hungary and Czechoslovakia points to the importance of *local* politics for the development of full-fledged anti-Semitic campaigns; in the case of Poland, 1967 was a "lucky break" for the Party faction struggling for power.

67. The regime propagandists appear to have been well aware of this "plausibility problem", as they would join the Zionists with the West German "revanchists" (demanding the return of territories annexed after World War II), in their own version of conspiracy theory (see: Lendvai, 1972).

68. K. Dejmek (1981/1983), the director of the play at issue—disputes the "Soviet intervention" theory, pointing to the warm reception his play had received from Soviet critics. The fact remains that rumors of such intervention were prominent at the time.

69. It definitely helped matters—from the authorities' point of view—that the two students expelled for participating in the demonstration against the closing of *Dziady* were both Jewish (Michnik & Szlajfer). It was, in turn, in protest against their expulsion that the university-wide demonstration on March 8th was organized, starting the whole chain of student unrest.

70. Bieńkowski (1971), an insider, while strongly opposed to the use of anti-Semitic means, is most explicit in reducing the 1968 events to an internal affair of the Party.

    Most significantly, perhaps, such was the position of the Church (see: Smolar, 1986).

71. It must be remembered that at the time, foreign travel, let alone emigration,

was extremely difficult for ordinary Poles. At an even more basic level, there were also numerous expressions of satisfaction with the now-open career opportunities—and apartments (see: Jelen, 1972).

72. Michnik (1977/79) sees the reasons for the Church indifference not so much in anti-Jewish sentiments as in a well-deserved reproach to the Polish opposition intellectuals in general for *their* lack of support of the Church during the early sixties in particular. [Poland's 1000th anniversary in 1966 was an occasion for especially horrific propaganda exercises.]

73. It must be appreciated that "raw" salary is by no means the most important indication of social status in Poland; access to low-cost, high-quality services often compensates for low income.

74. The appropriation strategy was not confined to history books, though. The figure of 6 million *Polish* victims became standard reference on posters and slogans widely distributed during Poland's many war-related anniversaries, for example.

75. The first edition of Gieysztor et al., *History of Poland* was published in 1968. The two paragraphs both refer to the Holocaust. In all fairness, though, the classic Polish history book published in the West (Halecki, 1961) is nearly equally silent on the Jews.

76. As late as 1980, a representative edition of a history of Polish culture (Suchodolski), available in French, English and German, contained only a brief reference to the literature about the Holocaust in the way of mention of Poland's Jews.

77. "Final chapter" indeed became one of the key terms used when writing about the 1968 campaign (e.g., Bauman, 1969) as well as the title of Vinecour's book (1977) on the remaining Jewish presence in Poland.

78. Reliable figures are difficult, if not impossible, to arrive at. The starting point, after all, is the security forces' creation, and the emigration figures do not include Jews who left the country through ordinary channels (i.e., not on an exit permit to Israel).

   According to a recent account from the senior officials of the Jewish community organizations in Poland, as many as 15 thousand Jews could still be there (Kirshner, 1983); included in this number is an unknown proportion of half-Jews, though.

79. Jerzy Urban was also on the staff of *Polityka* before being promoted to the post of the official government spokesman. It is, of course, impossible to tell to what extent selecting him was a deliberate strategy to incite anti-Jewish sentiment. When in Warsaw, I carefully "monitored" the very frequent references to Urban, made by people in very diverse positions; his Jewishness was *not* in any way emphasized. Anti-Urban articles in the émigré press are also free of anti-Semitic undertones.

80. As most analysts of the 1968 "exodus" point out, it was this compulsory de-Polonization which constituted the most humiliating part of the emigration experience (see, e.g., Jelen, 1972). Under the Polish law, even children of Poles born abroad are automatically considered Polish citizens. Depriving Jews of their citizenship meant that they would not be allowed to return. Years later, when many of these Jews—then as citizens of Western countries—wished to visit Poland, they were consistently being denied entry visas; the situation began to improve only in the 1980s.

81. Both Michnik (see: 1985) and Blumsztajn (1985) represent this position. It

should be kept in mind, though, that most Jews stayed in Poland for more pragmatic reasons (see: Bauman, 1969).

82. This is not to say that everyone was equally affected. To the best of my knowledge, those active in the Catholic circles (first or second generation converts) were not on the "hit list". Also, while in Warsaw. I was told of a fair number of cases of Jews who remain "invisible" to this day. Even being on the security forces' list did not necessarily mean being *publicly* identified as a Jew.

# 3

# The Breaking of Silence

It is late October, 1983; the days are becoming shorter. By the time the guests have arrived and our hostess lights the Shabbat candles, it is well past sundown. Following a blessing of bread and wine, we pass around a small dish with water for the symbolic washing of hands, accompanied by another blessing. The meal itself is simple and vegetarian. After supper, our hostess joins her two small daughters and a woman friend in singing Hebrew songs. Once the girls have gone to bed, our conversation becomes a debate. As the two women are in the process of preparing a Jewish cookbook, which is to contain an introduction on the basics of Jewish law, we first get into an argument about priority of action versus faith within the Jewish tradition. Later, as we talk about the different ways to be Jewish, another argument arises, this time about the best place to be a good Jew—is it Israel? The discussion then shifts to a recent article devoted to Jews and Communism. Though published underground, it strikes us all as unduly cautious in its treatment of the subject. But, we also all agree that this is an important first step. . . . For while we could be in any number of places, we are in Warsaw.

Is a chapter which was to be closed opening again? Yes and no. Yes, there are now young people, mostly in their thirties, who, together with their children, celebrate Shabbat and Jewish holidays, who gather to learn and discuss Jewish history and Jewish philosophy, who avidly read books by and about Jews, written in French and English and acquired by whatever means possible. They also teach themselves Hebrew as well as prepare and present smaller and larger research projects dealing with various aspects of Polish-Jewish history. And yes, for the most part and for now, these young Jews are set to stay in Poland; they are also set to remain visible and vocal, to take their search for Jewish heritage into the public forum (see also: Niezabitowska, 1986:77–111).

But no, this is not a revival of Jewish community life. When all are gathered together, for Passover or Chanukkah, these young Jews would at best number only a few dozen. And while they try to make an impact on the existing institutional structure, maintained as it is by the elders and controlled as it is by the state, their efforts do not meet with much success.

In part, it is a question of a culture gap. These young Jews have much more in common with young and not-so-young Jews in America or France than they have with the older generations of Polish Jews. Their experience of rediscovery of Jewish heritage is far more akin to the experience of an acculturated Western Jew in search of more meaning to his Jewishness than to the traditional ways of simply *being* a Jew in Poland. This younger generation does not, cannot speak the same language as Jews born into the large Jewish community and weathered by so many historical storms. They do not speak Yiddish, nor are they trying to learn it, Hebrew being their first choice as a link with Jewish culture.[1] Avid readers, they are more versed in modern Jewish philosophy and theology than they are in the Torah. And those few who made their return to Jewishness a return to Judaism were following a highly individualized and highly intellectual road, one which gave them little in common with Jews who had never left. Their religious observance does not easily fit into any existing categories. If they were in America, they would probably feel most at home within the Reform movement. This suggestion, however, is sheer speculation, for they *do* live in Poland where there is not much room for other than relatively orthodox forms of worship.

What renders that cultural gap ever more pronounced, though, is its political coloring. The community elders—the people in charge of the Jewish Socio-Cultural Society, the Yiddish Theater or the Association of Mosaic Faith, the people who tried during all the bumpy years to maintain some form of institutional Jewish presence in Poland—have all become strongly identified with the state itself. Our young "return Jews," on the other hand, have all been involved, some very actively, in the opposition (see: Wieviorka, 1984). There can hardly be much of a dialogue, for example between the director of the Yiddish Theater, a man who was elected a member of Polish Parliament in the 1985 elections, and people who campaigned for a boycott of those very elections. There is also much fear and suspicion on the part of those within the existing official organizations towards efforts to revitalize them. When calls for change come from opposition circles, then the very basis of those organizations' existence, namely the regime's protectorate, faces a particularly uncertain future.

In short, many older Jews believe that any serious challenge to the state control of Jewish institutions could spell the end to community life. And, for better or worse, the life of the remnants of Poland's Jews does depend on the state. It is the state which regulates all contacts with Jewish organizations abroad, including any financial aid. It is also the state which determines conditions for travelling abroad, of vital importance for people whose families are often scattered around the globe. In practical terms, the single decision of one minister can be a great deal more significant than all the work of these young Jews combined.

Yet another factor is at work here. My Shabbat companions are not alone in rediscovering their Jewishness. A good number of older people, perhaps as many as several hundred judging by attendance at the synagogue services as well as an increased participation in community activities, have rejoined what remains of Jewish life over recent years. At Warsaw's Jewish cemetery, after years and years of empty plots, there are now several graves marked with 1975, 1979, 1982. Who *are* these new-old Jews? For the most part, they are disillusioned ex-Communists and ex-fellow travellers, longing for the lost warmth of their childhood after their whole world collapsed in 1968.[2] Seeing their ideals shatter and being forcefully removed from the public arena, they have now retreated into what was left. But in trying to re-create a sense of the Jewish togetherness they once knew, they draw on memories of a traditional Jewish life, colored with much nostalgia. And so they too have trouble understanding and sharing in a very modern, very "Western" experience of the young.

Feelings are mutual, one should add. Among the young Jews, there is still a great deal of work before they really come to terms with their parents' past and appreciate the complexity of being both a Jew and a Communist in the 1930s, even more so, in the 1950s.[3] For the time being, a certain cynicism prevails, as they tend to explain the sudden swelling of community membership with one word: money. As it turns out, permission was granted to Jewish organizations abroad to provide small allowances— in hard currency, though—to all those who would enlist; it is no wonder then that the community halls are vibrant again.

Yet even if, in the end, the impact of my Shabbat companions on the future of the Jewish presence in Poland might prove slight indeed, their experience in and of itself has already proven significant. To appreciate its exact significance, however, we must look at it a little more closely.

I have said that this search for Jewish roots resembles a Western Jew's quest for identity. Make-shift ritual, philosophy readings, interest in history—these are all common expressions of a reawakened Jewish consciousness. [These are particularly common in France, where only a small minority of "returning Jews" takes the religious path to traditional observance (see: Schnapper, 1980; Rosenzweig, ed., 1979).] There are important differences, though. For one, as I talked to these young Jews in Warsaw about their sense of priorities, it became clear that their concerns do *not* revolve around points of central concern to Jews in the West. Israel, while important to them, is a very distant reality; they welcome an opportunity to learn more about life there, and they might wish to visit, especially now when such a visit is again within the realm of the possible. But they do not worry about Israel's problems day in and day out: "Quite frankly, our life here is so filled with trouble and danger, that we simply do not have the time."

These young Jews are not particularly concerned about the negative image of Israel offered by the official media.[4] It is something they have come to take for granted; treated as a part of the overall disinformation strategy, the regime's news and comments about Israel are seen as more lies to be dismissed together with all the other lies from that source. The anti-Zionist rhetoric does have a special meaning there, but it does not relate to Israel as Israel; rather, its intensity has proven to be a fairly good indicator of the official stance towards the *local* Jews. When read that way, anti-Israeli propaganda is important indeed, but it is also far removed from its ostensible subject matter.

Needless to say, there is no question of making financial contributions to Israel from Poland, either individually or through organizational channels. There is also no question of spontaneously rallying in the streets in support of—or in protest against—Israeli policies. And, perhaps as a sign of defiance, there is no question of making Zionism a focal point of one's rediscovered Jewishness, be it in private *or* in public.[5]

A second major element of modern Jewish outlook, or of what has been termed the governing "myth of redemption,"[6] is missing as well. The Holocaust, ironically enough, is much less of a concern for young Jews in Warsaw than it is, let us say, in New York. Or, more precisely, it is a very different concern.

As the "children of the Holocaust" in the West grew older, their experience, the experience of confronting the daily challenge of their parents' silence, has received much attention in North America (see: Epstein, 1980). It appears that while the individual stories vary, the majority of survivors adopted silence as a way of sheltering their children from the horrors they had experienced. Often, only the concentration camp number, tattooed on the arm, spoke of the past. Growing up not only without one's grandparents, aunts and uncles, but without the memory of their life and death, combined with a strong sense of being different from one's peers, would produce a great deal of anxiety, feelings of isolation and the need to know. Growing up laden with so much hope and importance by parents who had lost everything created a heavy psychological burden. It was difficult to break the silence, to start asking questions;

it is still difficult for the "children of the Holocaust" to come to terms with their own experience and the experience of their parents.

The story of Poland's "children of the Holocaust" is remarkably different; in contrast to those in North America, they grew up sharing in collective mourning, as it were. Many of their peers, Jews as well as non-Jews, came from families who had lost someone during the war, or from families with survivors of labor and concentration camps. With three million Polish war victims, martyrology was not a uniquely Jewish territory, nor was "survival" a word reserved for those who had escaped from the Holocaust.[7] A kind of World War II mythology developed into a powerful force behind much of Poland's post-war literature and film, gradually neutralizing much of the horror with some humor and some drama of adventure. And, memorials to the war victims became a familiar sight in Polish towns and cities; one walk down the streets in Warsaw, could serve as a history lesson. In short, being a "child of the Holocaust" and living in Poland carried little if any of the isolation and strangeness it would in America. It also meant being a part of a whole generation, the one born after the war and instilled with special hopes. The whole country, and not the Jews alone, would be healing wounds and rebuilding life on the ruins.

Yet, if sharing in grief spared Poland's "children of the Holocaust" from feeling alone, it also made it difficult for them to approach the Holocaust as a uniquely Jewish experience. This perception is changing (see: Krajewski, 1986; Śpiewak, 1986; List . . ., 1987), but the change is very much a part of the *general* shift towards a recognition of the uniqueness of the Holocaust. For a child—and I am now speaking about myself as well—hearing stories of the often miraculous survival of the Jews was not sufficiently different from learning in school or watching a movie about the risky escapades of the resistance, for example. And, bear in mind that the primary goal of remembering Jewish martyrdom was to reduce rather than to increase a sense of distinct Jewish identity. The memory of the Holocaust, even before it came to be appropriated by Poles, was not to set the Jews apart.

What makes the experience of Poland's "children of the Holocaust" truly different, though, is the quality of the *silence* they grew up with. More generally, what makes these young Jews different from their Western counterparts is the sheer length of their return journey. For some, the starting point consists of a realization that Jewishness does matter. For others, it was the discovery, often fairly late in life, that they were Jewish at all.[8]

When Alain Finkielkraut, a young French Jewish writer, described his and his generation's experience of a revived interest in Jewish history and culture, he coined an expression "Jewish on the outside, French on the inside" to designate their common point of departure.[9] An Americanized version of this combination of strong identification with Jews and weak cultural base for one's Jewishness could also apply to the experience of many a North American Jew at the outset of his or her journey of discovery (see: Porter, Dreier, eds., 1973). Put simply, a young Jew in the West knows that he is a Jew, knows that this is supposed to be quite meaningful, and yet has a sense that it is not, not when he looks at his daily life, his interests, his concerns. For some, this realization is not problematic; for others, it translates into an internal demand and a question at the same time.

If we were to apply this metaphor to the Polish situation, though, we would soon find that "Jewish on the outside, Polish on the inside" describes not the beginning, but in a way, the end of the journey, at least for the time being. For as I talked with these young "return Jews," I came to realize that the biggest step they have taken so far has been the very acknowledgment of their Jewishness, an acknowledgment to themselves and to the outside world. For those comprising the core of this small group, such an acknowledgment came in the form of shared, therapy-like experience during a series of sessions in 1979, organized as a follow-up to the visit of Carl Rogers (see also: Wieviorka, 1984). Maybe it was his particular approach, maybe it was their background in psychology, or maybe it was simply time to come to terms with 1968 and its aftermath; whatever the reason, it was during those sessions that these young Jews first broke the silence surrounding their Jewishness, first tried to formulate what exactly had been bothering them over the years, first tried to establish a bond with other Jews which would not by-pass the issue, but center on it.

Within only a few years, one of the "return Jews", Stanisław Krajewski was to be interviewed by an extremely popular and influential Catholic weekly, when he stated publicly and openly his reasons for returning to Judaism.[10] Characteristically, though, an equal emphasis was placed on his resolution both to remain Polish and to remain in Poland. Others, while they now celebrate Shabbat and hotly debate things Jewish, are equally concerned about the present and the future of Poland. Set on being highly visible as Jews, they have not abandoned or even diminished their commitment to the cause of democratic Poland. In a way, theirs is a struggle reminiscent of the early nineteenth century plight of Jewish assimilation-ists, a struggle for a Poland where one could be a good Jew *and* a good Pole at the same time. The main difference, however, is that these young Jews now have a much better grasp of Polish patriotism than they have of Jewish tradition—a reverse of the assimilation story. [Krajewski's own words, which served as a title of the above interview, summarize it best: (I am) a Pole who tries to be a Jew.''] They also have, (naturally enough, considering their upbringing within Polish culture and Polish values), an outlook on the world and an ethic which are essentially Polish. Their journey—so far, I stress—has not taken them outside that Polish territory, with their rediscovery of Jewish culture not replacing but *enriching* their Polish identity.

When I first heard of this small group of young Jews celebrating their Jewishness again—in early 1983, at the height of Polish media interest in things Jewish—my first reaction was a mixture of disbelief and awe at the sheer and irrational strength of that nearly undefinable bond of "feeling Jewish." When I first met them in the fall of that year, I was touched to see children again singing Hebrew songs by Shabbat candles *in Poland*. Neither I nor my Warsaw companions would have thought it possible even in 1973.

What puzzled me most, though, was not that this was happening. [After all, I too, having grown up far from any Jewish tradition, have later felt the need to explore it, if not to participate in the ritual or in community life.] What puzzled me most was how comfortable these young Jews appeared to be in their new role, or how much they seemed to feel at ease celebrating their Jewishness *there*.

This is not to say that their experience was problem-free; indeed, if anything, it had been a perpetual internal struggle, filled with strong doubts and very strong emotions, sudden turns and returns. But for all its psychological difficulties and for all its more pragmatic problems (such as where to find sources of information), this rediscovery of Jewish heritage did not appear to spell any kind of social outcasting; it did not make these young people suddenly strange or unacceptable. In fact, as I was to find out, their new Jewishness proved, if not fully comprehensible, at least quite attractive to their gentile friends.[11] In some cases, it was because of the direct prompting and curiosity of their gentile friends that the search for some substance to "being Jewish" began. Later, that search was to be shared by Jews and non-Jews alike; during the first two years, it took the form of privately organized seminars, seminars on various topics in Polish Jewish history, gathering as many as sixty to eighty people. This "Jewish Flying University," as it was called so as to parallel similar educational circles within the larger opposition network, was not to be active much past the birth of Solidarity in 1980—understandably enough, times being too vibrant and too absorbing for quiet learning. In part, too, it had run its course, the number of available speakers was never high to begin with. A meeting scheduled for December 1981 was to have focused on what could be done in the future. That meeting never took place; the imposition of

Martial Law made any such gathering illegal. But the learning process itself did continue, though in safer, more individual ways. And today, while the observance of Shabbat and Jewish holidays might indeed be reserved for the Jewish members of the group, the work on projects in Polish Jewish history, the public and private discussions and the very active interest in things Jewish involve *both* young Jews and non-Jews.[12] Most importantly, perhaps, they involve a set of *common* questions about Poland and its Jewish heritage.

Not being alone in their search, or indeed becoming a valued source of initiative as well as a kind of "live reference point" for queries about the Jewish presence in Poland, may account for the feeling of relative ease among my Shabbat companions. Their journey into a terrain ridden with many a tough question and many a blank spot is not only something they can share with each other, but something they can and do share in large part with their non-Jewish friends.

"Friends" is a key word here. Being among friends is not only what makes this return to Jewishness easier, it is also what can explain the most puzzling fact of all, puzzling at least from a Jewish perspective: their very resolution to stay in Poland. One could say that for these young Jews, just as much as if not more than for others within the opposition milieu, friendship is both a commitment and a resource.[13] On the one hand, sharing a cause makes them both stronger and more vulnerable. Stronger, as these young people have something which is very precious indeed—a sense that their lives matter, not just for themselves, but for the nation as a whole. More vulnerable, as they live under the constant threat of reprisals and a great deal of risk. On the other hand, being part of a veritable network of mutual assistance both lowers the risks and allows one to deal better with everyday problems, both in practice and in theory. It makes weathering the current economic crisis both easier and less important, for while these young people suffer from the same shortages and the same abysmal services as everyone else, they do not focus their lives on securing the necessities of daily existence. They can—or perhaps they must—see the everyday difficulties as incidental to what really counts: their cause and their friends.

Finally, and this is perhaps most important, the interest in things Jewish is very much a part of the larger struggle for a democratic Poland. A young Jew who was always involved in the opposition, but now does so more and more as a Jew, is not abandoning his old ideals or his old friends. His journey might indeed be a very private affair, his experience of Jewishness of necessity different from interest alone, but his questions about the Jewish heritage are at the very center of a very wide and public debate on democracy, pluralism and "Polishness." He can and often does feel that what is at stake is the future of Poland. Paradoxically, his efforts to be more Jewish may be rendering him more Polish at the same time, or at least even more committed to a Poland where his personal choices would indeed become a matter of personal choice.

In short, the decision to stay in Poland is not as strange as it might at first appear.[14] It is significant, though, well beyond the lives of the individuals affected. It does indicate that a new sense of belonging is now possible, one whereby a Jew is no longer silent and invisible. What makes it possible, I think, is the fact that in Poland today the Jew is no longer silent and invisible. And what makes *that* possible is the question we shall be exploring for the remainder of this chapter.

It might be best to begin with learning more about the people we have already met: the young non-Jewish opposition intellectuals, the friends and co-workers of our "return Jews." One might first ask what reason they could possibly have to devote so much of their free time, let alone of their professional careers, to learning about the Jew. And, why now?

The two questions, as it turns out, are very much related. For as I talked to some of those most involved in the "Jewish memory project", I would inevitably hear the word "sixty-eight". And it is not a coincidence that both they and my Shabbat companions all belong to what might be called the " '68 generation". As a category, the " '68 generation" reflects experience rather than demography, comprised as it is of people who vary in age, yet who share an outlook deeply marked, if not altogether formed by what they saw happening in 1968. Among today's opposition intelligentsia, some were old enough to be on the barricades then; others, like me, watched, listened and learned from that first serious encounter with the power of the regime. Actually, the drawing of lessons was to come later. At the time, concerns were much more immediate. There were friends jailed and/or expelled from university for taking part in the protest. There was a sense of isolation, a barrier between the attacked students and intellectuals and the rest of society (see: Lipski, 1983a). There was a profound feeling of shame in the aftermath of Poland's participation in the invasion of Czechoslovakia (which sparked only a very limited protest). And then, there were countless evenings of debating what it all meant, of decoding the power factions behind yet another smear campaign, of trying to prefigure the next move in this political game. Finally, there were the sad and rushed goodbyes at the railway station, as the trains to Vienna carried hundreds of fleeing Jews, torn from the country and the people they loved. At those moments, an explosion of anti-Semitic propaganda was no longer just a tactical maneuver skillfully—and successfully—

applied to subdue the growing unrest. It was a personal tragedy for those forced to leave and for those left behind.[15]

The 1968 exodus dealt a damaging blow to Poland's intellectual and cultural life with the departure of some of the most creative and promising people.[16] There was likely even more serious damage done. All those lies and slander and dirt thrown on people simply because they could be assigned some traces of Jewish ancestry (false sometimes), met with the general indifference of society at large. And even within the opposition itself, the reaction was often one of retrieval; as Kuroń was aptly to express it much later, "we did not all chant 'nous sommes tous des Juifs allemands' ".[17] Rather, Jewish activists were kept in the darkened background, so as not to give the regime additional fuel for repression *and* not to provoke a negative popular reaction against the opposition activities. Thus, although protests against reviving anti-Semitic sentiments were an integral part of the students' petitions at the time, the whole handling of this issue could still leave some people with an ambivalent moral aftertaste.

It has taken a good many years for these feelings to crystallize. To some, 1968 was and remains a purely political event, interpreted in terms of factional struggles and significant primarily for what it did for the development of ideas within the opposition movement. 1968 was the last time the protesters would be singing "the Internationale"; it was the end of the attempts to revise Marxism to make "real socialism" livable (Walc, 1981/83). To others, 1968 became more of a personal turning point. It was a time for taking definite sides, a time when plain human decency was at stake. These others, too, might at first have thought of the anti-Semitic campaign as a strategic tool applied from the top, or they treated it as a fair price for the Jews' having been in power for so long. But they also often refused to take it for granted. Disturbed by the very fact that it was seen as a useful tool—and that it had proven to be a useful tool—they would begin to question their own attitudes towards the Jews. A sudden explosion of the "Jewish question" into the public arena thus became a major personal challenge—morally, emotionally, and later also intellectually—for at least some of the members of the " '68 generation".

At the beginning, such a challenge was met mainly by extending support to one's Jewish friends, whatever their ultimate choices. It meant helping them through rough times, but also helping oneself by demonstrating in words and action that there indeed existed a different Poland.[18] Later, as everything was calming down, and the few Jews who did stay on were beginning to feel somewhat more comfortable, the collective and symbolic aspect of being a decent Pole gained in importance. As concerns moved outside the realm of immediate and individual problems, the whole experience of 1968 began to be translated into tough questions about Polishness and Polish history. And while feelings of empathy and sympathy with regard to individual Jews would not disappear, they would assume a secondary position in what was rapidly becoming an issue of collective self-definition.

It should be also remembered that while talking about the " '68 generation", we are talking about people born and growing up after the Holocaust, people for whom the first proper introduction to the "Jewish question" came in the form of an anti-Semitic propaganda campaign. In my talks about 1968 with some of the Poles most deeply involved in the "Jewish memory project," it was clear that just as significant as the events themselves was the very fact that they were rather suddenly exposed to the Jewish presence in Poland, only to realize how poorly equipped they were to make some sense of it all. To them, Jews had long symbolized martyrdom and suffering, but those Jews were figures of the past and not the present. The Jew they knew from literature, a mixture of sage, usurer and stranger, belonged to a past even more distant and less relevant. The symbolic Jew of a common stock of humor was a colorful abstraction. Most importantly perhaps, the real, living Jews they did know were all too much like themselves to provide any substance to the *difference* they were now asked to perceive. In contrast to their parents, then, these young people had no private memories of the Jewish community as it had once been. Theirs was the first generation which would need to rely primarily, if not exclusively, on Poland's collective memory for both knowledge of and sentiments about the Jew. Yet Poland's memory, as we have seen, accorded very limited space to the whole "Jewish question" and even less to Jews as Jews.

In short, though 1968 was felt and experienced very personally, it would prove not to be a personal problem in terms of conscience or interpretive efforts. From the outset, the problem touched on collective self-definition, collective behavior and collective memory. And while it would later present a good many problems in terms of resources, the very scarcity of these resources might also have made for a bolder, fresher, more critical, approach to questions beginning to emerge. That the " '68 generation" was the first with little, if any memory of the Jew may account for both its naïveté and its ignorance as well as its more open-minded look at the past.

Yet if being deeply bothered by the events of 1968 and their aftermath explains the *individual* motivation behind the breaking of silence surrounding things Jewish, it still leaves the question of why and how the silence came to be broken *publicly*. In other words, as important as these young intellectuals might have been for generating queries and ideas, their presence alone could not account for the recent explosion of public discussion and public exposure of the Jew. With the cultural scene in

Poland being what it was, the impact of a few, even a fairly influential few, producers of ideas within the opposition was by no means guaranteed, even within their own milieu let alone society at large. Yet by 1988, if we are to judge by the popularity of books, exhibits, films, and so on, devoted to the Jew, the interest in things Jewish appears to be widespread with no signs of diminishing. What happened?

What has happened, in essence, is that the Jew has acquired both relevance and presence within *all three* of Poland's "culture zones," at roughly the same time, although *not* for the same reasons. What has happened is that the interest in things Jewish of our "initiative group" has come to *resonate*[19] with much wider concerns within both the regime and the opposition. And, finally, it has also come to resonate with the concerns of Poland's progressive lay Catholic intelligentsia, securing a place for the Jew in that very influential realm of cultural production. [By 1986–87, in fact, the lay Catholic publications (and organizations) had become the *main* platform for discussing things Jewish.]

It is, of course, difficult to talk about such resonance with any degree of precision. Much of it remains—and will remain—hidden from the public eye, especially with respect to the involvement of official media and institutions; minutes of meetings in Poland's political chambers are not, after all, easily available. Much of it, although explicit, as with the Church pronouncements on the need to respect and learn more about Judaism—this "older brother of Christianity"—only raises further questions.

A good place to start examining resonance seems to lie within the very habitat of our "initiative group"—the opposition milieu. And here, a good point to start with is a realization that Poland's opposition is not a homogeneous entity, nor are the Jews within it a homogeneous group. Both of these factors are important, for both set the tone for discussing things Jewish and both set the limits to just how far such discussions can go.

Back in 1968, the situation was in many ways simpler. Both Jews and opposition were on the same side of the barricades, so to speak; the regime's tactics placed both on the defensive. In those days, it would have been unthinkable in public to raise the question of Jewish Stalinists, for example, without crossing the political divide. (This was not due to any in-group solidarity, but rather to the official propaganda tactic of "dumping" Jewish Stalinists together with revisionists, Zionists, etc., as well as emphasizing the direct parent-child links between them and the student leaders.) There was a definite sense of "us" against "them" as far as talking about Jews was concerned. Anti-Semitism, when officially sponsored and officially sanctioned, came to be identified with the regime and with the regime only. In early 1981, when the Association "Grunwald" made its first public appearance at a ceremony commemorating the Polish victims of Jewish Stalinists, people at the core of the democratic opposition saw this flagrantly anti-Semitic organization as yet another of the regime's inventions (they were right, but only partly) (see: Hirszowicz, 1981, 1982, 1986). They were also inclined to view all anti-Semitic brochures and tracts distributed country-wide at the time as yet another provocation of the regime.[20] Again, they were only partly right. By the time one of the main Solidarity activists spoke openly—and publicly—about "those Jews in the government" (in September 1981), they had begun to express some doubts (see: Weschler, 1984). They came to realize that as much as they might have preferred it to be otherwise, the opposition movement itself was not immune to genuinely-felt anti-Jewish sentiments.

That this was indeed the case should not have been surprising. With a movement as large and diverse as Solidarity, and as staunch in support of basic democratic rights, the appearance within it of people and groups carrying on in the best traditions of Polish nationalism was only natural. Indeed, one could argue that a real test of the principle of pluralism does not begin until there emerges a force challenging it. However, even Michel Wieviorka, an astute sociological observer of the Polish scene in general, and the "Jewish question" in particular, saw Solidarity's struggle for democracy the same as the struggle against chauvinism, anti-Semitism included. It is then less surprising that for people associated with KOR (Committee for Workers' Defense), people who in the words of one of them—a non-Jew—considered themselves all "honorary Jews," it took a good deal of time and effort to accept that theirs was also a defense of their ideological opponents.

Today, Solidarity having been crushed and the ranks of the opposition severely depleted, the diversity of views is still very much evident. In many ways, the blow dealt to the movement made it ever more divided, and the ongoing crisis almost guarantees its remaining so. What that means for talking about the Jew is at least two things. As the pros and cons of Polish nationalism are now hotly debated in what appears to be a more "balanced" fashion (that is, involving proponents of opinions spanning the spectrum of the Polish political tradition rather than skewed towards the Left as they were before), the question of Polish-Jewish relations can and does receive considerable attention.[21] It is difficult to discuss Polish nationalism meaningfully without at least some reference to Jews, a people long serving as the main target for nationalist antagonism. Thus for Poles today, although their relations with the Ukrainians, Czechs, Russians or Germans are a great deal more important in terms of immediate practice, their relations with the Jews possess what one might call a "theoretical" significance much closer to the heart of the problem. In reflecting on the meaning of Polish patriotism, the Polish tradition, and ultimately, Polish-ness itself, the position accorded to the Jew represents one of the better indicators of just how exclusive or inclusive "Polish" is to be.[22] In short, it can be said that the issue of Polish-Jewish relations, embedded as it is within a general historical framework for discussions of Polish national consciousness, might play an important role in the current intense national re-examination of the ways to be Polish. [23]

At the same time, however, we should not forget about the specific and immediate context of this whole debate. As democratic as it may be, it is still taking place within the underground and in opposition to the regime, making certain things difficult to say and others impossible. More impor-tantly for our analysis at this point, the debate is taking place within a milieu where the presence of Jews among its intellectual elite is still significant.

What that means is that any discussion related to the "Jewish question" can—and does—assume an undercurrent of direct personal relevance to the people involved (see: Cywinski, 1984), in turn signifying that, however important Polish-Jewish relations might be in the abstract, in practice, one would be inclined to minimize that importance so as to minimize the potential for tension and conflict.[24] Ultimately, one might prefer to remain silent on certain issues and about certain people, if only to avoid trouble.

Which issues, which people, what kind of trouble? The problem lies primarily with the past of a few prominent writers and intellectuals, a past marked by allegiance to the Communist rulers or at least, in the case of the younger ones, by principled belief in the virtues of socialism. As it happens, many of them are Jewish, though some by nomination only, and all, after "seeing the light", came to oppose the regime which in many ways they had helped to create. Today, no longer trying to reform the system from within, they are joined by people who never saw the system as redeemable to begin with, people who had always been against what it represented: a God-less, evil and foreign invasion of Polish national being. In short, yesterday's radicals, with a clearly anti-clerical outlook, are today's comrades-in-arms of the Catholics fighting to preserve Poland's national identity and moral integrity.

Coming from such very different backgrounds, such very different traditions, they are all now struggling—as *Poles*—to maintain some form of national sovereignty, to make room for independent thought, indepen-dent ethics, independent institutions (see: Michnik, 1977/79; Cywinski, 1970/85). Yet sharing a struggle does not automatically produce harmony and mutual understanding. Though the two sides increasingly speak the same language, concessions are both difficult and unavoidable. And one such concession, it seems, is a kind of "gentlemen's agreement" by virtue of which the problematic past of the secular wing is not to receive too much public attention. (Privately expressed opinions are another matter altogether.) When it does, it is likely to bring to the surface many of the old anti-Semitic clichés—"Judeo-Commune" not the least among them— and to rekindle resentments and tensions now dormant.

Since when has the Church in Poland been worried about generating anti-Semitism, one might ask, especially considering its past record of both actively promoting and passively condoning anti-Jewish sentiments and actions?[25] Is this a tactical change, now possible since the Jews no longer constitute any significant social presence? Or is it a change of strategy made necessary by the fact that the few remaining Jews are now on the same side? Is it perhaps more a real change of heart and mind with respect to the "Jewish question," a change in principle as well as action? And, if so, just how much of that change is of Polish origin?

With the Catholic Church in Poland a part of the universal Church, the first answer which comes to mind is "Vatican II." It was in 1966, after all, that the Church, in the voice of its highest authority, spoke against anti-Semitism in general and in its own teachings in particular. Twenty years or so later, the Vatican's directives specifically call for emphasizing the Jewish origin of Jesus Christ, while Pope John Paul II himself extends this new emphasis to apply to Mary as well, a dramatic change for Polish Catholics, who revere Mary in a cult-like manner. There are now efforts to open a dialogue with Judaism, one which would be based on mutual respect and which would offer a base for more mutual understanding. In the spring of 1986, on the historic occasion of the first visit ever by a Pope to the Rome synagogue, both sides expressed hope that such efforts would continue.

Although framed in explicitly theological terms, or as a dialogue between Catholicism and Judaism, these efforts are, of course, important for the relations between Catholics and Jews world-wide. In the Polish context, however, they do take on a different or additional role. To have meaningful dialogue, there first has to be a partner, but in today's Poland, the tiny group of religious Jews cannot possibly carry on the task of ecumenical communication. Thus while the Association of Mosaic Faith might be formally invited to represent Judaism at official Church functions, there has also been a less formal, less official invitation extended to Polish Jewry—a "memory invitation." It is now deemed important by at least some members of the Church hierarchy for all Polish Catholics to learn more about the partner they have known so little about—the Jew.

While these general developments within the universal Church are essential to what is happening today in Poland, the color and the direction which they assume there are also heavily influenced by a much more local—and much less known—movement within Polish Catholicism. In the interwar period, when the Church stood almost uniformly on the conservative side, with its reactionary ideas and practices, a small group of "progressive Catholics," many of them laymen, began to advocate a different model for Polish Catholicism, one centered on ethics and free of xenophobia and prejudice. In those days, these progressive Catholic intellectuals were a double minority, as it were: they worked outside the mainstream of the Church as well as outside the prevalently secular and rational ethos of Poland's intellectual elites. Some came from traditionally Catholic homes; others grew up in an agnostic environment (among them, a fair number were of Jewish descent). All fought for a closer and deeper alliance between faith and action as well as for a more open and sensitive approach to Poland's social problems (see: Michnik, 1977/79).

Under Communist rule, their fate seemed uncertain more than once, yet their influence grew, both in their numbers and, more importantly, in control over means of communication. Today, many of the Church-sponsored publications aimed at a wide audience originate with the lay Catholic intellectuals and convey their progressive view of Catholicism, far removed from a dogmatic and in some cases simply primitive approach to Church teachings.[27]

It is no accident that those are the very channels through which things Jewish have been presented to the Polish public in greatest diversity and depth (relatively speaking, of course). It is also no accident that it was the Club of Catholic Intelligentsia in Warsaw, one of several such centers of progressive Catholics, which initiated in 1973 what was to become an annual "Week of Jewish Culture." During that week, volunteers clean up Warsaw's Jewish cemetery, listen to lectures, and debate issues. And, finally, it is no accident that among the students at the "Jewish Flying University" were a fair number of lay Catholic intellectuals, extending their interest in things Jewish to include the more contemporary aspects of Polish-Jewish relations. Speaking more generally now, if the universal Church *rapprochement* with Judaism has meant a dialogue of faiths, that of the Polish Catholic intellectuals is a dialogue with the Jew, both past and present.

Translated into practical terms—and especially among the younger generation—such a dialogue is often a very personal affair. As I said before, from stories related to me by some of the "return Jews," as well as from the published accounts available (e.g., Blumsztajn, 1985), there emerges a picture of intense questioning, almost an insistence on the part of Catholic friends. The questioning of what it means to be a Jew, and the insistence on authentic Jewishness—both make for a kind of polite solicitation to stand by one's heritage, no matter how little of that heritage was actually at hand to begin with. It would often be from these Catholic friends that a Jew brought up in silence learned some basics of Judaism and Jewish history.

Why such insistence on preserving or rather on re-creating a Jewish presence in Poland? To some extent, it seems to be a way of making sense of the post-1968 confusion; in this context, the courageous stand taken by progressive Catholics in Parliament should not be forgotten.[28] But, for the most part, it is a result of a more general inquiry into the meaning of Polishness. Maybe paradoxically, these very Catholic Poles are also open to the idea of non-Catholic Poles. Theirs is a highly demanding, highly questioning Catholicism, a basis for moral, not national, integrity. In other words, it is a Catholicism which welcomes—at least in principle—the presence of people with different if not opposite views of the world. It is a Catholicism which leaves room for rationalism and agnosticism in the discussions it generates. It is a Catholicism which also makes room for the Jew (literally, too, by inviting Jewish writers to publish under the auspices of the Church, for example). In short, it is a Catholicism which guarantees at least a debate on the notion of ''Pole = Catholic.''

That such a debate should be of interest to, or indeed in the interest of, the state is not too surprising. It is, after all, at the very center of the regime's efforts to present itself as a legitimate *Polish* authority. And if, in the current situation, the equation ''Pole = Catholic'' has acquired a very real meaning, it not only keeps the discussion open but intensifies the issue. A great deal is at stake—from the point of view of the Communists in power—in demonstrating that not all Poles are or should be Catholics.

What was surprising was the regime's radical turn-about regarding its approach to the Jew. The rather sudden public appearance of many voices, either Jewish or highly sympathetic to Jews, combined with the great deal of ceremony and care devoted to the 1983 commemoration of the 40th anniversary of the Warsaw Ghetto Uprising—all made for a puzzling spectacle indeed. It had more than one touch of unreality to it: a country with only a few thousand remaining Jews, witnessing one of the largest celebrations on record of an event which not only belongs among the most glorious chapters of Jewish history, but also, potentially at least, carries many an unglorious implication for the Poles. There was also more than a touch of schizophrenia to it all, beginning with the participation of a PLO representative through a continuing stream of anti-Zionist rhetoric in the media and ending with the publication of some of the most viciously anti-Semitic texts ever to appear.[29] But in the main, there was a gnawing sense of something about to happen; all this attention paid to the Jews could spell only trouble, I thought. Confronted with people freshly out of Poland and firmly believing that there are still over one hundred thousand Jews[30] living there, I began to suspect that the media hoopla was merely a way to blow the significance of the Jewish presence out of all proportion, then *plausibly* to blame it all on the Jews. A Machiavellian scheme, perhaps, but one which did make some sense, considering how unsuccessful were the original attempts to lay the blame for the imposition of Martial Law, Poland's greatest crisis, on "Zionist perpetrators" (see: Hirszowicz, ed. 1981).

Discussing these matters in Paris with some of the most acute observers of the Polish scene, as well as with many ordinary Poles and Polish Jews, I was faced with another interpretation which, while no less Machiavellian, proved much more interesting. In Warsaw in the fall of 1983, that same interpretation was expressed again and again by people of otherwise quite different persuasions. That nearly perfect uniformity of views is as significant as the explanation of the regime's involvement itself. Simply stated, the government was seen as being "nice to the Jews" for only one reason: to get some badly needed credit from Western bankers. Did not General Jaruzelski himself express hopes for an improvement on the international credit front when talking with the representatives of Jewish organizations invited to the Ghetto commemoration ceremonies?

Old myths die hard, it seems. Yet if we put aside the unjustifiably high belief placed in the Jewish influence over world finance, the reasoning behind the regime's efforts begins to look perfectly rational. Poland is in very deep trouble, not the least because of the sanctions imposed by the West after the declaration of Martial Law. The state needs to regain at least some of its international standing, both politically and economically. With all the outcry against violations of human rights, what better way than to stage a demonstration of good will towards a minority everyone knows had been attacked in the past? At a relatively low cost, the regime's reputation abroad would improve, while the effect on the domestic front would be minimal (it should be stressed that in April 1983 most of the restrictions were still in place).

As it turned out, the plan, if ever there was a plan, did not prove a total failure. Once set in motion, the new policy of giving a "green light" to, if not actively encouraging, a public celebration of things Jewish, has not been a total loss either. For one, it did help, just as much as it was helped by, a gradual normalization of Poland's relations with Israel. Quietly but persistently, the once-broken ties between the two countries are now being reestablished, both on the diplomatic front and in terms of cultural and scientific exchanges.[31] Just how many of these efforts at normalization originate in Moscow is another matter. Whatever the story behind the scenes, a renewal of contacts with Israel, even on a limited scale and achieved at a time when the regime's acceptance by the West is still very tenuous, cannot hurt.

Besides being a part of the large international scheme of things, the official invitation extended to Jewish history and culture appears to have worked fairly well domestically. Once we notice that similar invitations were recently given to the whole subject of national minorities, all within a still larger framework of discussing "Polish national character," the inordinate amount of attention paid to the Jew begins to make more sense. And once we notice how gradually the emphasis in the official views relating to the Church has shifted in the direction of co-existence and pluralism, including the trial introduction of "religious studies" into high-school curricula as of September 1986 (where Catholicism is to receive an equal share with Buddhism, Judaism, Islam and atheism) the new emphasis on Poland's Jewish heritage seems in perfect harmony with the state's overall objectives.

Though rarely explicit, these objectives involve no less than a re-definition of what it means to be a good Pole. Faced with the formidable task of governing a nation whose overwhelming majority adheres to the Catholic Church, if not to the faith, the Communists cannot plausibly claim to represent it unless they appear convincingly as true patriots. In the past, this meant, more often than not, a forging together of the nationalist and the Party credos (see: Szafar, 1983); today, a somewhat different strategy is also being tried out, one no less "patriotic" in tone, but more in keeping with the realities of the ideological competition. The new approach stresses the *multiplicity* of traditions making up Polishness, thus aiming to undercut the hegemonic influence of the Church to make room for views which are secular, rational, pragmatic and not explicitly Communist.

It is no coincidence that the main platform of this so-called "liberal" view, the Party weekly *Polityka*, has also served as the platform for much of the officially sanctioned debate on Polish-Jewish relations. Over the last six years or so, *Polityka* has published numerous articles discussing—and popularizing—Poland's Jewish heritage: mini-studies by prominent historians and cultural critics as well as many smaller items, such as book reviews, essays and letters.[32] At times, the opinions expressed in its pages, as well as the quality of information revealed, make it seem as if we were in a free country, where a debate of the most controversial issues is not only possible but actually welcome.[33]

There is one catch, however. The long-time chief editor of *Polityka* was then Poland's deputy premier; the "liberal" journalists on staff were no less the regime's people than, let us say, those working in Polish television, which was subjected to a long-standing boycott by the country's most prominent artists and intellectuals. And, as mentioned before, most "court Jews" have a home there, some as weekly columnists, others as regular contributors; discussion of things Jewish is in large part their territory. No matter how unrestricted that discussion may appear, then, it is limited in one crucial respect: its public impact. For while *Polityka* does enjoy a wide readership among Poland's intelligentsia, it is still generally boycotted by people close to opposition circles. Among the "return Jews", for example, most no longer even bother to read *Polityka* (since its February 1982 reappearance under Martial Law), even when something of particular interest to them is being printed there. More generally, *Polityka* today, much as it struggles to "speak the voice of reason," or to occupy a kind of cultural middle ground, remains identified with the regime and its propaganda machinery, all its "liberalism" notwithstanding. The implication for our study is that *Polityka*'s own "Jewish memory project" is simply not on the same footing as the efforts made either within the unofficial cultural zone or by the Catholic intellectuals. [This weakness might be quite regrettable, in fact, considering the views on things Jewish it advocates.[34]]

The picture emerging from our analysis so far is complex, yet it is incomplete in one crucial respect. It could be argued that in all these considerations of resonance between individual interest in the Jew and his public presence, one element has been missing altogether: the *public* itself. Thus while we might now have a fairly good sense of the relevance of things Jewish in all three "zones" of Poland's cultural life, we are still talking about the concerns and actions of *opinion-makers*. And this, important as it may be, still leaves open the question of how these concerns and actions resonate, if at all, with public sentiments and interest.[35]

It is, of course, very difficult to assess the extent of public resonance, at least for an analyst who is not in charge of a large team of survey workers and interviewers. But some plausible suggestions are possible.

For one, it appears that the interest in things Jewish is indeed not restricted to the small "initiative group" at the "Jewish Flying University," or even to a wider, but still small group of opinion-makers and intellectuals.

In March of 1981, when the (then legal) opposition organized a week-long session on "March 1968" at University of Warsaw, several thousand people attended. The thick volume of *Znak*, a Catholic monthly, devoted entirely to Jewish topics and first published in the spring of 1983, saw an unprecedented second printing in 1984, due to popular demand. All the "Jewish books" which appeared officially would disappear rapidly from store shelves, with one exception: the huge (50,000) copy run of an obscure historian's (Orlicki, 1983) reflections on Polish-Jewish relations, which argued among other things, that the Kielce pogrom had been organized by the Zionists to further the cause of Jewish emigration. When *Fiddler on the Roof* was staged in Poland in 1985, it drew enormous crowds, becoming a veritable scalpers' bonanza. On a smaller scale, but of no smaller importance, are the public seminars on Jewish history and culture which accompany the annual "Jewish week" organized by Catholic intellectuals; these have been attracting several hundred people at a time. And then, as I was told with a touch of cynicism by a young, non-Jewish Warsaw oppositionist, Jews and things Jewish are now definitely "in" among elite intelligentsia circles (since then, kosher-style food became popular at parties).

It might well be that a good part of all this attention is simply a matter of fashion. Poland's cultural elite is not very different in this respect from other elites.[36] It might also well be that the tide will turn again. Among my Shabbat companions, there was some well-founded fear that the prolonged general crisis can lead only to yet another wave of anti-Semitic sentiments (see also: Morga, 1986).

Yet, there is one motif, running through *both* the public discussions and conversations with "people in the know," a kind of half-articulated *longing* for a different Poland, one which might eventually guarantee that the Jew, once re-invited, will remain. If talking about the often extreme polarization of Polish society and culture makes them appear very heterogeneous, one must remember that, deep down, as it were, Poland's is also an extremely homogeneous culture for the first time in the country's history.[37] It is only recently that some public forum has been granted to Poland's ethnic and religious minorities; even now, their impact on culture at large is minimal at best. Polish society today is virtually "pure" ethnically, and virtually exclusively Catholic, a dream come true for Polish nationalism. Or is it?

Is Polish culture really better off without "foreigners" in its midst? A culture cut off from the steady supply of different—and yet not too different as, for example, American—ideas and traditions, a culture ethnocentric in fact if not by design, a culture closed to opposites—is such a culture not in danger of becoming static and eventually boring? Finally, as a culture of national survival, is not Polish culture in danger of losing a universally human face unless it can regain some of the inbuilt universalism it once had?[38]

It does take time for a culture to feel the full impact of societal change. It took nearly forty years, in this case, for many Poles to begin questioning the virtues of a "purely Polish" Poland. At this stage, not much can be done to alter the demographics of the situation. But something *can* be done about altering the *symbolic* fabric of social discourse. And, an invitation extended to the Jew, it seems, is just one of the things which can encourage a more vibrant, more diverse culture. It is almost as if Poles, now deprived of their "natural" Other, need to re-invent the Jew.

## Notes

1. The choice of language is crucial here. Historically, Poland's Jews were very much divided on the language issue, with each preference (Yiddish, Hebrew, Polish, Russian) clearly indicative of a whole set of cultural as well as political values (see: Mendelsohn, 1983; Heller, 1980). Today, the revival of interest in Jewish culture among many young French Jews manifests itself—among other things—by a tremendous growth of *Yiddish* studies. *Not* learning Yiddish ultimately means a form of internationalizing one's Jewish identity—as opposed to maintaining the continuity of Polish Jewish tradition.
2. Not all inactive Communists have become ex-believers and joined the Jewish community. It is certainly not the case with some of the most prominent ones (see: Torańska, 1985); it is also not the case with a number of others I met while in Warsaw (see also: Wieviorka, 1984). Rudnicki (1987) reports on the opposite result of the Jews' sense of loss—the conversion of many to Catholicism.
3. The article on "Jews and Communism" (Kainer, 1983) is especially telling here. The plea for understanding the choices made by Jews is as much directed to the Polish readers as it is a personal statement by a child from a Jewish Communist family. It is, I must add, a statement made from the perspective of today's oppositionist, and not necessarily that of a Jew. In contrast to an often very critical re-evaluation of the Jewish involvement on the Left, taking place in France, where the ideological choices are now judged on the "is it good for the Jews?" basis, the efforts in Poland center on the universal, *moral* significance of being and/or supporting Communists.
4. It is perhaps ironic that people living with the continuous barrage of anti-Zionist propaganda are much less *personally* concerned about it than Jews in France or West Germany. It is understandable, though, in that they do not identify with the regime in the way that a French or West German Jew might wish to identify with the anti-Zionist Left (see: Finkielkraut, (1983), Zipes 1986).
5. It should be stressed, though, that while the interest in Jewish history and culture had been by 1983—generally speaking—encouraged by the government, the first *public* signs of a changing stand towards Israel appeared only in *1986,* in the form of neutral and/or favorable articles, frequently written as personal "journey reports".
6. The term is Neusner's (1981) and designates the basic premise of modern Jewish identity: the re-birth of Israel being the redemption after the horror of the Holocaust.
7. It should be stressed that while Jewish losses were *proportionately* so much greater, the "wide distribution" of Polish victims meant that nearly all Polish families were affected. Furthermore, with nearly one million victims of the Soviet occupation (including about 300 thousand Jews), "survival" meant much more than escaping the Nazis.
8. The borderline between the two is not easy to draw. Krajewski, for example,

describes going to visit relatives in Israel at the age of 14 and thinking nothing of it—"there are Poles in America, there are Poles in Israel. . . ."

9. The title of his book (1980)—*Le Juif imaginaire*—is in itself indicative of the combination between almost advertising one's Jewishness (for it makes the young person truly original) and being French to the core in terms of values, customs, priorities.

10. Niezabitowska's interview with Stanisław Krajewski appeared in *Tygodnik Powszechny* on April 24, 1983, that is, as a part of its coverage on the Warsaw Ghetto ceremonies.

11. With some exceptions, that is. While the interest in Jewish history and Jewish culture, including the ritual, could be shared, the "Jewish *angst*" could not. In other words, the more "authentic" aspects of Jewishness proved more appealing than the emotionally painful efforts of the search for authenticity. Also, as I was told, to be an observant Jew was definitely more acceptable than remaining an atheist, suspected of Communist sympathies.

12. It is not always possible to distinguish between the two; one non-Jewish person I met was effectively "passing" as a Jew in this group.

13. The importance of friendship ties is a subject which points to some crucial aspects of resistance to oppressive environments. (For an excellent report on the atmosphere within the opposition milieu, see: Weschler, 1984.) Michnik's writings offer a wealth of insights into the "defensive value" of fighting for a cause. Blumsztajn (1985) makes it explicit that the loss of the friends' network was very much behind his (unsuccessful) attempt to return to Poland. He is also more honest than most about the other side of the story, namely, the *self-esteem* derived from being part of an elite, self-esteem one loses when in the West.

14. That the decision to *stay* calls for an explanation is not only an outsider's view; as recently as April 5, 1987, Krajewski, again interviewed in *Tygodnik Powszechny* (Berberyusz), judged it necessary to spell out his reasons for staying.

15. Jelen (1972), Lendvai (1972) and Banas (1979) all provide extensive "phenomenological" accounts of the experience in 1968. It should be noted, though, that not all Jews felt their departure in 1968 or 1969 to be tragic; their story remains largely untold.

16. Among those who left in the 1968 exodus were many non-Jews, including such prominenent intellectuals as Leszek Kołakowski.

17. What Kurón (1981/83) was referring to—in his presentation at the Warsaw University—was the spontaneous reaction among the French protesters in May 1968 to the attacks on Daniel Cohn-Bendit, who was one of the students' leaders and a German Jew.

18. Solidarity with the victims was most pronounced in their immediate milieu, but efforts to disassociate oneself from the official policy were also made among the very officials handling the administrative side of Jewish emigration (for personal accounts, see: Jelen, 1972).

19. My analysis of resonance owes a great deal to discussions with Michael Schudson.

20. I rely here on insights gained from a member of KOR, interviewed in Warsaw. (see also: Steinsbergerowa, 1983.)

One must consider, though, that right throughout the legal existence of Solidarity, there was enough anti-Semitic propaganda in the official press to warrant giving security forces more credit than was actually due.

21. This is not to say that the issue is in any way central within the opposition's concerns. *Tygodnik Solidarność,* for example, in its existence from April to Dec. 1982, published numerous articles devoted to recent history, but only *one* dealing *directly* with the Jews: Kersten's account of the Kielce pogrom (Dec. 4, 1981).

22. Michnik's writings (1985) and, more recently, Cracow's *Arka* discussion of nationalism (nos. 10, 11, 1985; see also 1987 interview with the editors *(Redakcja 'Arki'),* make this point most explicitly; my own observations were based on the discussions within the "Jewish memory project's" initiative group.

23. Such a "generalized" significance of Polish-Jewish relations for *Polish* identity, it should be stressed, is in no way comparable to the very special and *central* position accorded to German-Jewish relations in the discussions of German identity (see: Rabinbach & Zipes, eds. 1986).

    On the other hand, the very fact that it is the *Polish* identity which is at issue here makes the examination of Polish-Jewish history very different from the otherwise parallel developments in France; bringing to light the dark sides of French Jewish history, which intensified in the 1980s, was primarily of import to Jews and *their* sense of identity (Finkielkraut, Wieviorka, personal communication, 1984).

24. A very good example of this "minimization" strategy is Lipski's book on KOR (1983a), where not once does he depart from describing Jews as "secular democrats".

    On another level, Karpinski's (1982) analysis of Polish upheavals, from 1956 to 1980, is also exceptionally cautious vis-à-vis the Jews; there, the only time he mentions the subject at all is in respect to 1968, and even then, only in terms of official pronouncements and general student protest.

25. The subject of the Church's role during the Holocaust in particular remains both controversial and impossible to study in depth (the archives are closed, see: Krakowski, 1984). While it is clear that the clergy *was* involved in aiding Jews, also by way of supplying false baptismal certificates essential for "passing", there is little evidence that devout Catholics were more likely to rescue Jews than others (Tec, 1986), and, by implication, that there was any massive appeal for such actions at the parish level.

    Among Polish sources, perhaps the most telling is the autobiography by a nun who heroically saved Jews during the war only to suffer scorn and ultimately ex-communication (Czubakówna, 1967).

26. According to my informants in Warsaw, Poland's Primate at the time—[1983]— was very receptive to the appeals from a delegation drawn from the core workers on the "Jewish memory project", appeals to ascertain that the teachings of Vatican II would be transmitted in all parishes in Poland. The very need for such an appeal testifies, though, to the slowness of the transformation within the Church.

27. "Progressive" in Poland should not be equated with "progressive" in the West, when discussing Catholicism. Both the weekly *Tygodnik Powszechny* and monthlies *Więź* and *Znak* contain writings of high intellectual caliber on subjects ranging from economics to cinema, together with a broad range of socio-cultural affairs. They do not advocate women's priesthood or the rights to individual choices in such matters as abortion. (For a discussion of the changing political situation of this group, see: Turowicz, 1973.)

28. The *Znak* group was *alone* protesting against the anti-Semitic campaign, subsequently to suffer itself from an attack. Even then, the Church remained silent (see: Smolar, 1986).

29. A series of articles by Bednarczyk in *Rzeczywistość* (April 10 & 17, 1983) devoted to his version of the ghetto struggles contained statements which surpassed even the worst excesses of the 1968 campaign. To take but one example: the Jews were said to hate Poles because it was the Poles who had witnessed the Jews' "total disgrace" (i.e., the Holocaust). Bednarczyk's pronouncements received harsh criticism from Passent in *Polityka* (April 23, 1983).

30. As unreasonable as it may appear, it is not necessarily malevolent; considering the long history of intermarriage with Polish aristocrats, for example, there is no way of telling how many people of—distant—Jewish descent there really are.

31. The number of such exchanges may still be small, but their symbolic significance should not be underestimated. In the Polish media, Israel is re-emerging as a country with strong cultural ties to Poland, one where many people still feel very attached to the Polish language, poetry, art (see: e.g.: Raczek, *Przegląd Tygodniowy*, no. 25 (221), 1986).

32. It is important to stress the value of *book reviews,* for they not only make certain views widely accessible, but also place a continuous emphasis on the need to consider the Jewish presence whenever one is considering Polish history. In a small yet significant way, these reviews further the overall goals of the "Jewish memory project".

33. For a good example of such a perception, see Rothenberg's (1984) review of Sandauer's work, which first appeared (in part) in *Polityka*. Puzzled by the paradox of the official publication of *very* unofficial views on the "Jewish question", Rothenberg passes over the fact that Sandauer—once a controversial literary critic—is now firmly on the side of the regime, a "court Jew".

34. This is not to say there are no "slips" in *Polityka,* only that its *overall* position is consistently critical of anti-Semitism.

35. The question here is quite different from the debates on the role of the media in the West, where commercial considerations are of utmost importance. In Poland, the official prominence of issues, artists, styles, etc., need not have any relation to their actual popularity; the system operates on policy principles, not on "staying in touch with the public" (recent efforts at reform notwithstanding).

36. In Germany, things Jewish are *en vogue* as well apparently on both sides of the Berlin wall, and also among Jewish and non-Jewish young intellectuals. I am grateful to Robin Ostow for bringing this subject to my attention.

In France, "Juifs á la mode" became a title of a perceptive analysis of interest in things Jewish (Scherr, 1980). Again, the difference is that there, it is mainly a Jewish fashion.

37. For centuries, Poland was a large kingdom, with an ethnically diverse population. Before World War II, Poland's population included fully a third of national minorities: Ukrainians, Byelorussians, Jews, Germans. In areas in the east— *kresy*—it was often Poles who represented a minority within the ethnic mixture. The destruction of the Polish Jewry, followed by a 1945 movement of the borders westward, with its massive migrations, left only about one-half million members of minorities in Poland today.

38. The longing for a different Poland finds one of its clearest expressions in the arts and especially literature devoted to *kresy,* the eastern lands. The world which will never be again, while not idealized to the point of denying ethnic conflicts, becomes a source of inspiration on the richness of cultural and social experience. The writings of Miłosz, Konwicki and Vincenz are probably the best examples here.

 While not part of the "Jewish memory project", strictly speaking, these are important testimonies to a persisting desire for openness within Polish culture. Significantly, these are also the only works where Jews—and Polish-Jewish relations—are not smothered with nostalgia.

# 4

# Memory Work

September 1986. In the *National Geographic* appears an article entitled "Remnants: The Last Jews of Poland", an excerpt from a book with the same title, published in New York in the same month (Niezabitowska). My first reaction, even though I have lived in Canada for over thirteen years is a mixture of bemusement and anger: have we indeed become so exotic that we qualify for the *National Geographic*? As I recognized pictures I had seen in Warsaw two years previous, I also began to appreciate how much their meaning had been altered by their journey to America.

There is a story behind the words and images of the "Remnants", a story which clearly illustrates the kind of work involved in the "Jewish memory project" as well as the difficulty of analyzing it. The story begins, appropriately enough, in 1968. A young girl, brought up in a traditional Catholic family, is suddenly exposed to the ugliness of anti-Semitism when one of her relatives, married to a Jew, unwillingly emigrates. Some thirteen years later, the girl, Małgorzata Niezabitowska is one of Poland's best young investigative reporters. She works on the staff of *Tygodnik Solidarność* (a weekly) while contributing important articles to other journals as well. *Polityka* publishes her long exposé of the organization "Grunwald," essentially an indictment of its open and not-so-open anti-Semitic theories and actions. *Tygodnik Powszechny,* a Catholic weekly, carries her interview with one of the young Jews rediscovering their Jewishness, a highly sympathetic piece. She is drawn more and more into Jewish affairs, trying to make some sense of a reality she finds both troubling and fascinating.

Gradually, Niezabitowska begins to establish contacts with Jews of older generations, and finds herself travelling across the country in search of "the last ones." Her husband, a talented photographer, accompanies her on most of these expeditions, building up a massive collection of pictures. In a way, the project grows on them as they meet more and more

101

people.[1] It also consumes a great deal of their time and energy, as well as money. And hopes for making it public are slim indeed, with her association with the now crushed Solidarity not helping at all. When I meet Niezabitowska in the summer of 1984, she is not optimistic about her career or about the fate of her "Jewish project." She does feel, however, that their work is valuable and important—the time is running out. Ideally, she tells me then, her stories of the last Jews of Poland, and especially the powerful pictures should attract some interest in the West.

Two years later they do. For a young Polish couple, it might be the ultimate in success stories: a fellowship at Harvard, a book in New York, publicity tours, the *National Geographic*. And it began when in the fall of 1985, a large selection of the photographs was exhibited, very officially, in a Warsaw gallery, drawing huge crowds and official acclaim.[2] The title of the exhibit was simply "The Last Ones," with "contemporary Polish Jews" added in small print. Included were pictures of my Shabbat companions and their children, a tiny light in an otherwise profoundly sad image of the end of what was once a vibrant presence.

As memory work goes, "Remnants" might be said to draw close to the ultimate limits of creativity. Not only is it a construction of a memorial to the past, but it re-constructs the present as the past. It creates its own raw materials, as it were, just as it presents them as *interesting*. Real and very much living individuals become *objects,* all the warmth of description and imagery notwithstanding. People become anthropological curiosities to be looked at with a sentimental eye. A culture becomes a piece of exotica, quite obviously capable of attracting a great deal of interest. Fascination mixes with regret as the last Jews of Poland go on display.

Am I being too hard on this project? After all, both journalism and photography are supposed to objectify people and experiences; that is what they do to communicate,[3] and, to communicate without appearing interesting is to defeat the purpose. Finally, is not the very granting of exposure to the long invisible Jews a worthwhile undertaking? Does it not offer an opportunity to meet—second-hand, but still more directly than ever before—those whose very presence has been the stock of myth and speculation? In short, does "Remnants" not perform an essentially enlightening function, making at least some Poles aware of the realities of being Jewish in contemporary Poland?

It might, but I also suspect it will not. The photographs, as powerful as they are, cannot tell the whole story. And the book is, after all, issued in New York, with its price tag alone making it an unlikely candidate for coffee tables in Warsaw or Cracow.[4] What began as a search and a query is now only a beautifully designed piece of nostalgia.

From an analytical point of view, this group portrait of the last Jews of

Poland is an interesting case of *combining,* albeit somewhat unusually the three *modes* of memory work within this "Jewish memory project." First, the actual effort which went into "Remnants" makes it an instance of a *critical* approach to memory: a way of remembering which is primarily about learning, asking questions (often very hard questions)—about the past, constructing a record, all for the sake of better understanding. The actual presentation, though, both in its general "look" and in its explicit focus, makes the "Remnants" part of what I call a *nostalgic* approach to memory: the Jew is interesting as a Jew; he is now being missed in all his *difference;* he is also **now** strangely beautiful and exotically attractive. In the last analysis, though, the memory work here might best fit into the *instrumental* mode, the mode which uses memory to serve ulterior purposes. In this case, for the author and her photographer husband, a memorial to the Jew becomes a ticket to a career and opportunities in the West. In most cases, instrumentality is much more *collective* in nature, in that the discourse about things Jewish serves the interests of particular political actors (with the government, not surprisingly, taking the lead), or, at the extreme, those of the whole nation, as in reassuring all Poles of the glories in their tradition, for example.[5] More often than not, memory in the instrumental mode is not about memory: it is about proving a point. In that sense, it is really no longer about the Jew, at all.

"Remnants" may serve as a good example of yet another combination, this time operating at the level of *memory production.* Very much of an individual initiative, the project was done under the moral auspices of the Church. Despite Niezabitowska's direct links to the opposition, the work eventually became a legitimate part of official discourse. The story does not end there, since it has by now become a kind of Western ambassador of Polish Jews. Is this an exceptional case? Partly, in that individual initiatives are rarely so successful. But not in principle, in that despite—or because of—all Poland's socio-cultured divisions, the ideas and actions of actual people rarely remain strictly within one particular cultural zone.[6] And, in the case of talking about things Jewish, perhaps even more than in respect to other areas of discourse, ideological distinctions cut across the political dividing lines. As a result, it would make little sense, if any, to introduce into our analysis such categories as "official discourse," for example.

Considering what we have already learned about the different concerns and motivations behind the recent interest in things Jewish, it should come as no surprise that critical memory work has been favored by people associated with the opposition. The stress on de-falsifying history, for one thing, makes quite natural an approach to the past which questions rather than confirms received knowledge. Similarly, the Catholic *rapprochment*

with Judaism is more likely to result in a nostalgic view of the Jew, if for
no other reason than that it is with the Jew that a now-advocated dialogue
is to take place. Finally, as cynical as it may sound, *all* the official publicity
accorded to things Jewish is ultimately instrumental in nature, be it for the
sake of money, reputation or legitimacy. But (and this is a *big* but) the
discourse itself, the words and images which find their way to the public
thanks to the government's extensive "green light," can and do *vary* in
terms of the modes of remembering the Jew.[7]

In a way, such an officially sanctioned discourse *must* vary. The "green
light" in and by itself takes on only a limited function within the whole
system of memory reconstruction, one of *distribution*. Now we have come
to an important feature of the work which goes into this "Jewish memory
project": the particular division of labor. Paralleling what one could
observe in other areas of cultural production, memory work consists of a
set of different tasks, often performed by different people and different
institutions. At its most immediate level, there are words, images, ideas or
objects being *created* by memory workers. The bits and pieces of remembrance, once available, may then become raw material again, this time to
be transformed, interpreted, *edited* (often literally) by what I would call
"secondary" memory makers.[8] This function is usually performed by
critics, translators, editors, but also by scholars and politicians. Finally,
whether in an unedited version—a memoir, for example—or in an edited
form, memory pieces do not become publicly accessible unless they are
*presented*, preferably through a medium of mass communication. This
might mean a lecture on television, a ceremony, a monument, a film; it is
less likely to mean an article in a scholarly journal read by specialists only.

The work does not end there, either. As important as these bits of now
*public* memory are, their entry into *collective* memory depends on how
they are received and retained by the public itself. And the public (even,
or especially, in this case) is not a *tabula rasa*. People in Poland do hold
individual memories of the Jews, be these memories from their own
experience or those passed on by the older generations, memories which
may or may not be in tune with the new elements currently offered. And
the people presenting the new offerings are perfectly aware of that; indeed,
they often say so. Some welcome direct challenge, while others prefer a
more gradualist approach to change—all have to reckon with the fact that
they are indeed breaking a long held silence which could only have affected
the realm of memory.

So far, the whole process, though quite complex in practice, looks fairly
straightforward to students of culture. Meanings are being produced,
arranged and re-arranged, presented (or not presented) to the public to
then become accommodated within the individuals' own systems of mean-

ing (see: Berger & Luckmann, 1967). An analyst who wishes to know what is being said and done on the "memory project" needs only to take into account the actual discourse at the various stages of memory production to gain a fair idea about the modes of remembrance. If he also wishes to know how the Jew *is* remembered, he is in for a far more difficult undertaking.[9]

There is a catch, however, or a strong *incongruity* to this project which renders both the project and the analysis a good deal more problematic. What we are dealing with here is a rather rare case of memory work using—for the most part—*someone else's material.*[10] Bits and pieces of Jewish culture, Jewish history, Jewish tradition are now being claimed by Poles as belonging to *their* memory, all by virtue of a shared historical experience. Ideas, symbols, in short, meanings originating in one very specific and very distinct system are thus being transposed onto another very specific and very distinct system. In the process, these meanings need both to retain their identity and to leave the host identity fairly intact. They need to be both interesting and *relevant* to Poles today. Remembering the Jew is seen as something which calls for *justification.* And "importing" meanings also often calls for translation. As a result, the job of memory reconstruction proves particularly taxing on those who under more normal circumstances might be restating the obvious: those people who introduce things Jewish into the public arena.[11] Not only do they select and interpret various memory products, they also have to make certain those are interesting and worth keeping, a task much less necessary when operating within *one* tradition. In other words, since remembering the Jew, at least in the sense of knowledge, empathy and respect is not exactly "natural" to Poland's memory, the work on this memory reconstruction project cannot be confined to memory production strictly speaking; indeed it has to rely heavily on editorial input.

To make matters slightly more complex, the role of memory distributors is also more pronounced than it is in a less divided society. The authority attached to words spoken by an opposition leader, a lay Catholic intellectual or an official critic is simply very different, quite apart from the fact that the words themselves may or may not be resonating with the audience's ideas. Thus, in addition to limits on what can be said, there are limits on what can be heard, closely related to the location of memory production. It could well be argued, for example, that the mere presence of an official stamp on so much of the "Jewish memory project" automatically cancels its impact on large segments of Polish society. For people who treat anything originating with the regime as suspect by definition, its "being nice to the Jews" might in fact turn into yet another valid reason to forget the Jew altogether. Time will tell.

Actually, at least in this case, time *can* already tell us a great deal. The very passage of years may ultimately account for the fact that things Jewish are today discussed in Poland at all. Historical time, in a sense akin to social location, exerts a powerful presence in the memory reconstruction process.[12] It is important to bear in mind just what kind of times we are talking about here. The "Jewish memory project" spans only a few years, but these years brought, in very quick succession, a period of great activity among the democratic opposition, growing tensions in society-at-large, the explosion of Solidarity, its exhilarating sixteen months of freedom, the rule of Martial Law, and finally, the regime's efforts at "normalization" when faced with a continuing economic crisis. These were all very different times, in terms both of individual concerns and of an alignment of social forces.

Time poses its own problems for the memory reconstruction job. In addition to importing meanings from a different tradition, the "Jewish memory project" uses, for the most part, materials produced in often radically different historical contexts, again calling for a good deal of translation.

Finally, it could be said that it was in large part thanks to a specific historical *moment* that the whole project could be launched on such a scale, that moment being exactly the 40th anniversary of the Warsaw Ghetto Uprising. It did take, of course, a decision at the top to commemorate the occasion in just such a way, but the story only begins there. Whatever were the reasons for staging the official ceremonies and for accompanying them with a wide array of publications, exhibits and a scholarly conference on genocide to boot, what actually happened during the spring of 1983 went far beyond the artificial. Indeed, what happened went far beyond commemoration proper. In all three zones of Poland's culture, the anniversary became very much of an *occasion* to celebrate the Jew—and to stake claims on the Jewish memory. With the nostalgic memory work at its most intense (nostalgic in the sense of remembering Jews as Jews), the officialdom, the opposition and the Church went on record as being the rightful keepers of Jewish memory. Whatever the intentions, the result was striking. Suddenly the Jew was everywhere.[13] A closer look at this peak time on the "Jewish memory project," may allow for a better appreciation of the *work* which went into remembering.

Preparations for the 1983 ceremonies were already well on their way in 1982. At the end of 1982, a beautiful edition of *The Polish Jewry* (Fuks et al) came off the presses—presses in Italy, to guarantee both the speed and the quality of publication. Combining a 100-page introductory text, prepared by a group of prominent Polish historians, with one hundred illustrations, the book portrays Jewish culture mainly through objects. There are a few reproductions of well-known paintings and a few photographs of Jewish cemeteries. There are no images of real, living Jews.

In spite of the very high price tag, the book disappeared very quickly from the store shelves. Its English edition was somewhat easier to obtain, but it too became scarce, as most of its copies were exported. Though clearly and explicitly aimed at Polish Jews scattered around the world, the book drew both interest and praise in the local press. Particularly appreciated were its aesthetic qualities and informative value. One reviewer, though, remarked that for this memorial to Polish Jewry to be really useful for contemporary Poles, it would have to contain a separate lexicon of foreign terms, "Jewish culture having become as removed from us as that of the Aztecs" (a.g., *Polityka,* Jan. 8, 1983).

In late 1982 as well, the finishing touches were being put on Warsaw's newly restored synagogue. Its official opening was to be one of the focal points of the anniversary celebrations in April of 1983. Invitations to attend were extended to all of the main Jewish organizations abroad as well as to some individuals from the world's Jewish communities. Inviting some Israelis to come, and making it possible for others to apply for a visa, was of special importance. It was the first time since 1967, and some feared it would be the last, that Jews from Israel could visit Poland at all. For those who were born in Poland and for those who had lost their families in the death camps, this was then an unexpected and welcome opportunity to share in the memorial. Some hesitated, though, as did many Jews in France and North America (there was never any question of inviting Soviet Jews beyond those included in an official delegation). Should they accept an invitation from a regime at the height of its repression of civil rights and freedom? Should they accept an invitation from the *Polish* government, in view of that government's record? The debate continued for several months. In the end, some Jews came; others stayed home in protest.

This debate was not without a local component. Marek Edelman, the only surviving leader of the Warsaw Ghetto Uprising who still lives in Poland, responded to the invitation extended to him with a widely distributed, though unofficial letter. Appealing to the basic sense of social and moral justice—and to the memory of his murdered people—Edelman staunchly refused to take part in or even lend his voice to the official commemoration of the anniversary. He also appealed to both Poles and Jews not to desecrate the memory of those who had fought for dignity and freedom, a desecration which was inevitable if the people participated in a propaganda display staged by those now oppressing these very values.

Edelman is probably the only genuine Jewish hero in Poland today, not the least because of his being involved with Solidarity and having been an elected member of the first and last Solidarity congress. His life and his views gained much publicity back in 1977, when a book-length interview with him, conducted by Hanna Krall (one of Poland's best journalists, herself a Holocaust survivor), quickly became a bestseller. Demystifying much of the aura surrounding the Ghetto fighters, frank to the point of cruelty, Edelman's ideas on life and death became perhaps the single most important guide to the "Jewish question" at the time. (see Krall, 1986).[14] Again, the time—1977—was just prior to the first breaks in silence among my Shabbat companions.

Edelman's appeal for a boycott of the official ceremonies became one of the reasons for the opposition's decision to organize its own commemoration. It was felt—and it was said—that if anyone had the right to lay a wreath at the monument to Ghetto fighters, it was the people who were today fighting for the same ideals and the same cause, namely Poland's suppressed opposition. [It should be kept in mind that, in the spring of 1983, many of these people were fresh out of internment centers.]

On Sunday, a day before the official memorial, some one thousand people, including prominent opposition members, gathered at the site of *Umschlagplatz*—the place where over four hundred thousand Jews had boarded the trains to Treblinka. Near a small memorial plaque, the crowd listened attentively to speeches delivered by two well-known intellectuals. Of the two speakers at this unofficial gathering—Martial Law was still in effect, remember—one, a non-Jewish Pole, was swiftly arrested, and the other, a Jew, let go—a fact which sparked a few ironic comments about reverse discrimination.

During the period of the anniversary celebrations, Edelman was kept under virtual house arrest. Lech Wałęsa, on his way to Warsaw to attend the unofficial memorial, was stopped by the police. The crowd itself was forced to disperse after about one hour. The next day, most major Warsaw newspapers carried a brief note condemning this "manipulation for political ends" of the Ghetto anniversary, referring, of course, to the oppostion. All of which did not prevent some five hundred people from laying flowers, or rather trying to, at Warsaw's Jewish cemetery that evening. The gates were closed, though, with the full cooperation of the cemetery's Jewish keepers. More generally, the opposition found itself alone in countering the officially staged events; none of the Jewish guests from abroad would join it. [For at least one Jew (and a Solidarity activist), speaking about the Ghetto anniversary (Anonymous, 1984), this lack of any participation by Jewish visitors was a particularly painful reminder of the lack of understanding on their part about who *really* represents Poland.]

There exists a fair amount of disagreement among the participants in those unofficial memorials as to the extent to which they were merely a platform for political protest. Whatever the intentions were—and many of the people I talked to described those as encouraging a genuine moment of remembrance and reflection—the outcome did carry all the signs of *competition* with the regime. A competition in which the opposition ultimately lost, one should add. In spite of a rather jarring incident during the official ceremonies—the appearance of a PLO representative claiming the Ghetto fighters to be very close to his heart, for "they were struggling for the same cause," which sparked protests from the Jewish organizations present—the message taken to the West was, after all, the regime's. Whether morally correct, the Jews' judgment of the situation did reflect the sheer pragmatics of it all. If there was any hope for a better future for the few Jews still remaining in Poland, it lay with the regime, or so it seemed when the candles lit up again in the Warsaw synagogue.[15]

What the Western visitors largely ignored, understandably enough, was that a much more significant development—from a Polish perspective—was taking place behind the politically visible front. The spring of 1983 saw the publication of perhaps the single most important work within the "Jewish memory project" to date: a special double issue of the lay Catholic monthly *Znak,* entitled "Jews in Poland and abroad. Catholicism-Judaism." With another special issue of the second most important lay Catholic journal, *Więź,* also devoted to Jewish topics, as well as with numerous articles in the widely read *Tygodnik Powszechny,* a Catholic weekly, it all made for an unprecedented introduction to things Jewish. Such an introduction, though timed to coincide with the official ceremonies, went well beyond a mere commemoration of the anniversary. It was as if the Church were again assuming its crucial role as a haven to voices countering the official propaganda. To be more precise, it was the progressive wing of Polish Catholicism which now provided both the resources and the encouragement to those genuinely interested in the Jew, with many of the contributions coming from members of the project's core "initiative group."

The special issue of *Znak,* a thick, more-than-four-hundred-page volume, opens with an article by its chief editor, one which could also be read as a joint editorial for all these lay Catholic efforts. It begins with the question of why a discussion of "the Jewish problem" is at all relevant today, considering that there are "no more economic or cultural or religious bases for anti-Semitism" (Wilkanowicz, 1983). For the editor, there are at least two reasons. One is that, in spite of the virtual absence of Jews, "there persist among many Poles remnants of an unconscious racism" (p. 171). Secondly, there also persists a "conspiratorial theory of society," which singles out Jews, and other groups as those "in charge of the world" (p. 172). Then, a much more extensive discussion centers on the universally experienced trend towards—and need for—*pluralism,* both cultural and religious. A dialogue with Judaism is only a part of this wider phenomenon, Wilkanowicz argues, but a part of special importance to Catholics whose understanding of their own faith can only be enriched by an understanding of Judaism, that "older brother of Christianity." Finally, the editor expresses some hope that such an increased understanding will provide some basis for dissipating those persisting and irrational ideas about the Jews.

Consistent with the "enlightenment approach" to the subject—and testifying to the fact that such enlightenment is indeed very much needed—is most of the material contained in these lay Catholic publications. What we have here are the very basic elements of Jewish tradition, from Talmudic quotations through descriptions of Jewish holidays and rituals to glimpses into Jewish modernity. What we also have are the foundations, or the beginnings of the foundations, for a better grasp of the Polish Jewish experience during the 20th century. It is reading these articles which makes one realize, perhaps better than ever before, just how much ignorance had surrounded the Jew.

Together with this emphasis on *knowing* comes a call for *remembering.* One essay in *Znak* is in fact entitled "The reconstruction of memory" and talks about the need to preserve and restore the material traces of Jewish presence in Poland (Jagielski & Krajewska, 1983). A round-table discussion on the Ghetto Uprising, reported in *Tygodnik Powszechny,* raises the whole issue of *how* to remember (*Samotność,* April 23, 1983). Bits of poetry as well as photographs speak directly to the collective memory, for these are the few well known images and words. Finally, there are two personalities being reclaimed by memory workers, though in opposite directions. The first is I. B. Singer, a Yiddish writer who grew up in Warsaw and still devotes most of his work to Jewish life in Poland. Completely ignored by the Polish audience, even *after* winning the Nobel Prize in 1979, he is now proclaimed as Poland's artist.[16] The second is Janusz Korczak, a Polish writer and educator, best known for his books for and about children, and revered for his courage and heroic death. In 1942, when the Jewish orphans under his care were led onto the train to Treblinka, Korczak refused to part with them, even though he was repeatedly offered secure asylum on the "Aryan" side. His real name was Goldszmit and the article about him is entitled "Janusz Korczak—a Polish Jew" (Lichten, 1983a).

Let us stop for a moment and look more closely at these two instances of memory work by reclamation," for we are now touching the very heart of the problems involved in this "Jewish memory project", indeed, I believe, the very heart of Polish-Jewish relations. Can or should the oeuvre of Polish Jews, understood in the broadest sense of their cultural production, be a *part* of Poland's memory? And if so, is it to belong there in all its Jewishness, or perhaps only insofar as it represents something of universal value? Or, perhaps, it should qualify only if it has directly influenced Polish culture? But then, should it not simply be considered Polish? Substitute the actual people for the work they produced, and what we have is a dilemma at the center of Poland's "Jewish problem" for at least 150 years. Can or should a Polish Jew be considered a Pole?

Answers in the past depended very much on just what kind of a Jew one was talking about and on who was doing the talking. By and large, though, the traditional Polish Jews, those living according to the precepts of Jewish law, speaking Yiddish and set on remaining a separate community, thought of themselves and were thought of by others as *Jews*. At most, among the more progressive circles of the Polish intelligentsia, and later the ruling class, Jews were to have an equal status with others, including Poles, as Polish *citizens*. For those Jews, equality under the law did not spell a breakdown of social barriers, indeed, they were doing their utmost to keep these barriers intact. Traditionally loyal to the authorities, they would often be perceived as disloyal to tne Polish *nation*.[17] In those days of partition and the struggle for independence, however, the "Polish nation" was still very much in formation. Peasants, for example, the single largest social group, were still very much on the outside (see: Thomas & Znaniecki, 1954; Davies, 1982). And the discussions about including the Jews in the Polish nation did indeed resemble contemporary debates on the "peasant problem," especially after the failed insurrection of 1863 (Cała, 1984). At issue was mostly enlightenment, or ways to bring the backward members of society into the realm of national culture and national concerns.

As we have already observed, some Jews did see the Jewish experience in those terms. Assimilationists, though nowhere close to forming a majority of Polish Jewry, did become an important voice in the Polish debates on the "national question" (see: Lichten, 1986). And, with their position as prominent members of the country's newly forming bourgeoisie and intelligentsia, their actions counted even more than their words. It is precisely from that period—the last decades of the 19th century—that one can date the major contributions made by Jews to Poland's cultural, economic and political life.[18] Those Jews, however, while firmly attached to Polish affairs and often seeing themselves as "Poles of Mosaic faith," were also still firmly attached to their Jewish brethren, if in no other way than as advocates of enlightenment.

The pogroms and unrest which accompanied the creation of an independent Poland in 1918 did not spell an easy future for the theory and practice of assimilation. With the increasing influence of nationalist discourse, if not the nationalist party, the earlier ideals of a Polish confederation of nationalities were rapidly becoming somewhat empty rhetoric. Jews, *all* Jews, were now finding themselves excluded from the Polish nation by virtue of definition: "Pole = Catholic" had gained currency. For traditional Jews, this exclusion did not, in itself, present a problem. Their concerns centered on economic hardships and discrimination, especially after Jews had failed to win the status of a *national* minority, becoming a religious one instead.[19] For large segments of the non-traditional, mostly secular Jewry, that exclusion from the Polish nation did not spell any psychological problems either. Both Zionists and Jewish nationalists as well as the socialist Bund struggled, though in very different ways, for a solution to the "Jewish question" on a *national* basis, that is defending the right of Jews as Jews to autonomy.

I. B. Singer may serve as but one example of that prevailing attitude among Polish Jews. Though attached to Poland and to Warsaw in particular, his was an attachment to the Jewish Warsaw, to Yiddish language and culture. He had never "aspired" to be a Pole to begin with, and his decision to leave for America was based on his tragically accurate foresight of impending disaster, *not* on some broken dream of full acceptance into Polishness.[20]

The case of Korczak is, in many ways, more complex, just as was the experience of the assimilated Jews during the interwar period. Estimated to number some two hundred thousand (thus not even 10% of the total Jewish population) and concentrated in the arts, sciences and free professions, these "Jewish Poles," as one might call them, came to face a terrible burden—psychologically, emotionally, morally. Korczak himself, though trying to work with both Polish and Jewish children and espousing a universal humanistic ethos, could not but notice that his Jewish background was becoming more and more of an obstacle, even a stigma (eventually, he was barred from a popular radio program, which had been featuring him under the non-name of "The Good Doctor," in 1935 as perhaps the most painful of blows). Korczak wrote in Polish, he worked in Polish, he thought in Polish, yet he was increasingly being defined as a Jew whose influence could only damage the Polish soul. He too almost left Poland in the late thirties—for Palestine. In the end, though, his commitment to those most needing his help, the Jewish orphans, prevailed.[21]

For years, following the war, Polish children would be reading many of his books and learning about his heroic death. What they were not learning about were all Korczak's terrible difficulties in the thirties or his Zionist sympathies—or his experience as a Jew, for that matter. In effect, what happened to Korczak was what happened to many Polish Jews who perished in the Holocaust: they were accorded *post mortem* acceptance as Poles. And what is beginning to happen to Korczak's memory, especially after a monument to him found a home at Warsaw's Jewish cemetery, is what is beginning to happen to the memory of other Polish Jews: their Jewish identity is being restored. It could even be argued that differences of modalities and tone notwithstanding, *all* the memory work on this "Jewish project" is about making Polish Jews Jewish again while inviting them to inhabit Poland's collective memory.

Yet if Polish Jews are now to be remembered *as Jews,* the whole mechanism of exclusion/inclusion which had operated before is put into question. Not surprisingly, there is then a fair amount of confusion about the nature of the *relationship* between the Jew and Poland's memory, confusion, it seems, that is only compounded by the fact that the few Jews whose voices still count offer quite different, if not contradictory, models for such a relationship, both in words and in action. In short, although re-inviting the Jew into Poland's collective memory is a *symbolic* undertaking, its dynamics cannot be divorced from the existing practice of Polish-Jewish relations, however insignificant a minority might be involved.

As we have seen, the "return Jews" are a recent arrival on the Polish scene. Their very presence challenges many of the assumptions that had for decades gone unchallenged, but it does not automatically make them disappear. Among the Jews who are prominent among the country's elite, and especially among those active in the opposition, it is still the older, universalistic ethos of secular Polishness which prevails. Even for someone as "evidently Jewish" as Blumsztajn, an opposition activist for close to twenty years and a convenient target for anti-Semitic attacks with his "custom-made" name, being Jewish bears no relationship to his outspoken identification with Poles and Poland (1985; also, in Wieviorka, 1984). Michnik, one of the leaders of the democratic opposition, though never denying his Jewish background, talks about himself and others like him as members of Poland's "secular tradition." His works, published in the late seventies, were perhaps the single most important force behind a *rapprochement* between that secular tradition and Polish Catholicism; again, not a word there about a possible impact of Jewishness on any of this.[22] Indeed, the very decision to *stay* in Poland after 1968 was for both Blumsztajn and Michnik, as well as for many others, very much an act of defiance, a protest against those who were denying them the *right* to be Polish.

The confusion is much in evidence in the very language used by the memory workers. Standard in the current discourse are references to "Jews and Poles of Jewish origin" (or nationality, or descent). Less frequent, but also present are references to "Jews-Poles." There are "Polish Jews", but no "Jewish Poles"; there are "Jews from Poland" but also *"nasze Żydki,"* a term roughly similar to "our Yids," an expression still quite popular among common people. In some texts, one encounters such anachronistic usages as "Israelites" conferred onto the Jews in Poland today. In many of the Church publications, Jews become "Poles of Mosaic Faith," as if to counteract the "Pole = Catholic" definition.[23] All in all, none of these terms does justice to the complex personal sense of identity of every individual. And all of those terms reflect the fact that an objective definition is still only a definition.

There is more to the story, though. The Polish word for a Jew—*Żyd*—is not a neutral one. For some people, even today, it is a difficult one to pronounce, especially in the company of a Jew. The words "I am a Jew" carry such a heavy emotional load that speaking them is, in itself, an act of defiance. To say "he is a Jew" hardly ever conveys simply a piece of biographical data. [One of the best discussions of the emotional load attached to the "discovery" of someone's Jewishness is a brief satire by a leading Polish dramatist, Mrożek (1985).] There is a tremendous amount of uneasiness associated for all concerned with *talking* about Jews, an uneasiness which diminishes but does not disappear when writing about them.

At issue here, of course, is more than language. The centuries-old mostly negative connotations attached to the word "Jew" are not easy to drop, even for those speakers who do not share the view behind them. The idea that being a Pole is somewhat "better" than being a Jew is not far from the surface. At the extreme, though not a rare one, being a Jew becomes simply less human than being a Pole.[24] In part, this is a legacy of folk tales and superstitions, of myths surrounding the Jew in all corners of Europe (see: Cohn, 1967). And in part, it might be the fresher legacy of the war times, times when Jews *were* actually excluded from membership in the human race. We cannot forget that the pogrom in Kielce in 1946 was sparked by a charge of ritual murder, and that the killings which took place all over the country were not met with the objections one might have expected. It was as if the equation between "Jews" and "death" needed some time to dissipate. Today, the equation between "Jews" and "problem" still needs more time to lose its grip on Polish discourse.

As we have seen, even such a well intentioned text as that of the editor of *Znak* refers simply to the "Jewish problem." In other texts, it may be the "Jewish question," though more and more often the emphasis shifts to "Jewish themes" or a "Jewish problematique", or, more correctly, to "Polish-Jewish relations."[25] At issue, again, is more than language; it is the very way of seeing the Jew. And, again, talking about the "Jewish problem" does not come easy. What we have here is a situation where the very act of talking feels problematic. Whether this is the legacy of the past, or the legacy of silence, or both, discussing things Jewish in Poland calls first for a "normalization" of discourse (see also: Niezabitowska, 1986). In other words, the first, if not the major challenge in remembering the Jew lies in rendering him "normal," in making talking about him into something similar to talking about a Pole, an American or a Greek.

It could, of course, be argued that this is a kind of challenge that only time can meet. Any profound change of attitudes which relies on changes in everyday discourse cannot occur overnight.[26] A repeated exposure to the new idiom, its repeated use—indeed, in this case, the very repetition of talk about the Jew—might eventually make such "normality" something as taken-for-granted as the "problem approach." When I visited Warsaw in 1983 and thought back some fifteen years, I was struck by just how much easier it had become to talk about things Jewish. But I spent most of my time with people already involved in the "Jewish memory project," hardly a representative sample of Polish society at large. Still, it was hard not to wonder whether such ease would eventually prevail.

As difficult as it would be to answer such a question, to raise it helps us understand the present. It allows us, for one, to see how the different modes of memory work meet the challenge of "normalization" and how they indeed do it differently. Also, it again highlights the issue of resonance with popular sentiments and attitudes, a crucial issue for this study.

Let me begin here with the critical mode of memory work. Its very nature as an inquiry and a search for "truth" makes it advocate a definite *cooling* of emotions. Acknowledging the problems inherent in discussing things Jewish in general and Polish-Jewish relations in particular provides a standard opening for many a piece here. And, more often than not, it is followed by a recognition that the passage of time together with the disappearance of the actual "Jewish problem," now even from the political arena, provides the necessary *distance* for the subject to be approached *objectively*. In a call familiar to any scientist, even the works of journalists appeal to the same principles of cool objectivity. To normalize discourse about things Jewish means, in this version, to examine and re-examine the past as if there were no more taboos and no more "blank spaces". Previous silence is also often condemned not only for creating those "blank spaces" in historical awareness but for reinforcing prejudice, misconceptions, stereotypes, and so on (see: Łukaszewicz, 1983). The idea, at least in principle, is that an open and cool inquiry into the shared Polish-Jewish experience is now both necessary and possible, with "truth" alone capable of working wonders with popular attitudes.

Memory work in the nostalgic mode operates on an almost opposite premise. The appeal here is made to *warm subjectivity,* as it were, or to feelings of regret and curiosity, to sentimentality itself.[27] Often philo-Semitic in orientation—in contrast to the critical mode which, in principle, takes no sides—nostalgia beautifies the Polish-Jewish experience from a distance which is now both chronological and cultural. Once the Jew is both different, interesting and "pretty," it is possible to talk about him in very warm terms indeed.[28] His very exoticism allows for a normal discourse, in the sense that talking about Greek culture, or the Polish peasants for that matter, is normal. Those breakers of silence working in this mode may occasionally refer to the decades of silence as something very regrettable; more often, they set out simply to repair the situation. There is little if any looking back, by way of self-examination in this nostalgic approach to Poland's Jews.[29] Normalizing discourse is thus also a way of *neutralizing* it. It is as if nothing particularly problematic or touchy could come to the surface now that one works with the long gone and "innocent" past.

The past is anything but "innocent" for the memory workers approaching it instrumentally. In fact, if one were to measure the "emotional temperature" here, the discourse would be quite *"hot."* Things Jewish are being discussed not because, objectively speaking, they should be, or because, subjectively speaking, they are fascinating, but rather because the discussion provides *immediate returns*. As we saw during the Ghetto ceremonies, such returns need not be confined to the interests of the regime. Indeed, apart from the on-the-spot returns, instrumentality works on memory in a much more sophisticated fashion. The grandest and longest-lasting of such returns lies with the "defense of the honor of the Polish nation," something close to the hearts of patriotic Poles in all segments of society.[30] The idea here is that if the "Jewish problem" is to be publicly discussed at all, if the Jew is to be remembered, all should fit within the frames of collective memory already in place. In a sense, then, normalizing discourse becomes a translation job, a way of bringing meanings in line with what is known and felt, thus also making talking easier. There are times when such translation calls for treating Jews as Jews. There are times when it is best to treat Jews as Poles. There are other times still when the Jew has to become a "person." And, if there are no clear cut rules, there is a clear imperative to do what is judged best *at the moment*.

If Korczak could be celebrated for years as a Polish hero and if today he becomes a Jew again, the whole operation may look awkward indeed, just as it seems perfectly natural for the people involved.[31] Staging a lavish memorial to the Ghetto fighters and inviting the guests to visit Treblinka, only then hardly to mention the fact that it was the Jews who had been murdered there,[32] may too seem strange until one considers the context of both events. And the context was the "Month of Martyrdom" (Polish martyrdom, of course). More generally, one would look in vain for any logical consistency to this philo-Semitic turn of today, just as one would with the 1968 anti-Semitic campaign. It seems that the instrumental discourse governs itself by the logic of *myth* instead. "Anything goes," as long as it serves the purpose.

Ideotypical as these three models of memory work are, they best reflect what happens at the level of memory production itself; that is, they reflect the ways in which *new* meanings are created, new ideas put forth, new images put together. Yet even there, as we saw in the case of "Remnants," the work and the result need not be in the same memory mode. The slippage between a cool inquiry and a warm appeal to remember is not uncommon, either, especially when the materials one works with invite it.

The many years which took Monika Krajewska across the country in search of the remaining traces of Jewish memorial art could have resulted in an indictment of forgetting. The decay and abandonment which come across in the photographs gathered in her album *Time of Stones* (1983) may indeed speak for themselves. But the author, herself an artist rather than an historian, speaks about the symbolism of this memorial art, of the universal aesthetic value of Jewish memory markers, of the need to safeguard that part of Poland's heritage. The texts which she chose to accompany the images in her book carry many memorial themes. The tone, all in all, is nostalgic. [Krajewska's involvement with the preservation of the memory markers makes her book (and other presentations), though, an important means to an end. It is quite likely that a sharply critical voice would not be half as effective as the artist's.]

On the other hand, there are also materials which invite another kind of slippage, this time from a cool inquiry into a heated debate. It is quite inconceivable, for example, to be nostalgic about anti-Semitism. One can study it, one can condemn it, one can also pretend it never existed, but one can hardly reminisce about the "good old days" of social and economic discrimination.[33] The issue is touchy, perhaps one of the most touchy among those involved in the "Jewish memory project," it is never touching, though. Similarly, the debates surrounding the role of the Jews in establishing the Communist regime in Poland can be cool or hot, but not warmed with a glow of regret and fascination.

At issue here is what I would call a division of *memory space*. Certain areas, such as those of traditional Jewish customs, rituals and beliefs, appear to be inherently suitable for nostalgic remembrance. They can be— and they are—deemed interesting in and by themselves, their strangeness proving of great value. Where an outside observer might think it peculiar to see young Poles become versed in the Hassidic tales or the Kabbalah, there is perhaps nothing really peculiar about being "into" Jewish mysticism. Other young Poles, after all, are "into" Eastern religions. Nostalgia, as we said, tends to neutralize the "Jewish question." It is quite natural, then, that it applies best to areas which are already fairly neutral from the vantage point of Polish-Jewish relations.

The areas which are not neutral, on the other hand (and this is true for the majority of topics in the history of Polish-Jewish relations), appear to invite *both* critical and instrumental memory work. Potentially at least, an objective examination of what actually happened during World War II would be as likely as a heated debate on the extent of Polish aid to the Jews. Both could bring the whole period into new relief within Poland's collective memory. Potentially, the notion of "Judeo-Commune" is as likely to be subjected to a critique as it is to stand in the background of a discussion on Stalinism. Potentially, the position taken by the Church on the "Jewish question" during, let us say, the first years following the Holocaust is as likely to become a matter of public record as it is to be glossed over with a standard "condemnation of violence" epithet. In short, there are no rules of foreclosure inherent in the materials themselves, no *a priori* reasons to make critical memory work impossible. The fact that the past *is* problematic, in other words, does not by itself predetermine the ways in which it could enter collective memory.

In a situation where the "Jewish memory project" stems from the interest and initiative of people for whom much of that past is the past (something they wish to make sense of but also something outside their personal biographies), one could indeed expect the critical inquiry to prevail.[34] Whether it actually does or where—within the memory space— it is applied is something we shall want to make some sense of for much of the following discussion.

Why such a stress on the critical memory practice? Does not much of what I have said here indicate that this mode of remembrance is subordinated within the whole "Jewish memory project"? There are two reasons for such attention. First, from a moral point of view, I would argue that all this renewed interest in things Jewish will be of little significance *unless* it carries at least some examination of conscience, an examination possible only in the critical mode. That is, if this re-invitation extended to the Jew to become a member of Poland's heritage deprives him of a voice, the whole undertaking becomes nearly identical to the past practices of keeping him silent. And that is also, now from an analytical point of view, the second crucial question. Just how much of a *change* are we witnessing as we listen to all the "noise" suddenly surrounding things Jewish? Is now remembering the Jew any different from once forgetting him?

# Notes

1. Niezabitowska tells her own story in the Introduction to the book (1986:9–25). An element she stresses there, much more so than in our conversations in Warsaw, is a certain similarity between her experience as someone with nobility heritage to that of the Jews: both worlds no longer exist in Poland.
2. Tomaszewski's exhibit opened in Warsaw on Nov. 6, 1985. I owe thanks to Paweł Śpiewak for sending me the invitation to the exhibition as well as a report on its contents and its success.
3. Photography has a special affinity with memory work; on a social level, preserving memory is its main function. (For a very insightful discussion, see: Bourdieu, et al., 1965.)
4. $35, even at the official rates, is roughly an equivalent of 10 days' wages.

   All this is not to deny the *documentary* value of *Remnants*. I had no hesitation to use it as resource material; I am only arguing that the people it will reach are not the people who could benefit the most from learning about Jews, that is Poles in Poland. Except for her interview with Krajewski, the "return Jew", only a short fragment of Niezabitowska's work on Lublin appeared in *Więz* in 1983.
5. Under more usual circumstances, that is when the people remembering and the people remembered are one and the same, the distinction between nostalgic and instrumental modes is likely to disappear, leaving the opposition between critical and instrumental memory work. Stürmer, a German historian (quoted in Craig, *NYR*, Jan. 15, 1987), talks about it in terms of a continuous tension between "de-mythologizing" the past and "investing it with meaning people can identify with".
6. The work of Julian Stryjkowski, a Polish Jewish writer who still lives in Poland and who still writes on Jewish themes, spanning many historical periods, offers another good example here. His novel *The Great Fear* (1982)—dealing with Jews and Communism—was published underground. At the very same time, he was cooperating with Kawalerowicz on the film adaptation of his novel *Austeria*, a very official undertaking. Stryjkowski is also a recipient of a special prize from the lay Catholic circles and an author of a well-publicized statement of joy and pride over the election of the Polish Pope.
7. Two examples may best illustrate this. The film *Austeria* had its world premiere at the Chicago Film Festival in 1982; *Polityka* sent its film critic to Chicago for just a day (which is, by Polish standards, unheard of and which was this critic's *first* trip ever to the United States); Kałużyński then went on to report in a page-long review (again, a rarity) on how the film was received, stressing the director's emphatic assertions as to the appropriateness of Poles' filming the *Hassidim* (Nov. 27, 1982). Quite clearly, then, *Austeria* was both an "ambassador" and an important component of the regime's celebration of Jewish culture, which does not make it any more or any less of an artistic expression of nostalgia.

   During the Ghetto anniversary ceremonies, another of *Polityka*'s reporters joined a group of the invited Jews on their tour of Poland. Her account (Pietkiewicz, May 28, 1983) is one of the warmest texts ever to appear, as it portrays—very realistically—the feelings of Jewish survivors towards the country where they were born. It brings out the whole complexity of emotions involved, thus countering one of the best entrenched images in the propaganda lexicon, that of the "ungrateful Jews". Again, the fact that this article appeared as a result of a very deliberate "staging" of the ceremonies does not take away from its important message.

8. This memory editing work is often a very creative process. The Yiddish poetry collected and translated by Łastik and Słucki (1983/1986) was not a "memory piece" before they transformed it into one.

The "editing" can also come in stages; Czerniakow's Warsaw ghetto diary, prepared for publication by Fuks (ed., 1983), became a source of reflections for Zimand (a Jewish literary critic), resulting in a small book of its own (1982). (The importance of editing of the original Jewish memory works is not confined to Poland; the English edition of Ringelblum's essay on Polish-Jewish relations during World War II (1974), for example, contains editorial notes by Krakowski and Kermish which often counter or contradict Ringelblum's own interpretations.)

9. The problems here go well beyond the logistics of conducting a large survey. For it might be argued that the very act of asking a question, *any* question about the Jews cancels the possibility of uncovering the dimensions of forgetting. Lanzmann's *Shoah* illustrates this difficulty, or the effects of direct intervention, in the most acute of ways. Time and time again, Lanzmann asks Polish villagers and townsfolk to convey their memory, using both the very open and the very leading questions. It is *his* solicitation which brings the memories to the surface. Whatever they are, warm, cruel or indifferent, we still have no way of knowing their actual relevance to people's lives or, for that matter, their "original" form outside the artificial situation created by the filmmaker.

10. Though it is too early to draw any definite parallels, there are indications that another "Jewish memory project" is in the works in Spain; reports from the April 1987 international symposium on Spanish Jewish culture and history speak of "breaking five centuries of silence" and of an extensive interest in things Jewish in the Spanish media (Boukhobza, 1987). In a country where for so long any references to Jewish ancestry of its prominent artists are barred [see: Gilman, 1972], it is indeed striking to see people seeking to ascertain their roots among Jews forced to convert under the Inquisition.

11. Memory workers operating within a well-established tradition may also have a problem justifying their endeavors; it is, however, of a different kind. They need to show that their work adds something new to the ideas and images in place, in other words, it is their *individual* effort which is to be judged as worthy of public attention, not the very principle of remembering.

12. The subject calls for much further inquiry. On the one hand, time often brings a new generation onto the scene, a generation with no direct memories, yet with a keen sense of the past. This was the case in West Germany, when youth began to question Nazism in the late 1950s and 1960s [see: Rabinbach & Zipes, eds., 1986]. On the other hand, time helps those with painful memories to overcome the difficulty of talking about them, as was the case with numerous Holocaust survivors (see: Wiesel, 1968; Hemmendinger, 1986). Finally, time, or a sense of time's "running out" may be responsible for a renewed effort to record the experience of direct participants in an historical event; again, oral history projects on the Holocaust are but one manifestation of this "urgency" function of time.

13. In my survey of the press, I came across articles devoted to Jews in *all* of the

popular weeklies, including such special interest ones as *Kobieta i Życie* (Woman and Life). Warsaw dailies, through much of April 1983, would not only provide coverage of specific events but include longer features as well. This "explosion" of talk extended to television and radio for the duration of the commemorative ceremonies.

14. Edelman countered many an established notion of what constitutes "honorable death"; it was the first time that Poles were told so forcefully about the heroism of those Jews who did *not* fight.

15. I rely here on my interview with Olga Lengyel, an Auschwitz survivor, now with the Holocaust Library in New York, conducted shortly after the commemoration ceremonies she attended.

16. I use the term "Poland's artist", for in discussing Singer, there was no effort to make him "Polish" in the sense of identity, only in the sense of being a member of Poland's cultural heritage.

17. Loyalty to the authorities was not unique to traditional Jews, though. For an in-depth analysis of how assimilationists in Galicia became the chief devotees of the Austro-Hungarian empire, see: Mendelsohn (1969). The importance of this factor for the Poles' attitudes towards Jews is consistently stressed by Polish historians (see, eg., Kieniewicz, 1986).

18. Hertz (1961) points out the important function of Jews in the earlier periods—they were the main transmitters of *information*, both between the nobility and the peasants and from the outside world. Shatzky (1972) shows that even the Hassidic Jews were among the (virtually all Jewish) booksellers in Warsaw who throughout the 19th century performed much of the task of keeping Polish culture alive (with educational institutions missing). But it was not until the latter part of the 19th century that Jews became a *major* force in the economic development (see: Marcus, 1983), and a major "supplier" of Polish intelligentsia as well as political activists (especially on the Left).

19. The difference was not semantics. By that time, a great many Polish Jews were secular in outlook. The protection of minority rights, when restricted to religious matters, was ineffective in such key areas as employment (see: Korzec, 1980). Polish authorities were not consistent in their own definition of a Jew; population surveys, for example, had first relied on questions about religious affiliation to then switch to one on "mother tongue" (which, incidentally, accounts for often wide discrepancies in the estimates of the total number of Jews in Poland; see: Goldscheider & Zuckerman, 1984).

20. Apart from Singer's works, which make this rather clear, an explicit statement of his position may be found in *Conversations with Isaac Bashevis Singer* (Singer & Burgin, 1985).

21. I rely here on the "Dossier Janusz Korczak" at the *Centre de documentation juive contemporaine* in Paris, which contains materials published by different Korczak associations around the world, including one in Poland.

22. The one important exception to Michnik's otherwise silent Jewishness is his 1982 essay on Piłsudski (1985:201–223), where he explicitly points to his Jewish roots as the source of great respect for Piłsudski's non-nationalistic Polish patriotism.

23. Turian (1983) used the term "Żydek" in his brief reflections on the "innocence of jokes". In one publication (Trzeciakowski, *Polityka*, July 21, 1984) the term for Jews was actually "Judejczycy"—roughly, the inhabitants of Judea—which was then transformed to "pochodzenia judejskiego" (origin from . . .); all this

in a review of a book by Sandauer who openly writes as a Jew. This may be an instance of pure linguistic invention. The one term which is *not* used publicly is "parch", a very derogatory designation fairly common in the past (see: Hertz, 1961, for a discussion how "żydek" was a positive term by comparison). It should be stressed, though, that the naming problem is not unique to Poland. In France and *among* Jews, there is still some confusion if the word should be "Juif"—signifying nationality—or "juif"—referring to religion; both are commonly used.

24. Again, perhaps the best expression of this comes from Mrożek, in his short tale about the Nose (1984). Apparently autobiographical, it is a story of a non-Jew who, as a teenager, suddenly develops a large, uncontestably Jewish nose and who tries to accommodate the resulting suspicion by others to his own sense of Jews as very strange creatures Mrożek points out that this view of Jews as *outside* the common social universe is not anti-Semitism; the Jew is merely deprived of any *relevance*. His utter foreignness does not make him an enemy, only a "fish with bird feathers".

25. An essay on anti-Semitism by Ryszka (*Polityka*, April 16, 1983), in which the notion of the "Jewish question" was taken to its logical conclusion, i.e., an examination of what was wrong about the Jews, did provoke a sharply critical reaction from Toeplitz (KTT, *Polityka*, May 7, 1983), stressing the need to reverse the inquiry and to look at what was wrong about the anti-Semites. To the best of my knowledge, it was the only time the implications of the notion of the "Jewish question" were so explicitly brought to light. In a very important departure from the standard, London *Aneks* (41/42, 1986) published a series of articles on the subject under the common title "Jews as a Polish Problem".

26. An illuminating parallel here could be drawn with the emphasis on language by the advocates of women's equality, especially in the area of socialization. The term "Ms", to take the most obvious example, while popular, is still neither universally used nor universally accepted.

27. It is in the nature of this nostalgic mode that it incorporates, if not relies on works by Jews, art more often than commentary.
     Rączka's book on Cracow's Jewish quarter (1982), which includes over one hundred photographs, is perhaps the best example of a Pole's regret and remembrance; the juxtaposition of past and present produces peculiar results, though, as in images of Hassidic Jews on the streets of Cracow *today*, as if they still belonged there.

28. "Talk" should not be understood too literally; an important role here is played by the visuals. And the visuals in the book *Polish Jewry are* pretty, so is the the movie *Austeria*, or the stage set of Singer's *Magician of Lublin*.

29. Matywiecki's unencumbered appeal (1983) to "fill the void" surrounding the Jew is a typical one here. There are, I should stress, exceptions to such unreflexive nostalgia. Wóycicki (1983), while he too appeals for memory work to "fill the void", warns against slipping into exoticism; remembering the Jew should be *work*, not mere fascination. His own contribution to what he sees as an important part of the project—learning about the *contemporary* Jewish life—is the introduction of Polish readers to the philosophy of Levinas (1983b). Raczek, who is *Polityka*'s drama critic, while praising three theater productions on Jewish themes, including the first one of *Fiddler on the Roof* (July 17, 1983), opens his review with a brief *critical* note on the attitudes towards the Jew, past and present, relying heavily on Hertz' work, and focusing on the all-

inclusiveness of the "Jew = problem" notion. Far from being a full-length critical study, this is nevertheless a significant departure from the "straight" nostalgic path.

30. Honor, both individual and national, figures prominently among the most cherished values of the Polish ethos, in part due to the strength of the nobility's tradition. It is a question both of self-esteem and of reputation. In contrast to America, where it might be perfectly honorable to reject the prevailing values (though, we should remember, individualism is one of them), the Poles' tolerance for open dissent is rather low. Artists who, like Gombrowicz, mocked Polish self-delusions, or like the Romantic poet Norwid, bitterly criticized them, were not easily accepted into the national Pantheon. This is not to say that Polish culture has no self-critical component to it; it does. But, speaking very generally now, it is a culture very, very sensitive to the opinions by others, a culture easy to offend and difficult to criticize from within.

31. With some exceptions; the decision to place Korczak's monument at the Jewish cemetery sparked protest from people who felt that this symbolically removes him from Polish memory (see: *Pomnik . . . , Polityka*, Jan. 15, 1983; March 5, 1983). One of the tasks of the "Jewish memory project" would be to assure that it does not.

32. In contrast to Auschwitz, Treblinka today is not a museum, but a vast field of stones, with inscriptions of names of *places* the victims came from and a tall *menorah* at one end. According to Olga Lengyel, members of the Jewish delegation were rather divided on the issue; for some, being in Treblinka was too powerful an experience to pay attention to the Polish authorities' handling of the ceremony, others openly expressed disdain. The press coverage of this particular memorial service emphasized the theme of "struggling for peace", as indeed was true of most of the reports on the "Month of Martyrdom".

33. I speak here of the discourse *within* the "Jewish memory project". It is quite conceivable that members of the openly anti-Semitic organization *Grunwald* or those in the security forces responsible for distributing anti-Semitic posters on the eve of the declaration of the Martial Law would in fact speak of the "good old days". . . . (I owe this point to Kurt Jonassohn.)

34. In this respect, it is significant that some of the most critical voices to date on the subject of Polish-Jewish relations during the Holocaust come from Poles who were *children* during the war, people who remember with a great deal of pain their own helplessness and who are now prepared to face the past Kuroń, 1986), or those who now try to make sense of their innocent childhood, experienced next door to the Jews' deportation (Rymkiewicz, 1988).

# 5

# Challenges to Memory Work

*Remnants: The Last Jews of Poland* is a meticulously edited book. Printed in Italy, it is one of the most beautiful albums I have ever come across. In Poland itself, nothing of even half the quality would have been possible. In Poland, could the contents have even passed the various stages of censorship control?

The answer is "yes"—they probably could, with some rather minor modifications. The photographs themselves were, as we know, exhibited in an official gallery in Warsaw a year before. And, although Niezabitowska's text is written without any concern for the censor—she speaks freely about the glories of Solidarity, for example—it is a text that could be toned down to accommodate officialdom without losing its main strengths. Comparing the interview of one of the young "return Jews" to the text published in 1983 by *Tygodnik Powszechny,* one notes that the only significant loss to the censor's scissors then was a fragment dealing with 1968.[1] This is an important cut, but not one that seriously detracts from the significance of this part of the book. Similarly, a chapter featuring the director of the Yiddish Theater in Warsaw, a controversial figure by any standards, presents no outright attack on his servility towards the regime. We could run through the whole text, looking for such sensitive points and we would still arrive at the same conclusions: *Remnants* is not a dissident work defying official rules.[2] It is simply a work quite correctly aimed at the international market.

I am again using the example of *Remnants,* for it again very well illustrates points essential to our discussion of what can and cannot be done on the "Jewish memory project." First, it sensitizes us to the fact that not all or, in this case, not even most of the existing barriers have to do with *censorship.* And that is a significant point, significant because it goes against one of the prevailing myths about cultural discourse in Poland in general, and discourse about Jews in particular, a myth that has the government censorship elevated to an all-explaining status of an omnipotent decision maker, responsible for any and all silences.[3] That this impression is simply a myth is a point we shall discuss here at some length.

Secondly, the work on *Remnants* exemplifies the importance of a much more mundane factor, one sometimes lost in analyses of "totalitarian culture",—*money*.[4] This, too, is a point deserving our attention, especially as we are talking about a project relying to a large extent on imports from abroad. Finally, as we begin reading the essays closely, or even just the captions accompanying the images of *Remnants,* we can uncover quite a few examples of *self-censorship* at work. We may immediately wonder why certain things remain unsaid, even when no outside restrictions apply. This is also an issue I spoke about with some of the editors and authors operating within the unofficial zone, an issue which led me to question still further the *inner* restrictions on discourse. In this respect, *Remnants* offers us a rare opportunity to see what the "Jewish memory project" might look like if it were to be conducted in a less politically dense context.

As it is, though, the memory work we study here is done almost exclusively within Poland's politically dense context. It is that density, rather than plain powers of the state, which may account for the directions taken and *not* taken by memory workers.

The forms of cultural discourse in Poland today are no longer determined at the top. Yet the very existence of the extensive network of underground publishing together with the increasing importance of Church sponsorship—in short, the steady development of cultural institutions outside the control of the state—does not make for any loosening of the grip of politics on culture. If anything, it could be said that now, when Poland's culture producers are no longer doomed to work within the officially sanctioned system, the political significance of their voices is greater than ever before. A poem about bees and flowers may become a political statement, solely by virtue of *where* it appears. An abstract painting, exhibited in a private gallery, becomes a sign of protest. Even feature films, which are forced to by their production requirements (such needs as capital and equipment) to be made within the state-controlled structures, can now acquire an opposition flavor through the director's post-production manifestos.[5]

Closer to home, being interested in the Hassidim used to be identified as an anti-regime action, and the singing of old Hebrew songs was once a sign of defiance.[6] Exploring Poland's Jewish heritage began, after all, at the underground "Flying University," while the caring for Jewish cemeteries was first undertaken by a group of Warsaw's Catholic intellectuals. [It is thus extremely important that the 1987 in-depth discussion of Polish-Jewish relations took place within the lay Catholic journals, thus moving

the center of gravity of the "Jewish memory project" again into the sphere
of independent culture.] Re-inviting the Jew into Poland's collective memory stood, even ten years ago, in opposition to the official efforts to make
him disappear forever. There was, then, a sense of being on the right side
just by virtue of talking about Poland's Jewish heritage.

The sudden turn-about in the government's position surprised many of
those genuinely interested in things Jewish. Coming, as it did, in the midst
of "Jaruzelski's war with the nation"—as the martial law was popularly
called—it came on the heels of a renewed effort to blame it all on the Jews.
The Stürmer-like anti-Semitic posters which plastered the streets of Warsaw and other cities on December 12, 1981, accompanied by media attacks
on "Zionist perpetrators" were replaced only a few months later by the
elaborate preparations to celebrate the heroic Jews of the Warsaw Ghetto.

As we have seen, the opposition reacted by staging their own ceremonies
and by trying to make sure that no one forgot what this regime had stood
for. Yet, what was possible on one specific *occasion* could hardly be
maintained in the long run. Even the most steadfast oppositionists had to
recognize that the government's "green light" to the Jew was actually
helping their cause of public recognition for Poland's Jewish heritage. A
dilemma still existed, however. Should one be a party to officialdom, even
if it proved the only possible route to exposure? Should one be a party to
officialdom when it guaranteed merely greater exposure? In short, should
one jump at the opportunity to publicize things Jewish better, forgetting
that the providers of that opportunity might, at any time, reactivate the
weapons of anti-Semitism?

This was more than just a moral dilemma. The core of the memory
workers, the producers, and expecially the Jews among them, could never
be certain—as they still cannot—whether the policies of the regime would
remain in their favor. Signals from the top were and remain mixed indeed.
On the one hand, with respect to the more international side of Poland's
"Jewish politics," the government has been taking an increasingly relaxed
stand, lifting many of the restrictions on travel, on scholarly and artistic
exchange, on financial aid from abroad. On the other hand, within that
same government, the Minister of Interior Affairs, would, even in 1985,
refer to opposition activists under investigation for "crimes against the
state" as "Jews," pure and simple, thus breaking its own tradition of
offering euphemisms such as "Zionists" or "cosmopolitans." Reports
from people subjected to security measures also indicate that the young
recruits of the repression machine are still being trained on anti-Semitic
manuals (see: Poleski, 1985; Morga, 1986). And, as I have said, anti-
Semitic texts did not disappear from the official media, even at the very
peak of publicity surrounding the Ghetto anniversary. It is no wonder,

then, that the group initiating this "Jewish memory project" must operate with caution. They could, at any moment, become targets of an attack, with their innocent gatherings and debates transformed into the basis for major conspiracy charges.

What does such caution imply for actual memory practice? As it turns out, not a great deal. Not signing one's own name to a particular piece or not advertising a private meeting with visiting Israeli scholars may be important as precautions for the people involved, but it little changes the contents of what is being said. Indeed, if anything, the assurance of anonymity makes for a more open discussion, one where ideas do not have to be hidden between the lines. It is an altogether different matter, though, as one leaves the confines of the underground. What matters here is not so much personal safety as personal loyalty. Thus even when given an opportunity to operate officially, many memory workers choose not to, preferring instead to go public under the auspices of the Church. As strange as it may seem to an outside observer, it is on the platform supplied by the Church—often literally—that much of the "Jewish memory project" reaches the public.[7]

There are, of course, gains and losses inherent in such sponsorship. A clear gain, from any point of view, lies in the fact that anything said within this semi-official zone carries far greater authority than the officially-sanctioned discourse. One might even argue that it carries more authority than the words coming from the underground, for it appears as less politically motivated and less concerned with the present. Thus if one wants not only to reach a wider public but to be listened to, Church patronage is particularly valuable to cultivate.

On the other hand, patrons are not generally open to much direct criticism of themselves. Thus, while we might find a tremendous variety of topics discussed in lay Catholic journals or during meetings at the Clubs of Catholic Intelligentsia, that variety does *not* include critical evaluations of the role of the Church itself in promoting anti-Semitism.[8] In the special issue of *Znak* that we have already noted, the only memory piece which might be strictly classified as critical deals with the prevalence of anti-Semitic beliefs and stereotypes among Polish students (Łukaszewicz, 1983). The results of a sociological study conducted during the seventies reveal a rather sad state of affairs, with most of those questioned carrying a strongly negative image of the Jew.[9] Yet while the author explicitly condemns the years of silence for both producing the ignorance and not producing any changes in the traditional patterns, she also says nothing about the possible influence of Church teachings on it all. Even the section of *Znak* explicitly dealing with the history of Catholic-Jewish relations has almost nothing to offer in the way of insights into that past, devoted as it is to what these relations *should* be in the present and in the future.[10] In short, amidst all the breaking of silence and calls for a dialogue with the Jews, one would be hard put to find any serious examination of an issue which is, after all, crucial for an understanding of Polish-Jewish relations.

What happens when the issue of Church promotion of anti-Semitism is raised on the *other* side of the political divide may best be illustrated by the "Urban episode." In 1983, Jerzy Urban, the government's spokesman and, as such, the most prominent of "court Jews," delivered a speech in which he attacked the prestigious *Tygodnik Powszechny*. There would have been nothing out of the ordinary about this rather standard rebuttal of one's political opponent, except that Urban chose the occasion for reminding the public that the Church in Poland had not always stood for just and liberal causes. And he chose to do it by bringing to public record the viciously anti-Semitic statements crowding the Church publications of the 1930s. As it happens, the editor of those publications was none other than Maximilian Kolbe, a priest who was later to sacrifice himself in the stead of a fellow Polish prisoner in Auschwitz, the deed for which he has only recently been canonized.

Urban's speech sparked a fury of protest, culminating in calls for his resignation by Catholic organizations and prominent individuals alike. *Polityka,* in an effort to restore calm—Urban used to be on its staff— published both a letter in defense of freedom of speech and opinion by Poland's then deputy premier (and *Polityka*'s former chief editor) as well as a large selection of extracts from Kolbe's pronouncements on the "Jewish question".[11] In the end, Urban's political career was spared. The debate itself was closed.

It could be argued that were it not for this peculiar combination of a "court Jew" and a saint, the subject itself would have received a fair hearing. It is a possibility, yet an unlikely one. If one judges by discussions taking place in Polish émigré journals, for example, this is simply a subject not yet ready to be heard.[12]

To be fair, the government as a patron scores only slightly better on the self-criticism scale. Even during the heyday of Solidarity, when official media became a forum for wide and open debates, *Polityka* scorned the attempt, arguing that to discuss 1968 was both premature and ill-timed considering the grave problems facing the country. It did, however, publish an open letter appealing for such a discussion, one signed by prominent intellectuals. Over the years, references to 1968 have become less and less oblique. There is still no question of any full accounting of—or for—what happened, but it seems perfectly acceptable today to restore the reputations of at least some people attacked back in 1968 or to talk about the "forced internal exile" of others.

It is now also perfectly acceptable to criticize one's adversaries *within* the official zone. Again, *Polityka,* with its liberal line, is in a continuous debate with the Party "hardliners" of strongly nationalistic persuasion, a debate which touches on anti-Semitism as well. Thus, for example, the Association "Grunwald," which many believe is sponsored by the nationalistic Party faction, has been consistently attacked and ridiculed in *Polityka,* with its "Jewish conspiracy" theories receiving particularly harsh treatment. And, along similar lines, the book accusing Zionists of organizing the Kielce pogrom to further their own goals did not pass unnoticed, with *Polityka*'s reviewer making a point of bringing its lies to public attention (Tomaszewski, Jan. 7, 1984). In short, far from being monolithic, the regime's own media do now allow for some critique of its past and present policies regarding the "Jewish question".

As is true of any government decision, the motives underlying this one are difficult to assess and the policy is subject to change, both in view of internal politics and in line with international policies. It is only very recently, for example, that one may find favorable—or at least neutral—articles dealing with Israel in the official press. But I suspect that the Kremlin might not allow any references to the plight of Soviet Jewry for some time to come. Still, restrictions from the top are not the main barriers to the work on this "Jewish memory project." After all, the history of Polish-Jewish relations does not begin in 1945, and, as significant as the 1968 campaign was, its place within that history is relatively minor. In other words, once the "green light" has been officially given to discourse about things Jewish, the spots which remain lit in red, as it were, are fairly few.

The fact that today's regime *can* plausibly disassociate itself from the pre-1945 period has a great deal to do with the fact that relatively few topics remain officially taboo. It might explain, for example, why the government decided, after initial loud protest to the French authorities, to screen Lanzmann's *Shoah* in Poland, and on T.V. at that.[13] The image of Poles emerging from that film is truly horrifying, and it must even have intensified when, out of 9½-hour movie, about ninety minutes dealing directly with Poles were spliced together for a T.V. presentation. That presentation, to make matters worse, did not include the only redeeming feature of the film as far as Poles were concerned, namely the interview with Karski, the Home Army courier who carried the message about the plight of Polish Jews to the West.[14] But, if Lanzmann's portrait of Poles-as-witnesses-to-the-Holocaust is a tirade against Polish anti-Semitism, he also makes it clear that the responsibility lies with the Catholic Church.

In a scene closing the series of interviews with Polish peasants and small town people—and closing Part I of *Shoah*—Lanzmann sets his camera on the steps of a church which once housed Jews being readied for deportation. The day is special: Mary's birthday. It is also special in that Lanzmann brought to Chełm its sole Jewish survivor, whom all warmly remember as a teenage boy with a beautiful voice (he was forced to sing by the Nazis). After the service, he and the local people crowd in front of the church. The verbal exchange, initiated by Lanzmann's questions, is particularly powerful, even within a film filled with emotionally charged moments. What we hear is a story told by one of the town's most respectable citizens in which a rabbi, at the very moment of the Jews' being deported, explains their fate with the standard "Jews killed Christ". And a woman who just a few moments before shed tears while reminiscing about the treatment of the Jews is now the first to repeat this age-old "truth" in visible anger.[15]

At issue here is the question of why the film was shown. It seems reasonable to argue that the government saw it as an arms-length opportunity to voice its own criticism of the Church. The film, after all, contains very few direct references to the post-1945 period; indeed, the very fact that large portions of it were shot in Poland, with the help of a Polish interpreter, might be seen as indirect testimony to the regime's good will. Even the absence of the word "Jew" from the Auschwitz memorial is passed over in silence by Lanzmann. *Shoah,* then, could and probably was treated by the regime as an exposé of the forces of darkness (read Catholicism) contrasting with the forces of enlightenment (read the Communists). [I am speaking here of the parts of *Shoah* relating to Poles; not of the film as a whole.] It is especially significant that the television screening in the fall of 1985 was accompanied by a long discussion and, later, by a large scale debate in the press rather than by a simple editorial comment to the effect of "look at how Jews are again smearing our reputation."[16] In the past, the few critical voices from the West which would reach the Polish public would always be presented as evidence of the "anti-Polish" campaign instigated by the Jews. (This idea, I should add, has a long history of its own, going back to the nineteenth century.) While with *Shoah* this element was by no means missing, there was also at least some attempt to make Poles *listen* to what Lanzmann had to say.

It is, of course, impossible to know the exact motivation for this unprecedented opening in the wall of silence surrounding anti-Semitism *during* the war. It is possible, however, to give it some perspective by looking at the censorship rules in the not-so-distant past. A set of internal censors' instructions, issued in 1973/1975, smuggled to Sweden and subsequently published (*Czarna . . . ,* 1977) offers a unique glimpse into this secret realm. Interestingly enough, together with what one would expect— stops put on all mention of pollution or of large industrial accidents, for one thing, and blacklisting of intellectuals—come the instructions *not* to publish tests with *overt* anti-Semitic references (Curry, ed., 1984:364). A series of internal memos further clarifies this general rule: one censor is reminded that anti-Semitic expressions in a novel dealing with the beginnings of the 20th century should pass, these are, after all, a matter of historical record (p. 365). By the same token, as another censor points out, special care should be taken with writings moving closer to the present to avoid creating the impression that Poles are anti-Semitic. On the other hand, though, when the "Jewish question" is treated in a neutral or philo-Semitic manner—which, for the censors at least, was the case with Wajda's film *Promised Land,* a film widely criticized in the West for its anti-Semitic undertones[17]—the discussion should be limited to brief mentions of that particular element, with any further elaborations to be strongly discouraged (p. 410). Why? Because, in this case at least, dwelling on "Jewish themes" was seen as potentially damaging to the desired impact of the whole film or to the message of the "historical importance of the class struggle," a message which censors were advised to promote cautiously. Why? Because any emphasis on philo-Semitic aspects of Wajda's work might, as far as the censors were concerned, spark a negative popular reaction.

What we have here, then, are two quite different concerns, each working against talking about things Jewish. First, there is the concern for Poland's international reputation, not surprising when one considers that these instructions were issued only a few years after the 1968 campaign. Second, there is the concern for the popular impact of the official propaganda line, with "being nice to the Jews" judged, perhaps correctly, as not helping the cause.

For a more complete picture, we should also remember that just as these censorship rules were being laid down, officially sanctioned Polish historiography was making its greatest strides in erasing the Jew from Poland's past. The disappearance of the Jew thus went hand-in-hand with the disappearance of most records of past anti-Semitism and with an implicit acknowledgment of its persistence in the present.

Much has changed since then. Or has it? The guiding concern for Poland's international reputation, although it is no longer putting a stop to discussion of anti-Semitism, is still firmly in place. Indeed, it might well be the driving force behind the official sanctioning of the "Jewish memory project." What about the concerns about the internal ramifications of "being nice to the Jews"? For one, it seems that the regime has not fully abandoned the idea that its anti-Semitic campaign against the opposition may bring in some much needed popular support. In that way, the possible negative public reaction to its sudden outpouring of affection towards the

Jews may work in its favor by keeping anti-Semitic sentiments alive. It looks like a contradiction, but it might well be the understandable result of different factions trying out different strategies. It is simply much too early to tell whether the regime is ready to have its international interests define the thrust of the internal ones with respect to the Jew or, concretely, to drop its own anti-Semitic tools (see: Hirszowicz, 1986).

What one can already tell is that all the good—or bad—intentions notwithstanding, the actual work on the "Jewish memory project" can only go as far as *resources* allow, especially concerning the nostalgic remembrance of Jews as Jews. To restore even a small portion of Jewish cemeteries takes a great deal of money. To provide a structured learning environment for young people who wish to pursue their interest in Jewish history and culture—in university, for example—also takes more than simple willingness. In 1983, there was no opposition *in principle* to establishing "Judaic studies" at Warsaw's university. The problem was not a political one but rather a question of how to provide a decent level of scholarship when so few specialists are available.[18] At that time, it was possible to learn some Hebrew and some Yiddish through a combination of self-teaching and private instruction; clearly, this method would be inadequate if a large number of students were involved. Furthermore, it is hard to conceive of respectable "Judaic studies" without the establishment of exchanges with centers of Jewish scholarship throughout the world. And here again, though there might be fewer and fewer restrictions on cooperating with the Americans or even the Israelis, the success of such cooperation would depend on more than the government's granting exit and entry visas. Any prolonged study abroad, for example, calls for expenditures well beyond the present means of individuals or of the state. In effect, then, without outside funding little can be done.

Cultural endeavors share this predicament with the academic ones. If *Fiddler on the Roof* had to wait until 1985 to be staged in Poland, this was apparently not a matter of censorship. It might have taken some encouragement from the top as well as some sense of a favorable popular climate, yet the key lay in being able to convince the show's authors to donate their royalties—in Polish currency, at that—to the cause of preserving Jewish historical monuments in Poland. Quite generally, Poland cannot afford to import much culture from the West, not when its huge foreign debt makes it difficult even to import essential medical supplies or equally essential replacement parts for key industrial sectors.

In this light, the money already spent on celebrating things Jewish is, in itself, an important signal of the regime's current priorities. It could be argued that the funds allocated to Jewish organizations or to such a facade as the Yiddish Theater—where many actors and the audience no longer speak Yiddish—are merely an *investment*. Propaganda may cost money, but it yields tangible returns. Indeed, as one writer argued in *Polityka,* the whole question of restoring the physical markers of Poland's Jewish heritage should be viewed from a purely economic perspective: "Would not such memory markers attract the attention of Western tourists?" he asked (Płużański, March 10, 1984). After all, the culture of Polish Jewry could draw people to Poland—and make them leave behind the much needed hard currency.[19]

As much as such reasoning is rarely made explicit, it is, as we have seen, implicit in much of the government effort to bring the Jew back into the public arena. Nevertheless, the potential for an influx of Jewish tourists is only secondary to the more important returns expected here or to the "good word" put in for Poland on international money markets. All may be well if these hopes for improving the country's credit standing turn out to be justified. If, on the other hand, "being nice to the Jews" offers only limited returns, it may quickly forego its fairly high place on the list of investment priorities. (We must also not forget that current policy may be—at any time—overruled by orders from the Kremlin.)

We are left, then, with those aspects of the "Jewish memory project" which are not generally dependent on officially distributed resources. Volunteer work by members of lay Catholic organizations, individually pursued research initiatives, seminars set up at the Catholic University, the "Committee for the Protection of Jewish Historical Monuments" itself—all draw only minimally on state support. They rely on the regime's tolerance, not on state funds. Still, it would be inaccurate to say that they do not face financial problems. The work that went into *Remnants* or into the photo documentation of Jewish cemeteries took many years of hardship and perseverance, not the least because of the costs. To gather even the most rudimentary library, young "return Jews" rely primarily on gifts from abroad. To spend time exploring the "blank spaces" in the history of Polish-Jewish relations more often than not means being unable to spend time securing one's livelihood. In short, however enthusiastic and devoted to the cause, members of the project's "initiative group" have to reckon with obvious limitations on their energy and resources.

They too have to establish priorities. The difference, however, between the regime's deciding where and how to invest and the decisions of those young people is that they rarely, if ever, think of memory work as an "investment." A young Polish scholar describing the mixed response to researching Polish-Jewish relations within the university framework revealed more than a touch of shame that, in the end, this pursuit of individual interest had "paid off" in an academic degree. [The circumstances of this case were such that this was indeed a valid concern, beyond the ethical considerations of one's commitments.] There is a sense that other memory workers consider any immediate rewards for their efforts ethically unacceptable. Their work, after all, has grown out of a deeply-felt moral concern and not a cold calculation of means and ends. Indeed, if at times these people see themselves swept into a public political confrontation—as was the case during the 1983 Ghetto ceremonies—many feel particularly uneasy about it. They might all be making a statement of what *independent* Polish collective memory should be about, but they are also concerned not to draw the Jew into current political disputes.

This, as we have already seen, is easier said than done. As much as one might wish to believe that the "Jewish question" is no longer significant in Poland today, the facts speak otherwise. And as much as things Jewish are now being discussed—through the underground channels or within the lay Catholic ones—as if there were no longer any "Jewish problem," the very ways in which this discussion proceeds testify to a prevailing concern that such might not be the case at all.

One of the better illustrations of such double-edged talk comes from the junction between the unofficial and the semi-official zones. Bogda Cywiński is one of Poland's foremost Catholic intellectuals. In 1970 (1985) his analysis of the roots of Polish opposition—first published officially and then reprinted abroad—marked the beginning of his career; the book became something of a Bible for the whole Solidarity generation. He remains one of the most respected observers of the contemporary scene. In a lecture delivered at the 1984 meetings devoted to Polish-Jewish relations at Oxford (subsequently published with some other materials from that conference by the underground journal *Puls*), Cywiński outlined his view of the present significance of the "Jewish question" within the opposition. After stating and restating that there was *no* "Jewish problem" in today's Poland, he went on to describe how the conflict between two visions of Poland's recent past might be misconstrued as a conflict between Jews and others.[20] In essence, he argued that anti-Jewish pronouncements by some opposition activists were not anti-Jewish at all, but rather anti-ex-Stalinists, anti-intellectuals and so forth.

Two aspects of Cywiński's reasoning deserve closer attention, as they re-emerge, albeit in different forms, in much of the democratic opposition's discourse. First, there is the taken-for-granted notion that the very absence of Jews spells the end to the "Jewish problem." Read in reverse, it does imply that the presence of Jews poses one. Secondly—and of greater significance for our present discussion—there is the strong condemnation of anti-Semitism combined with an effort to show that such anti-Semitism is no longer *viable*. If few informed observers of contemporary Poland would altogether deny that anti-Semitism persists, as a carry-over from the past, the thrust of the democratic opposition's arguments is to discredit it both morally *and* tactically (see, e.g.: *Szum* . . . , 1985). In saying that the "Jewish problem" is of no relevance to Poles today, one is also saying that it no longer makes much sense to attack Jews, for it is no longer with them that any real power over Polish affairs lies.

Should not such observations be obvious, we might ask, in a country with about five thousand Jews and only a handful of them in positions of any power? The very need for such an argument seems strange indeed to an outsider, or it might testify to the mysterious strength of anti-Jewish sentiments. Inside, though, there is nothing strange or mysterious about it. The argument made by the democratic opposition reflects fairly accurately the realities of current political battles. On the one hand, it is directed straight against the regime, the regime which persists in using a theory of "Jewish conspiracy" to attack its opponents. And even if the strategy is proving less and less successful in terms of popular response, there are good reasons to believe that it might someday enjoy a revival. As the general crisis deepens, so does the need to blame Poland's misfortunes on somebody—and Jews are a traditional target and an abstract one. Here again, as one of the members of the "Jewish memory project's" initiative group said in the summer of 1986, the government's "being nice to the Jews" carries the potential for yet another wave of popular anti-Semitism, if only because its niceness cannot solve Poland's economic problems. To prevent a recurrence, a number of opposition intellectuals take to rational logic in addition to their ethical principles. Anti-Semitism has to be shown not only to be wrong but also to be equivalent to playing into the hands of the regime.

The task of the democratic opposition intellectuals would be fairly easy, though, were it not that they also have to deal with an internal opponent. Poland's opposition is not homogeneous; with time, a resurrection of some of the darkest sides of Polish nationalism acquires both strength and permanency. In itself a rather curious phenomenon, in that most people involved in the underground movements of nationalistic orientation belong to a generation which was not to know, let alone espouse, the ideas of Dmowski and his National Democracy, the return of the Right goes well beyond the organizational structures set up in the 1980s. When looking at the lists of underground publications, for example, one is struck by just how much room there is for publicizing the older and the newer forms of nationalism. When we add the less documented facets of this veritable publicity campaign—articles in the small underground journals or leaflets distributed at various occasions—the exposure given to the Right is impressive indeed. The debates which filter through the émigré channels to the West show that the opposition's divisions on ideological issues surpass any unity offered by being an opposition.

To all those perfectly legitimate signs of a maturing movement, of a training in democracy, must be added manifestations of reactionary ideas which take even the most ardent advocates of polemics unpleasantly by surprise. As the August 1986 issue of Paris' *Kultura* reports there are now at least four *parishes* in Warsaw alone which regularly distribute leaflets, brochures and booklets accusing the Jews of being in evil control of the world, while saying very little about the evils of Communism (Morga, 1986). Although the *Kultura* author stresses the marginal nature of this phenomenon, he is deeply troubled about the potential spillover from the margins into the center. He too, just as the editor of *Znak,* believes there remains much fertile ground for planting "conspiracy theories," theories which almost always invoke Jews and theories which can only gain momentum as the general *chaos* of the Polish situation prevails.[21]

It should perhaps be stressed that the "Jewish conspiracy" theory, like other mythical constructions, does *not* need Jews to exist. Historically as well as today, its function has been to explain the troublesome reality faced by non-Jews, a function it performs quite well with or without real Jews posing any threat to the established order (see: Cohn, 1967; Wilson, 1982). When considered comparatively, the blaming of all Poland's misfortunes on the Jews is not as illogical as it might at first appear. Ruled by its own logic, a "conspiracy theory" draws strength from the depth of problems and difficulties people experience yet cannot easily understand, precisely the kind of situation many Poles find themselves in today.[22]

Although I would not claim that the progressive opposition intellectuals think in just those terms, I would argue that they act upon them. A concern for the possible fueling of popular anti-Semitism in general and the "conspiracy theory" in particular is very much on the agenda when things Jewish are to be discussed publicly by them. As far back as 1968, leaders of the student protest made a point, albeit not always successfully, of diffusing the connection between Jews and opposition by keeping Jews in the background. Later on, the "Jewish question" was only the subject of polemical attacks on the regime's propaganda productions. In 1981, when all kinds of previously silenced issues exploded into the public arena, a collection of essays dealing with the "Jewish question" was all ready for publication by the underground press, controlled by KOR. At the last moment, the editors decided not to publish it, at least not then, for fear that it might only add substance to the increasingly heated arguments within and without Solidarity as to the extent of "Jewish influence" there. *Tygodnik Solidarność,* the Solidarity weekly which began appearing in April 1981, generally shied away from the "Jewish problem," although it carried a long exposé on the Kielce pogrom in its second-to-last issue. As its chief editor later suggested the main reason for such caution was the desire not to exacerbate an already sensitive situation or not to cause any more anti-Semitism.

What is it in particular, one might ask, that is perceived as best left unsaid? What specific issues are avoided due to such well-intentioned self-censorship? Where lie the self-imposed limits to *critical* memory work?

Broadly speaking, anything which can *directly* give substance to the "Jewish conspiracy" theory as it affects the democratic opposition must remain a topic for private conversations only. By extension, any advocacy of "Jewish causes" or critique of anti-Semitism in Poland's past and present becomes a highly delicate undertaking. The article, for example, that my Shabbat companions and I were discussing in the fall of 1983 was the *first* attempt to deal with the subject of Jews and Communism objectively. Written under the telling pseudonym of "Abel Kainer"[23] by someone identifying himself only as a child of Jewish Communists, the text is indeed extremely cautious. Just as it aims to counter the prevailing stereotype of "Judeo-Commune" by citing some facts of the matter—that Communists were only a tiny minority within the pre-war Jewish community, for example—it also tries very hard not to offend anybody in its defense of the people it talks about. This quasi-sociological analysis of the Jewish involvement in the Communist movement and, subsequently, the Communist regime is essentially a plea for understanding and forgiveness. It is not, as it could have been, considering the historical realities, an all-out attack on anti-Semitism in interwar Poland. It says nothing at all about the post-Holocaust anti-Jewish atrocities, beyond the by then acceptable mention of the Kielce pogrom. In short, it treads a thin line between truth and silence.

Similarly, the presentations at the widely attended session devoted to March 1968, organized at the University of Warsaw in March 1981 (these presentations were subsequently published by the underground press), do not move far beyond a critique of the *official* anti-Semitism at the time. Except for Kuroń (1983), whose position might be easier because he is not Jewish (although he was ready to accept such an identity in prison), the long-time opposition activists shedding light on the mechanisms of 1968 either leave the issue of popular anti-Semitism dormant or explicitly minimize its significance. Thus, to take but one example, in a very revealing insider's report on the attitudes of industrial workers—people who were crowding the factory halls chanting "down with the Zionists"—the whole question of how much such "spontaneous" gatherings reflected genuine feelings turns into an issue of strong anti-intellectual biases prevailing in those days, biases which were eventually to give way to cooperation within Solidarity, without, however, disappearing altogether (Bujak, 1983). Again, just as in Cywiński's analysis, anti-Semitism as such is not at issue here. And again, its existence, while not altogether denied, becomes diffused in a much larger context of anti-intellectual fears and resentments.

*Is* anti-Semitism still an issue?

It is true that while in the past nationalistic discourse was almost by definition also anti-Semitic in thrust, the connection today is both much weaker and much less apparent. To illustrate: the "sociological intervention" analysis of Solidarity, conducted by Alain Touraine and his co-workers and published in France in 1982, makes frequent intriguing references to "nationalism" with no further explanation. The transcripts[24] of many long discussions generated by the French-Polish team in various centers of Solidarity and including comments by a wide variety of its members, offered few specific expressions of this rather abstract "nationalism". In most cases where "national" issues were on the agenda at all, the target of direct attack would inevitably be the Russians. On the other hand, when the "Jewish question" was brought up by the researchers themselves, as in a debate following the infamous statements by Jurczyk on the "Jews in the government," it was clear that at least for those involved in this study there was more to these words than political lunacy.

As other observers pointed out, the rank-and-file of Solidarity did not feel completely at ease with the presence of "experts"—many of whom were Jewish. They seemed to fear that the movement could come to be manipulated by the intellectuals for their own purposes, purposes not necessarily in agreement with the workers' aims (see: Touraine et al, 1982; Ash, 1985; Weschler, 1984). Yet if Jews were not attacked as Jews but as intellectuals, their being Jewish did constitute a major reason for suspicion. In one telling dialogue between a low-ranked Solidarity activist and Zbigniew Bujak, Solidarity leader in the Warsaw region, the question of Kuroń's identity comes up: "Is he Jewish?" Bujak first dismisses the question as irrelevant, then points out that Kuroń has in fact some Ukrainian ancestry. The issue is quickly dropped, as if such a query made in front of the visitors from France was not in keeping with the *image* of Solidarity as a democratic movement (see also: Wieviorka, 1984:36).

We have now come to what I believe is at the heart of the matter: the question of *reputation*. If anti-Semitism as such is only marginal in actual terms, its symbolic significance, as a blemish on Poland's good name, is still very much a concern in terms of collective definition.

Poles today are quite aware that popular world opinion has them portrayed as "eternal anti-Semites" at best and direct accomplices to Hitler's "Final Solution" at worst. They have heard it repeated again and again ever since the 1967 anti-Zionist campaign began, repeated, that is, by the official media. Those familiar with the émigré publications can see that view confirmed by independent writers. Those who travel to the West often encounter—and report—such negative images on a personal level.[25] Having spent over a year close to the Polish community in Paris and having witnessed many a heated debate, both private and public, on the topic of Polish-Jewish relations, I can say that there are few, if any, equally sensitive issues. There are few, if any, equally raw and emotional moments as those when the question of anti-Semitism in Poland is raised. Even when the discussion takes place in the context of cool scientific inquiry, it is often high-pitched.[26] It then comes as no surprise that people whose voices are to be *publicly* heard—such as Solidarity activists—take great care not to *appear* as anti-Semites. At a time when so much depended on Western support for the movement and its goals, Solidarity simply could not afford anything less than a morally pure image. What in another context could be a sign of a perfectly healthy and well functioning democracy, in Poland, any traditionally anti-Semitic expression needed to be toned down, if not suppressed altogether. Such expressions might not have disappeared from private conversations, as Michel Wieviorka points out in his account of the "Jewish question" within Solidarity (1984), but they certainly had to disappear from the public sphere.

The very fact that they are now re-appearing within the opposition zone, essentially unaltered by any concern over reactions from outside, might mean that Polish opposition politics have turned inwards again, with policies and tactics aimed to win popular support rather than Western backing. In a sense, then, the present situation within the opposition comes to resemble that within the official zone, with some people still trying to make anti-Semitism useful while others are trying to make it disappear, if only for the sake of Poland's international standing. People opposing anti-Semitism do not do so merely for its damaging effects on Poland's image. It is, however, nearly impossible to find in Poland statements on anti-Semitism which would not contain concerns over reputation.

As we have seen, the situation within the Catholic Church and laity is not monolithic either. While anti-Semitism is now clearly and loudly condemned at the highest levels, it still quietly perseveres among the lower clergy. And while the lay Catholic channels serve as an important platform for discussing Polish-Jewish affairs, this discussion is not oriented towards self-criticism. Indeed, if there is one topic badly missing on the agenda of the "Jewish memory project," it is the question of the role in creating and maintaining anti-Jewish sentiments played by the teachings and the practices of Christianity in general and of Polish Catholicism in particular.

When speaking about the Catholic Church, it must be stressed, we are no longer speaking of people concerned with their political fortunes while talking or not talking about anti-Semitism. The Church neither gains nor loses its popularity in Poland because of its stand with respect to the Jews; at the most, it can re-affirm its status as an oasis of serious moral reflection or, conversely, re-appear as the traditional refuge for Polish nationalism. Its interest in a dialogue with Judaism and Jews, however central to *our* analysis, is only a small part of its overall spiritual mission.[27] On the other hand, its lack of interest in promoting a critical inquiry into its own past counts for a great deal in making the present discussion of Polish-Jewish relations what it is—an "objective" study of the "Jewish problem".

At issue here is not another form of "conspiracy theory," this time with the Catholic Church as a culprit. I do not think anyone could claim that the Church exerts some direct pressure on the Catholic intellectuals, let alone the more secular ones, the pressure to stay away from topics it might consider "inconvenient." I will argue, though, that unless the Church—in Poland[28]—changes its present position, the critical approach to Polish/ Jewish history will remain a very painful but not very illuminating effort. Without theology, without metaphysics, there can be no tenable explanation for why, forty years after the Holocaust and nearly twenty years after the expulsion of virtually all of the remaining Jews, it is still perfectly legitimate to hold the Jew responsible for his own fate.

### Notes

1. *Remnants* includes an updated version of this interview (for a *full* text, as it read in 1983, see: *Moment* (April 1984) ), with the new elements not likely to suffer from cuts either.
2. This is particularly true of the last chapter, an interview with Szymon Datner, an historian and a survivor, where some of the most painful issues in Polish-Jewish relations are being discussed quite openly. The *text* is not any more controversial than that by Sandauer (1982), published very officially; the principals, however, are.
3. The "explosion of memory" during the times of Solidarity offered a very powerful confirmation of this myth; with censorship nearly gone, Poles were able to discuss their *real* history.

    While I do not minimize the significance of censorship for silencing Polish historical experience, I am arguing that discourse on Polish-Jewish matters followed its own dynamics.
4. The notion of "totalitarian culture" presupposes that most, if not all, of the resources are at the disposal of the state. Directly or indirectly, it is the state which controls culture producers, not the least because of the financial control involved. What can easily be overlooked here is that the state itself does not have unlimited resources—a rather obvious point for a country in dire economic straits.
5. The situation within the film industry is particularly telling in that censorship

applies even to the idea for a future film, let alone its script. Once the film passed through all the stages of state controls, the last one at the point of distribution, its very presence testifies to the "liberalism" of the regime. It then takes some "ideological work" (Berger, 1981) to place the product again within the oppositional discourse.

6. Some of this anti-regime spirit still persists in that students looking at the Jewish resistance during the Second World War (particularly in the ghettos, where it took the most diverse passive forms) relate their knowledge directly to their own efforts at passive resistance vis-à-vis the regime.

7. What was true in 1983–84 is even more true in 1986–87, when much of the *discussion* on Polish-Jewish relations in particular takes place within lay Catholic journals as well as at meetings sponsored by lay Catholic organizations. The state, on the other hand, remains the main sponsor of cultural events and scholarly exchanges; both are areas where it generally exercises much greater controls.

8. In 1987, there were signs that this uncritical position vis-à-vis the Church might be slowly changing. An issue of the lay Catholic monthly *Więź* (no. 7/8), prepared in 1986, but which reached the stands in 1987, contains a long discussion among the journal's regular contributors and editors on an essay by Śpiewak (also there) proposing a theological interpretation of the Holocaust as the "killing of Christianity." Among many points raised in that discussion, there were also questions as to the Christian roots of anti-Semitism, both in institutional and in theological terms, questions, however, not yet comprising any coherent focus for analysis.

9. The sample consisted of 250 students in various faculties (social sciences and physics); the survey was conducted in 1975–1982.

10. Included is a long article by Lichten (1983 b) (a representative of B'nai B'rith in Rome and a Polish Jew) on the dialogue between Catholics and Jews. He explicitly prefers to by-pass the questions about the past as injurious to the general spirit of reconciliation.

11. *Polityka's* regular columnists frequently point to the strength of reactionary positions among the clergy in the inter-war Poland, usually in response to the Church publications which completely silence the issue.

12. The most explicit illustration of this reluctance to delve into the Christian roots of anti-Semitism in Poland comes in the form of a reluctantly published discussion around Grynberg's book *Prawda nieartystyczna* (1984.) [Unartistic truth] in *Kultura*. The book, a collection of essays essential for any understanding of Polish-Jewish relations (written by a Polish Jewish author, now living in the U.S.) was rejected for publication by *Kultura's* editor. A review of it, published at the author's initiative (Szulczyński, 1985), while generally favorable, strongly rejects Grynberg's argument on the responsibility of the Church with respect to the Holocaust. While publishing an exchange between Grynberg and the reviewer, making this point ever more explicit ("Polemiki", 1985), *Kultura's* editor admits to doing so not to be accused of anti-Semitism by the overly sensitive Grynberg and, then, categorically cuts off any further discussion on the subject. It should be added that while *Kultura* has, over the years, published several essays and letters dealing with the "Poles and Jews" questions the brief discussion of Grynberg's thesis is the closest it has come to raising the issue of the Church's responsibiity.

13. To put it in some perspective, I should point out that *Shoah* has been presented

on French T.V. in June/July of *1987*. Lanzmann himself explains the Polish government's decision with an observation that while Polish peasants are anti-Jewish, they are also anti-Communist (quoted in Alaton, *Globe & Mail,* June 13, 1986).

14. I rely here on the reports by two viewers in Warsaw. The sections dealing with Poland in *Shoah* exceed the period of T.V. presentation by about one hour. From the discussion which appeared in the press, one can gather, though, that the most damaging scenes *were* included in the T.V. selection.

15. The impact of this particular scene is all the greater for its apparent spontaneity. In contrast to a number of exchanges with Poles earlier in the film—where Lanzmann probes, asks questions and very much "directs" his respondents—this one is a rare instance of his low interference.

16. The "anti-slander" thrust was not absent from the press coverage of *Shoah.* A fair amount of attention, for example, was devoted to the manipulative tactics used by Lanzmann while filming in Poland, with the general conclusion that he had intentionally created an anti-Polish picture (see, e.g., Chłopecki, *Prawo i Zycie,* Nov. 16, 1985). Watching *Shoah* made me realize that Lanzmann's approach was manipulative beyond what might be expected from an artist. And while I personally have no objections to manipulation vis-à-vis the Nazis interviewed in this film, I cannot accept the idea that the end justifies the means as far as the treatment of his other subjects is concerned (which includes Poles, but also some Jewish survivors, pushed to the psychological limits of endurance).

17. *Promised Land* is a film based on a novel by Reymont, depicting the 19th century developments in Łódź, a city where both Jews and Germans plays a crucial role in the textile industry. It is the only major literary work on the subject. In France, where the film was also shown on T.V. (I saw it in Paris in the summer of 1981), Wajda's portrayal of Jews was judged as so negative to badly affect the reputation of this well-liked director. I think the critics were too harsh; no one, especially the Polish capitalist, comes across in a nice light in the film.

18. As of 1986, an Institute of Jewish Studies was in fact established at the Jagiellonian University in Cracow. (*Soviet Jewish Affairs* regularly publishes updates on the research activities, including Poland.)

19. In 1987, the state administrators were very supportive indeed of the various initiatives on the part of a privately established Nussenbaums' Foundation (now a major source of funding for the restoration of Jewish memory markers).

20. At issue here is continuity of Polish history after 1945. Jews in the opposition are more likely to dispute it, to see the pre-1956 situation as qualitatively different (especially in terms of political choices) from the later period. This is then perceived by their opponents as a self-serving justification for not opposing the regime from the very beginning.

21. In fairness, *Polityka* regularly publishes critical "reviews" of the oppositional anti-Semitic discourse as well, beginning with Bogusławski's (Sept. 12) 1981 appeal to prosecute Solidarity for printing parts of the "Protocols of the Elders of Zion", through the 1983 warning against conspiracy theories by Groński (Feb 26), to the most recent one, also by him, about the situation in the Warsaw churches (May 23, 1987). The longest of such expositions was rather intriguing. Jerzy Urban published elections from a book attacking him—as a Jew and as a government spokesman. If authentic, that book is a remarkable piece of the worst kind of anti-Semitic garbage (March 29, 1986).

22. It should be re-emphasized here that the "Jewish conspiracy theory" has been a prominent feature of the *official* discourse ever since 1967, a characteristic which may further add to its potential. To claim that the official propaganda has no effect whatsoever would be to engage in especially misleading wishful thinking. It is also to forget that—at least in 1968—it proved quite effective.

23. The pseudonym draws on the Biblical story of Cain and Abel, conveying the duality of Polish-Jewish experience.

24. I am very grateful to Michel Wieviorka for his extensive assistance in this matter. The original transcripts were both in Polish and in French; fortunately, the sections of most interest to me preserved the Polish wording.

    For M. Wieviorka's own interpretation of the same materials, see his *La Pologne, les Juifs, Solidarność* (1984).

25. There is now a Polish American *sociologist* doing a discourse analysis of the anti-Polish slander (Niedzielski, 1986), much in the same vein as the less sophisticated but equally offended Poles.

26. Among the meetings I attended, a scientific colloquium on the impact of the Warsaw Ghetto Uprising (held on April 24, 1983) gave rise to perhaps the most emotional reactions on the part of Jewish survivors, while on Dec. 15, 1983, a discussion of Polish anti-Semitism at Centre Rachi—of high intellectual caliber but framed more publicly—became a scene of over one hour of an impossible-to-moderate outpouring of emotions on both sides.

    On this continent, the controversy surrounding Norman Davies' treatment of Polish-Jewish relations has also reached well beyond academic points. In this case, stakes are particularly high, since his books have rapidly become standard reference for students of Polish history, students often ill-equipped to object to Davies' minimizing the significance of anti-Semitism in the name of "objectivity."

27. During the Pope's most recent visit to Poland, in June 1987, he held a 15-minute meeting with eight representatives of Polish Jews (including Szymon Datner, an historian, and Stanisław Krajewski, *the* "return Jew", together with officials of the religious community). *Tygodnik Powszechny,* which reported extensively on the visit and published many of the homilies (June 21 & 29, 1987), stressed the importance of this meeting. The Pope's visit lasted one week. I think the "time relation" here is a fairly exact reflection of the significance of Jewish affairs.

28. The position taken by the Polish Church is crucial not because it is radically different from that of Catholics in other countries, but simply because it alone can influence Polish Catholics.

    *The Storm Over "The Deputy"* (Bentley, ed., 1964) is a good lesson on the universal Church's reluctance to confront its past. I should add, though, that the only time—in Poland—that a member of the Church hierarchy spoke *directly* of its responsibility for the fate of the Jews during the Holocaust was— to the best of my knowledge—when the then Archibishop of Paris, Jean-Marie Lustiger, prayed in Auschwitz in 1983 (he had joined the Pope during his summer visit to Poland). Jean-Marie Lustiger, though, was born a Polish Jew and his mother perished in Auschwitz.

# 6

# Neutralizing Memory

From the outside, the current interest in things Jewish in Poland may indeed appear puzzling. Even after one tries, as I have done here, to piece together the different interests in and behind this "Jewish memory project," one still wonders why the Poles seem so *keen* to invite the Jew into their memory, their heritage.[1] Even as we begin to appreciate the significance of this invitation for the pluralist vision of Polish society, Polish history, and ultimately, Polish identity, and to understand that this significance may be so great as it is precisely because it *is* symbolic, there still remains one query. Considering just how difficult it is—still—to talk about the Polish-Jewish past, and considering just how problematic that past *is,* why would anyone in Poland want to discuss it?

There are two ways to answer this question or, more precisely, two parts to one answer. It seems reasonable to begin by arguing (as some people in Poland have done)[2] that Poles must, for the sake of national moral health, come to terms with their history vis-à-vis the Jew, no matter how difficult the process.

The history of anti-Semitism in Poland in particular is then something of a "locked box" that has to be opened and aired out, if only to ensure the health of the future generations. As a corollary to the purification of the *collective* self, there comes the urge to normalize the conception of the Jew, for the public rejection of anti-Semitism is not seen as enough to make it disappear. Unless Poles know more about the Jewish tradition, Jewish culture and philosophy and about the Jews themselves, there can be no meaningful reconciliation. Polish-Jewish relations, even if primarily symbolic, must be based on mutual respect and understanding. And since Poles and Jews have lived together for much of Poland's history, this mutual respect and understanding must apply, by the nature of things, to their shared past as much as to their separate present.

The key word here is *mutual*. As much as this fresh and often critical approach to a Polish-Jewish past challenges many of the long-accepted ideas about the Jew, it is seen as no less of a challenge to many of the long-accepted ideas about the Pole. Unless everyone, and especially the Jews, recognizes that being Polish is *not* equivalent to being anti-Semitic and recognizes that Poles too suffered greatly during the Nazi occupation, there can be no reconciliation.

Poles, then, have a memory obligation to Polish Jews, but they also have a memory obligation to themselves. And the "Jewish memory project" is an attempt to fulfill both of these obligations. It is an effort to honor the Jew in all his Jewishness, but it is also an effort to honor Poland as the home of Europe's largest Jewish community before the destruction. First of all, though, it is an effort to learn from past mistakes.

And here we come to the second part of our answer. For what Poles define as these "past mistakes" is what structures their present efforts to rectify them.

Our own map of the territory of Polish-Jewish relations is not a good guide here, though. What I and others may see as serious moral wrongs—the exclusion of Jews from the common universe of discourse, the resulting indifference of most Poles to the fate of Jews during the Holocaust and most of all, perhaps, the murder of hundreds of survivors—are not "automatically" defined as wrong by the Poles themselves. Thus, the fact that the Polish-Jewish past is so publicly prominent today cannot properly be understood unless we understand the dynamics of *neutralizing* memory.

We begin by listening to the voice of one of Poland's most respected intellectuals, a man whose life and work qualify him perhaps more than anyone else as the spokesman of the Poles' moral conscience—Jan Józef Lipski. A prominent historian and one of the co-founders of the Committee for Workers Defence (KOR), Lipski is the most outspoken among the opposition intellectuals on the question of nationalism. His essay on two kinds of patriotism, widely circulated within the underground in 1981 and even discussed in the official media with some degree of respect, became one of the most important, almost programatic expositions of the humanistic ethos of democratic forces in Poland. Lipski attacked with great vigor and candor anything with any connection to xenophobia and prejudice, including, very prominently, anti-Semitism. During the existence of KOR, and especially in its later period when there were serious differences of views on the "national question," Lipski remained on the side of those who defended a highly morally conscious and all-embracing humanism, a patriotism free from resentments. Not always popular, especially for his position regarding the Germans and the Russians,[3] Lipski was always highly respected and his personal integrity never questioned. Though perhaps a little idealistic, his is a model position of morality in politics, a position shared with other members of KOR and one he was to describe extensively in his work (1983a) on the ethics of this unique group of people.

In April 1983, Lipski spoke about Polish Jews at a special mass commemorating those who "died and were murdered during the war," a mass celebrated at the time of the official ceremonies marking the 40th anniversary of the Warsaw Ghetto Uprising. Lipski's exposé, published later in 1983 (b) by both the underground press and the émigré journal *Kultura,* was to become one of the focal points for discussion on the subject. It is then worth looking at in some detail.

The presentation is fairly brief. It begins with homage to the Ghetto fighters who "fought not to win but to die with dignity," followed by homage to the position taken by Edelman (the refusal to participate in the officially staged ceremonies). Lipski, however, goes further to point out the dangerous corollary implicit in such homage—it is a "dangerous moral wrong" to see the other Jews as people dying *without* dignity; this is a point often lost in both the official and the unofficial commemorative spectacle.[4] Stressing that the heroism of the Ghetto fighters should not overshadow the death of millions killed without resistance, Lipski stresses: "For us who were watching the death of both, there remains, alongside the duty to remember and to respect, a compelling necessity to answer a number of bitter questions and memories, for a kind of statement of our own national conscience" (p.4). To strengthen his appeal for a critical look at the past, he asks: "If not in the armed struggle, then in the work of aid and salvage, did we do as much as was possible?" Then another question: "Did we all do what was possible, or less, or nothing—at a time when dying people and our own moral norms were calling for more than the possible?" (p.4).

Lipski leaves these questions without an answer. Only indirectly, in the paragraph which immediately follows, does he address the issue of responsibility. He begins by pointing out that it is "doing of harm to the Poles" which comes from generalizing too far about the cooperation of some Poles in hunting or blackmailing Jews. He then points out that an "amoral margin exists in all societies," therefore Poles have the right to reject any "irresponsible generalizations" made about them. And, they should reject any generalizations harmful to other nations. "Anti-Polonism is nothing morally better than anti-Semitism or anti-Ukrainism."

Moving into the history of Polish-Jewish relations proper, Lipski emphasizes both the traditional Polish tolerance and the sharing of Poles and Jews in the struggles for independence.[5] But he also talks about the "venom of anti-Semitism which began to poison our national ethos in the middle of the 19th century" as well as the events in independent Poland which "we cannot remember without shame: anti-Semitic units, pogroms, the hatred so great that it had made its Catholic proponents beat up a Catholic priest in a Catholic church just because his ancestors were Jewish and he considered himself a Jew, all the anti-Semitic propaganda." Here, he poses a critical question: "Who knows how many more Jews would have survived on Polish soil were it not for that poison?"

Rather than answer this key question, Lipski rapidly moves to a brief mention of the pogrom in Kielce in 1946 which, provoked or not, could never have succeeded without fertile soil. Then, he acknowledges that the success of anti-Semitic propaganda in 1968 was "unfortunately not nil." For Lipski, though, both 1946 and 1968 form only a part of a general pattern which still prevails: Anti-Semitism does service in the struggle against Poland's fight for independence and freedom.[6] During the Stalinist era, such anti-Semitism had naturally gained in strength, although, for Lipski, "Jews in the security apparatus were exactly the same kind of Jews as their Polish colleagues from the same apparatus were Poles."

Lipski makes a final appeal, this time for what he calls a "partial judaization of our culture," or for such an enrichment of Polish culture as would allow for learning about and understanding "all that was great in the culture of Polish Jews." This, he says, may "lessen the tragedy of an ultimately all too little fertile co-existence of our nations over the centuries;" in other words, it might help to undo at least some of the "tragedy of the lost chance."

The "Jewish memory project" as a way to make amends? Before answering, we should consider just what kind of memory work has been performed here. Lipski may have gone further than perhaps anyone else in Poland then in *raising* the issues of responsibility. He may also have gone far in countering some of the popular misconceptions, first in his comments about death and dignity, and later in his remarks about the Stalinists. But, and this is a big "but", he did feel obliged ultimately to *reassure* his audience that Poland's bad reputation was not only unjustified but the work of hostile forces "in the world"; in an earlier statement (1981/83), Lipski identified those forces simply as Jews. And, for him, no one can be held responsible for the "criminal margins" of any society. Poles have reason to be proud of their tradition of tolerance, they should also remember that anti-Semitism has always been used as a *tool* against their struggle for freedom. Notice, there is not a word here about the basis for such manipulation by foreign powers; there is not a word here on the role of the Church. After all is said and heard, even the tough questions about the Holocaust are overshadowed by innocence that such direct delegation of blame encourages. What remains is regret that two peoples living so closely had so little in common. And *this* is the "tragedy of the lost chance," which can now at least be partially repaired. What began as a critical examination of conscience ends on a call for nostalgia. What began as soul searching ends in self-reassurance. What began as homage to the memory of the Jew ends in homage to the Poles' *collective self-definition*.

Lipski's views might not be at all representative of such a collective self-definition. If anything, his views lie at the edge of self-criticism and moral outrage over the darker sides of the collective self. It, therefore, makes a lot more sense to consider his position than to look at the ample examples of the less critical variety.[7] What we have here are precisely the inner limits to memory work as defined by the conception of collective self. What we also have is a good illustration of just how well nostalgia towards the Jew can simultaneously satisfy the need for self-examination and neutralize it. The very act of remembering the Jew as a Jew, far from disturbing the collective self, is now said to enrich it; this newly reinvited Jew though, must remain in the past. When the Jew becomes the Jews "staining Poland's honour," memory work cannot but shift into the instrumental gear.

There is perhaps no better illustration of how this shift occurs than the outrage which became the Poles' first and then most common reaction to Lanzmann's *Shoah*. From outright denunciations of the film as slanderous and offensive, through a whole series of articles dealing with anti-Semitism in Lanzmann's France, to a call for responding to *Shoah* with a true picture of Poles (the one of them as extensive helpers of the Jews), the Polish media were filled with anger and fury. This was not the first time that Poles felt they had to defend their "good name," but it was the first they were challenged so directly. Again, it might be best to listen to the few voices of serious critical reflection rather than the uproar of self-congratulatory protest if we wish to understand how even the impact of *Shoah* could be neutralized.

Andrzej Grzegorczyk, a Catholic philosopher who frequently contributes to the official media, took part in the television debate immediately following the screening of the "Polish sections" of *Shoah* in November 1985. Not satisfied with the debate itself, he then wrote a long article for *Polityka* (Nov. 16, 1985), entitled "The Jewish Question." Arguing that it was necessary to "de-ideologize" the discourse about anti-Semitism and seemingly accepting the challenge presented by Lanzmann's attack on the Church, Grzegorczyk went on to sketch what he saw as the essence of the *conflict* between Jews and Catholics. To a reader even vaguely familiar with Western Catholics' writings on the subject, this Polish account appears more than a little strange. In fact, the largest section of the article was devoted to an explication of sources of distrust and also hatred felt *by*

*Jews* towards Christians. Only towards the end did Grzegorczyk even mention that there had been some reasons for negative attitudes in the opposite direction. All in all, he was careful to emphasize and reemphasize that in this centuries' old conflict, Jews were as much to blame as Christians for all the layers of mutual misunderstanding and resentment. And, equally careful to point out the differences, Grzegorczyk ended by echoing the appeal made by Polish bishops to the German people in 1961— "let us forgive and ask forgiveness."

The appeal did not pass unnoticed. In letters to the editors, common people protested loudly against such an outrageous formulation; to them, Poles had nothing to be forgiven for in the first place. *Polityka* itself was to become a forum for a debate set in a very different mode. The first reply to Grzegorczyk came from KTT (K. T. Toeplitz), a well known culture critic and columnist, but also a well known "court Jew" (he is, in fact, only a descendant of a famous Haskalah family). Toeplitz (Nov. 30, 1985) also expanded on the views he had expressed during the post-*Shoah* debate. He strongly opposed the whole of Grzegorczyk's argument, accusing him of "standing the problem on its head." "What on earth should the millions of Jews murdered by the Nazis be forgiven for?" he asked, as he went on to clarify some of the most pronounced misconceptions about Judaism found in the "conflict approach." The title of this article was "This is an Ideological Question"; the headline emphasizing its main point read "one ought not to forgive those who are sowing the seeds of hatred between people, faiths and nationalities." To support his position, Toeplitz too used an historical overview, reminding the readers just how difficult it was to be accepted as an assimilated Jew and how even after the destruction of Polish Jewry, the problem did not go away. Citing the pogrom in Kielce in 1946 and the 1968 campaign as examples of "a marginal phenomenon but still . . . ," Toeplitz insisted that these were facts not to be omitted in any discussion on the subject. The formula of "mutual forgiveness" might sound attractive, he concluded, but it was also dangerously close to making allowances for racism and intolerance.

The second reply came from another prominent culture critic, a frequent contributor to *Polityka,* well known for his anti-clerical views. Kałużyński (Dec. 7, 1985) was also the only writer to follow up on the controversy stirred by Urban's attack on Church anti-Semitism with a thorough examination of available sources. A "court journalist" but not a Jew, he took on the unpopular role of a surveyor of national faults. "I refuse to forgive," he declared at the outset. His article was not only a response to the views of Grzegorczyk but, more importantly, a reply to the most influential of Catholic intellectuals, Jerzy Turowicz, the editor of *Tygodnik Powszechny* (Nov. 10, 1985). What angered Kałużyński most was the fact that both these Catholic writers had delegated responsibility for anti-Semitism away from the Church and onto the Polish people themselves. This he called a "miracle or a gift for forgetting (the role of the Church as an institution in promoting anti-Semitism)." To forget, he argued, was to go well beyond Lanzmann's explicit critique in *Shoah;* to appeal for "mutual forgiveness" was to seal forever this obnoxious substitution of responsibility. Here the argument was based on two quite different logics. First, the readers were given a lecture on documentary filmmaking and investigative reporting, a defense of Lanzmann as a director. Then, they were offered a guide of sorts in the techniques of manipulation, as Kałużyński surveyed how the Jewishness of Jesus had been dealt with in Catholic teachings. The critic seemed to have gone out of his way to provoke the public without caring very much whether he could convince anybody.

He certainly did not convince Grzegorczyk himself. In a reply to both critiques, though, one saw a new element which had a pronounced effect on this Catholic philosopher's reflections. After his original statement and before the one officially closing the debate on the "Jewish question," Grzegorczyk (*Polityka,* Dec. 21–27, 1985) saw *Shoah* in its entirety. And as his comments reveal towards the end, the film moved him so much that he was forced to reach beneath his established view of man in the world. His position became one of retreat, a retreat to a far more reflective and philosophical humility towards the Holocaust. As a result, he would now be able to say that he and other Poles had not met the challenge posed by the mass extermination. In the end, he would repeat his appeal for a mutual forgiveness but reverse the order—himself being the one to be forgiven first.[8]

*Polityka* was not the only journal to devote space to *Shoah,* but it was the only one to devote so much to views which were not in line with the popular response.[9] Indeed, before the Polish government even decided to screen the film in Poland, *Polityka* published two articles arguing that seeing *Shoah* was a necessity for any morally and intellectually decent understanding of Polish history. On their own, both of these[10] were statements of the highest moral values, well thought out and well presented. There was one problem, however. The articles were written by A. Sandauer and J. Rem—in other words, by a prominent literary critic long associated with the regime and the government's official spokesman, thus by two of the most visible "court Jews." When read together with those which followed the T.V. presentation, they could leave a distinct impression that the only people *critical* of Polish anti-Semitism in general and the role of the Church in particular were indeed "court Jews," with the exception of one anti-clerical "Journaliste-provocateur." More importantly, perhaps, these voices of critique all came from one source, namely the cultural officialdom, a source which is not, as we have already observed, credited with a great deal of social or moral authority.[11] Their significance as voices of conscience might therefore have been very small indeed, all the critical impetus notwithstanding.

But what about those people with credibility? The position taken by Turowicz, the editor of the most influential Catholic weekly, was not very far from that of a less rebellious Catholic intellectual writing in *Polityka*. While acknowledging the "national sins" of the interwar period for which Poles still had to search their conscience, he too refused to acknowledge any connection between the Church tradition and anti-Semitism after 1939 or between anti-Semitism during the war and the final outcome of the "Final Solution." Turowicz, in fact, went on record internationally, in reply to T. Garton Ash, whose perceptive analysis in *The New York Review of Books* branded such a refusal of facts as "nationalism of the victim." Turowicz made his views plain: ". . . the conception and the execution of the "Final Solution" was exclusively the doing of the Nazis, and I do not see why anybody else should be burdened with co-responsibility for it" (May 8, 1986).

It should be stressed that Turowicz's own credentials on the "Jewish question" are impeccable. His weekly has long represented the most progressive side of Polish Catholicism, the one attacking nationalism of all varieties, including anti-Semitism. He takes pride in the accomplishments of his journal in *changing* the face of Polish Catholicism, a fact which Ash is quick to note later, for it does represent a second-hand acknowledgment that "something else" had characterized the Church in the past (*NYR*, May 8, 1986). In short, the refusal to accept *any* responsibility for what happened to the Jews of Poland during the Holocaust comes from someone who is not only highly respected but also highly respectable for his own work on improving Polish-Jewish relations.

At this point, one may ask whether such a whole-hearted refusal is representative of Polish public opinion. A survey[12] of the audience response to television programming, conducted shortly after the T.V. screening of the "Polish sections" of *Shoah* offers a rare glimpse into popular attitudes. It shows that the majority of respondents did watch both the film and the discussion which followed. Of those, some sixty-six percent found the film "offensive to Poland." Fifty-six percent thought that Lanzmann had made a "tendentious and one-sided" picture expressly to discredit Poland. And, for many of the viewers of the T.V. debate in particular, the call for "mutual forgiveness" proved totally unacceptable; there was *nothing* in the history of Polish-Jewish relations, they felt, which would warrant such an appeal on the part of the Poles.

Nearly a year later, the results of yet another extensive survey, this time a sociological study of "historical consciousness" among Polish youth, were made public in *Polityka* (Olszewska, Oct. 25, 1986). Of relevance is the fact that among all the different aspects of Polish history that this broad sampling of young people felt should be subjected to critical re-examination, the whole area of Polish-Jewish relations was missing. In-deed, in spite of calls by many prominent intellectuals on both sides of the political divide, the whole area of Polish relations with national minorities was missing from the list of concerns. It is true that this survey asked no direct questions regarding the Jews; one nevertheless suspects that had such been posed, the answers would not have deviated from those voiced in response to *Shoah*. In short, it is reasonable to think of the question of responsibility for the ultimate fate of Polish Jews as a "non-question" as far as most Poles are concerned.

Of all the limits to the critical inquiry into the Polish-Jewish past, this is definitely the most imposing. It is also the most demanding from the point of view of analytical interpretation. To understand this so effective of neutralization strategies, I believe we ought to begin by considering Auschwitz as a symbol of the place accorded to the Holocaust in Poland's memory.

For many years, a visitor to Auschwitz, or, more precisely, to a museum in the stone buildings remaining on the site of Auschwitz I—the concentra-tion camp—would have a very hard time appreciating that it was there that hundreds of thousands of Jews were murdered solely because they were Jews. In most of the pavilions and on all the memorial tablets, the very word "Jew" was missing. Walls covered with pictures of prisoners pro-vided the backdrop for enormous piles of human hair, shoes, glasses, luggage. What had happened to the people who had left these behind was clear—they had been gassed. What was not clear was the *difference* between being a Polish or a Russian or a German inmate and being a Jew directed straight to the gas chambers. In part, the difference was literally beyond the visitors' vision, as nearly nothing remained of Auschwitz II, the site of systematic extermination. In part, the difference was silenced by the overall emphasis on the universality of the Nazi crimes against *humanity,* silenced, it should be stressed, not solely by the Polish authori-ties in charge of the Auschwitz memorial.[13] In 1961, for example, Alain Resnais, a famous French filmmaker, produced *Night and Fog,* a film serving for many years as the ultimate documentary on the horrors of the camp. There, the only indication of who—not why—was systematically put to death in Auschwitz comes in the form of two brief images of people wearing the Star of David and being hurried off the train.

In 1978, Polish authorities did open a small "Jewish Pavilion" at the

Auschwitz museum. Yet even then, as Susan Sontag commented after her visit there, its out-of-the-way location together with the very fact that the materials it contained were available only in English or French, meant that its impact as a memory marker would be limited at best.[14] In 1979, When Pope John Paul II officially visited Poland his itinerary included Auschwitz. Stopping before a memorial tablet with a Hebrew inscription, he paid homage to the "sons and daughters of a nation destined for a complete extermination." A few moments later, now in front of a tablet with the inscription in Polish, the Pope said: "six million Poles perished during the last war, one-fifth of the nation."[15]

In April 1983, Auschwitz was again a center of considerable media attention. This time, the visitors were scholars, some Holocaust survivors, on a tour which followed their meeting in Warsaw, the one devoted to the subject of genocide and scheduled to coincide with the ceremonies commemorating the Warsaw Ghetto Uprising. Once again, in paying homage to the millions who perished in Auschwitz, they would be honoring the *Polish* victims of the Nazi genocide.[16]

For years, many Jewish visitors to Auschwitz were taken aback by its silence (see esp.: Vidal-Naguet, 1981). But, in 1986, a number of Jewish organizations in the West, together with some Christian groups made a passionate appeal *for* silence. Upset by the plans to install a retreat for Carmelite nuns next to the camp site, or rather by what they perceived as plans to make this retreat a part of the Auschwitz museum, they protested to both the Church and the Polish government. Auschwitz, of all places, should be left in peace, they argued. For Catholic prayers to be said at this massive Jewish graveyard would be to desecrate the memory of the dead. Fearful of the efforts to "convert" the victims and resenting the very presence of the Church at a site so central to the memory of the Holocaust, the Jews appealing for silence were now reclaiming their *right* to Auschwitz. On the Polish side, the responses were equally emotional. For the Poles, Auschwitz is also a symbol; but it is known by its Polish name Os'więcim, and it commemorates Polish death and Polish suffering during World War II. It is a symbol of Nazi terror and inhumanity to man. For the Poles, then, it is not—and it has never been—a symbol of the Jewish Holocaust.[17] The nuns, as far as Poles were concerned, would be doing only what should be done at a cemetery—meditate and pray, pray for all the victims but especially for those who were Catholic. What possible harm could be caused by quiet devotion?

Efforts to reconcile the two sides of this memory dispute culminated in a meeting in Switzerland, where an agreement was reached at least to respect each other's position and to engage in further negotiations (by that time, only the Church was involved on the Polish side). In an effort to explain this whole debate, one of the most outspoken of Poland's young "return Jews" went on record in the Catholic weekly *Tygodnik Powszechny* (Krajewski, 1986). As a Jew, he wrote in defense of the nuns' retreat. While appreciating the symbolic value of Auschwitz for the world Jewry, he argued that the nuns' prayers might actually *remind* visitors of the Jewishness of most of the victims, a valuable reminder in and of itself. While appreciating the Jews' concern about the effects of Church teachings on the popular attitudes towards the Jew—the paper's editor was quick to point out to readers that such teachings had been "often misinterpreted" prior to Vatican II—the author also appreciated the power of prayer, *any* prayer, in lieu of the often noisy bustle of tourists.[18] Considering his voice uniquely equipped to speak for both sides, this young "return Jew" was calling for *mutual respect* for the memory of the victims, Polish and Jewish alike.

In February 1987, after about two years of negotiations, representations of the Polish Episcopate and leaders of the European Jewish community came to an agreement (see: "Deklaracja", *Tygodnik Powszechny,* March 15, 1987), that Auschwitz would not house a Carmelite retreat on its grounds; instead, the Polish Church, in co-operation with other European churches, would within the next two years, establish an "information and reflection" center to assure that the significance of Auschwitz is not forgotten. The declaration that both sides signed stresses the element of *mutual recognition:* in Auschwitz at least, the memory of both the Jewish and Polish victims must be honored together.

When one reads the ensuing commentaries in the Catholic *Tygodnik Powszechny* (Musiał, March 15, 1987) and the French Jewish *l'Arche* (Sulzbach, 1987), one can better appreciate why the compromise was possible. To the Polish Catholics, the very acknowledgment that Auschwitz is not solely a symbol of the Holocaust was crucial. To the Jews, the very acknowledgment that Auschwitz is also a symbol of the Holocaust was a promising enough development in light of the long years of silence.

What this unprecedented memory dispute brings into sharp relief is just how far apart Polish and Jewish memories really are. Indeed, it brings into focus the deep gulf separating the presence of the Holocaust in the Western "after Auschwitz" consciousness from the Poles' sense of what Auschwitz demands.

We are now back in Auschwitz, Auschwitz—the symbol of an ultimate challenge to our faith in and understanding of humanity, the ultimate challenge to imagination, to language. Not to minimize the significance of all the other facets of 20th century experience, it is still in Auschwitz that our confrontation with "civilization" begins. Theologians and philosophers of language, poets and historians, survivors and their children, social scientists of many orientations, filmmakers and painters—all have tried to make Auschwitz real.[19] In so doing, some have searched for its universal meaning. Many, though, have asked a more concrete question: why the Jews?[20]

To ask that question is not to deny the death and suffering of others, it is to attempt an understanding of what made Auschwitz possible. And if there is one argument which immediately becomes suspect when reflecting on the Holocaust, it is the idea that Jews are to blame for their own misfortunes. It did not make the smallest difference whether one was an "enlightened" modern Jew or even a converted one, or a ghetto Jew or a Zionist or a French patriot. It is only when we think of the totality of the Jews' death sentence that we can make any sense at all of "humanity" and "civilization" with regard to Auschwitz (see, for example: Steiner, 1971, 1987; Lifton, 1986).[21]

"What man did to man"—such was the motto of one of the most moving works in Holocaust literature, a collection of short stories by a Polish writer, Zofia Nałkowska (1956). "What man did to man" could also serve as a motto for much of the literary and scholarly treatment of the "Univers concentrationnaire" in Poland since (see also: Grynberg, 1984b). For some, especially those less philosophically inclined, the issue translates into one of what Nazis did to the Poles and other peoples or into questions about German history and German politics.[22] It is an Auschwitz without Jews, one which poses a challenge to understanding in a way very different from Auschwitz with Jews. Auschwitz without Jews allows one to think past the Holocaust, or, more precisely, to think of genocide as a fate *shared* by Jews, Poles, Russians, and so on. At the least, it allows one to think of Poles as the "next in line" on the extermination list. At the most, it makes their experience during the war identical to that of the Jews. Both Jews and Poles become *victims* of a murderous regime.

This last perception is, of course, historically correct. Yet it also hides the essence of historical reality—the difference between the living in terror and being sentenced to death. In more concrete terms, it turns the experience of Poles in Warsaw and that of Jews in the Warsaw ghetto, for example, into two instances of oppression, varying in degree perhaps but not in quality (see: Korboński, 1983).

As we know today, the Nazis did their utmost at the time to perpetuate this version of events. As we know today, a number of Jews inside the ghetto walls thought, to the very last, that deportations indeed meant "resettlement" in the East, while some of those advocating active resistance identified the Jews' struggle with those of all other nations in occupied Europe and Poles in particular (see: Gutman, 1982). To appreciate the full meaning of the "Final Solution" *then* was very much an exception rather than the rule. Yet what is true of 1943 becomes difficult, if not impossible, to maintain forty years later.

It is the exceptions which offer us the most telling lesson here. There are very few non-Jewish accounts of life in the ghettos, understandably enough, since the ghettos were by definition off limits to most Poles. The ones which are available, such as Karski's description of Warsaw (1944) or a Polish pharmacist's memoirs of Cracow (Pankiewicz, 1947/1982) make it clear that the life of a Jew during the war *was* completely different from that of a Pole.[23] It seems that for people who got sufficiently close, the combined blinding effect of Nazi propaganda and Polish fear for the Poles could indeed give way to full empathy and understanding. Those, however, were the exceptions.

As we observed before, Jewish martyrology, far from being forgotten, did become an important part of the overall record of *Polish* suffering. In the process, the crucial question "Why the Jews?" moved further and further away from the foci of remembrance. "Reflections on the Holocaust" as they are understood and undertaken in the West have been nearly absent from both Polish historiography and Polish literature.[24] Though Nazi atrocities against Jews were uniformly condemned, there was very little effort to bring anti-Semitism into the focus of analysis. And, while murderous anti-Semitism became identified with Nazism, the full extent of that connection could not come to the fore, blurred as it was by a persistent emphasis on *Polish* victims. Finally, as more and more would be written about all the sound historical reasons for the emergence of fascism in Germany and for Germany's urge for territorial expansion, the Jewish aspect of the matter, escaping as it does most scientific explanations, entered into the category of "ideology," a category secondary by far to that of socio-economic and political forces.

We should keep in mind that when talking about Polish historiography, especially in the version designed for mass consumption, we are talking about a fairly crude and basic Marxist interpretation of history. To assign absolute priority to economic factors often results—not only in Poland and not only with respect to the Holocaust—in a serious misunderstanding. In this case, seeing Nazism as a phenomenon which really had very little to do with Jews has a way of informing the past with rational sense so as not to disturb the established order of things. It also makes the "Final Solution" incomprehensible. [The key here is to realize that implementing "Final Solution" was a severe drain on the Nazi war effort (see: Steiner, 1987).]

In another way, though, Poles also perceive Nazism as having a great deal to do with Jews: it is Nazism and Nazism alone which is responsible for the "Final Solution." This view may also be understood as a legacy of the past, or as one belonging to Poland's collective memory by virtue of both experience and memory work. During the war itself, what was happening to the Jews was in fact so closely identified with the Nazi regime that a large segment of the Polish underground felt completely at ease discussing the appropriate solutions to the "Jewish question" or the fate of Jewish survivors in the future Poland (mass emigration being the favoured choice). The fact, often quoted in support of the "noble" version of Polish-Jewish relations during the war, that a number of prominent anti-Semites were engaged in efforts to save Jews may also be read as evidence of this very special status accorded to things Jewish at the time (see: Tec, 1986).

In the words of Zofia Kossak-Szczucka, a prominent Catholic writer and one of the key initiators of the organized effort to aid Jews, Poles had a moral and Christian duty to oppose the Nazi atrocities against Jews, all the while remembering that the Jew was still Poland's *enemy* (see: Smolar, 1986).

The idea of the "Final Solution" *was* a Nazi idea, from conception to realization. Physical violence was not beyond the notion of acceptable means for Poland's pre-war anti-Semites, extermination was. This point is important, not solely for moral reasons. If Poles to this day do not perceive their role during the Holocaust as any kind of major challenge to their national conscience, it is in large part due to their absolutely correct sense of an abyss separating the Polish proposals to solve the "Jewish question" and the Nazi policies (quiet satisfaction at the results notwithstanding see esp. Brandys, 1983; Hillel, 1985).[25]

The persistence of this virtually unchallenged identification between "presence of Jews" and "problem" owes a great deal to the ways the Holocaust entered *both* the experience and the memory of Poles. As an experience, the destruction of Polish Jewry was kept at a *distance*. It was something that could be and was *bracketed* out from within the totality of Polish-Jewish relations, both for better and for worse. Furthermore, when Jews were being herded into the ghettos and then systematically murdered, theirs was an experience which could not be and was not shared, yet it did seem not altogether different from what Poles were subjected to in the course of Nazi occupation. Later, the memory of Jewish suffering was to be put again on a par with the memory of Polish victims, testimony to the evils of Nazism. And as it became more and more "Polonized," the Holocaust lost its potential to undermine the existing structure of beliefs about the Jew. The message it imprinted on Poland's memory was a universal one; it was also one which could be fitted into the overall "victimological" vision of the national past. Bringing Jews *and* Poles together as victims left no room, intellectually and emotionally, for considerations of the Poles' moral responsibility (see also: Mendelsohn, 1986). It also left very little room for an inquiry into the roots of anti-Jewish phobias. With the question "Why the Jews?" never truly on the agenda, memory of the Holocaust, just like that of Auschwitz itself, was freed from its conscience-troubling aspects. And the very horror of the "Final Solution," when identified solely with the Nazis, only strengthened the Poles' conviction that "we have nothing to account for."

To accept no responsibility for the ultimate fate of Polish Jews is important not just in moral terms. One should not, of course, minimize the significance of a number of Poles admitting guilt, a number steadily growing as the most recent discussion of Polish-Jewish relations during the Holocaust continues, now in a tone which is much more reflective than that of the debate surrounding *Shoah*. Set off by an article on "the poor Poles (who) watched the ghetto," an article written by prominent literary critic Jan Błoński and published in the Catholic *Tygodnik Powszechny* (Jan. 11, 1987), this discussion too has seen its share of anger at slandering Poland's good name and its share of appeals to balance the record by talking about Polish aid to the Jews. But both Błoński and others (see especially: Berberyusz, Feb. 22, 1987; Jastrzębowski, April 5, 1987) have openly admitted to a "sin of omission" in respect to the Jews, a sin which greatly troubles their conscience and which they see as "haunting" Poles into silence. The journal's editor, Turowicz, went on record with a statement which is much more self-critical[26] than the one following *Shoah* (April 5, 1987). Most importantly, though, he made it possible for two key witnesses to speak to the Poles about what really happened. Jan Karski, whose testimony in *Shoah* was not seen on T.V., and whose written reports were not previously available in Poland, talked at great length about the conditions in the ghetto (*Tygodnik Powszechny*, March 15, 1987). Teresa Prekerowa (March 29, 1987), a historian who wrote extensively on the actions to aid the Jews, then provided some much needed numbers, estimating that about *two percent* of Poles could be said to have helped Jews in one form or another during the war.[27] Her article was also a critique of the still very prevalent stereotype of the "passive" Jew, sharp criticism of anyone attempting to legitimate the Poles' inaction by blaming the victims.

Testimonies like these count for a great deal more than the admission of sin. Most readers who replied to Błoński's article were, not surprisingly, outraged at his formulation. [The angered reader is, however, much more likely to respond than someone prompted to reflect.] Yet Błoński, and later Turowicz, talked only about "omission," *not* co-responsibility. The problem here is not whether this is enough, nor whether the public will agree. The problem is that the religious language of sin and atonement may very easily lead to *closing* the critical inquiry in general and that most needed one—into the role of the Church—in particular. As we have seen, the current dialogue between Polish Catholics and Jews is only rarely about the past, with the statements against anti-Semitism displacing self-examination. And this is the most powerful of all neutralization strategies, for it allows the greatest spiritual comfort.

Let us now turn to a lesson in how comfort, psychological comfort at least, has already been achieved in an area where it might appear impossible. Let us turn to a lesson on silencing the silence.

For some thirty-five years, the 1946 pogrom in Kielce was not publicly discussed. It was something that the Jews in Poland might have discussed in private, but even they felt somewhat uneasy talking about it, since, after all, they had nevertheless stayed. Surrounded by so much speculation, the events in Kielce could prompt some Jews to leave while making others even more supportive of the authorities, the only protection they had, or thought they had. To the average Pole, Kielce was a non-event until 1981, when the second-to-last issue of the weekly *Tygodnik Solidarność* published a long article by Krystyna Kersten, a historian, on what happened there (Dec. 4). Often cited in the West as well, for even here the complete story of Kielce is yet to emerge, Kersten's study was not the only one to break the silence. A few months later, *Polityka* published a series on the "situation of Polish writers of Jewish origin" by A. Sandauer (1982)—he too mentioned the Kielce pogrom as dramatically influencing, in real and symbolic terms, Polish-Jewish relations during the post-war decade. However, not only did Kersten's article deal with the events at much greater length and depth, but it was in all likelihood read differently, since it had the authority of Solidarity behind it. Indeed, it was the local chapter of Solidarity which initiated a memorial to the victims of the pogrom in 1981, not without sparking a good deal of controversy (see: Wieviorka, 1984).

By 1986, the 40th anniversary of the pogrom was being commemorated in both the official media and by the Church. A special mass was said, with the homily published by the Catholic weekly *Tygodnik Powszechny* (*Msza* . . ., Aug. 20, 1986). Excerpts from the 1946 comments made in the journal immediately after the pogrom appeared on the anniversary itself (*Zbrodnia* . . ., July 6, 1986). *Przegląd Tygodniowy*, a fairly popular official weekly, carried a page-long article devoted to the events in Kielce (Morawski & Pytlakowski, Aug. 10, 1986). On all fronts, a call was being made to assure that, as painful as it might be, "July 4, 1946" would become a date in the standard memory lexicon, standing as a reminder of the "dark forces of chauvinism". With a united voice, the Church and the regime now stood firmly against any and all anti-Semitism. And *both* insisted that their position *at the time* had been the same.

To a reader unfamiliar with the *reaction* to the pogrom—and most Poles would be—the regime's proclamations likely seem suspect. While the truth about Kielce might never be fully known, there do exist solid grounds for speculating that the whole "affair" had been provoked by the Communists to discredit Poland's pre-war authorities and to divert international attention from the power struggles taking place then (at the time of a crucial national referendum). This was the thrust of Kersten's interpretation as well. The odds are, though, that no parallel mistrust would be evoked by the Church. Not only is the voice of the Church highly regarded in general, but, in this case, the very *selection* of words could easily pass unnoticed. *Tygodnik Powszechny,* for one, while quoting a very moving and self-critical statement made by one of the prominent Catholic intellectuals in 1946, did not cite the comments made by Poland's Primate, who shared the view that Kielce was an abhorrent yet *justified* expression of popular anger towards Jews cooperating with the Communist regime. This ommission does create the impression of a perfectly clean record indeed.[28] The very call for remembering Kielce, progressive and humanistic as it might be, also has a way of reading into the past something that was just not there: an unconditional condemnation of anti-Jewish violence. In that sense, talking about the pogrom becomes a powerful method for silencing its moral implications.

There is another aspect of this renewed concern with the Kielce pogrom—a kind of "monumentalization" of memory—which is equally disturbing. That pogrom *was* by far the most tragic in the whole series of violent outbursts against the Jews during the first two years following the liberation. But it was only a part of the whole. If forty-one victims are worthy of a memorial, so are several hundred other Jews murdered in those years. To commemorate Kielce alone is like erecting a monument beyond which one does not look and does not see. It is true that such a pogrom may demand more attention than the killing of one or two people here and there. And yet, precisely because of its magnitude and thus the questions it raises about *political* responsibilities, Kielce acts as a symbol to obscure the much larger issue of *moral* responsibility. To talk about Kielce today as if that were all there were to talk about is to break the silence only to strengthen its hold. It is again to raise questions only so that some reassuring answers prevail.

So effectively to close the chapter on the years immediately following the Holocaust is much more serious, in my view, than all the avoidance of confrontation with the Holocaust itself. Indeed, unless what happened after the Holocaust is confronted, there can be no meaningful confrontation with the past at all. Why? Precisely because the killings came *after*. How could it happen that Jews were being murdered by Poles after Auschwitz?

Here, there is no recourse to the general conditions of terror imposed by the Nazis. There is no recourse to the general human response to exceptionally trying circumstances. Here, the questions are only about Poles and Jews, questions which are often still too painful to be posed, even by people who were there. There is no "post-Holocaust in Poland" literature, to take but one indication.[29] As Nechama Tec openly admits in her book *Dry Tears* (1984), a brief post-script describing what happened after she survived, and written at the prompting of her editor, was all that her emotions could manage. For all her intellectual desire to know—and she went on to conduct a sociological study of aid to the Jews—she could not face *that* memory. Could it be that this is the silence which will never be broken? If, forty years later, there are so few eye-witness accounts, will it not become a chapter forgotten altogether? And if it is remembered, will it be believed?

The last question is not as hypothetical as it might seem. It is to the credit of one Polish researcher that some of the terrifying details of those post-war years have been uncovered. Alina Cała[30] stumbled on the topic almost by accident. In 1974, she had conducted an ethnographic study in the south-eastern part of Poland (once a region with a high proportion of Jews, on the extent to which the age-old myths and stereotypes of the Jew still held among the peasants. The results proved quite striking; it seemed very little if anything had changed after the Holocaust. Ten years later, now aided by a team of student researchers, she went back to the original villages as a follow-up to see how the younger generations would respond to the same questions. She was also interested in following up stories she had heard before but could not then focus on, namely tales of death. In most of the sample communities, there would be at least one story relating how the returning Jewish survivors had been killed after the war. Now told in much greater detail, at the researchers' prompting, these stories were narrated quite matter-of-factly, as if there were nothing particularly problematic about murdering Jews at the time. Cała, was understandably shaken by the findings and cautious about making them public.[31]

Cała, however, did not wish to remain silent. In the spring of 1984, immediately following her study, she took part in the annual "Week of Jewish Culture," organized by Warsaw's Club of Catholic Intelligentsia. In a three-hour lecture, she described with great eloquence what she and her students had uncovered. Her audience responded with voices of rejection and disbelief. Some people questioned her methodology; others,

her integrity as a scientist. Those who accepted her findings all felt that
the phenomenon was necessarily *marginal*.

What does it all mean for our analysis of the *limits* to memory work?
From one point of view, that of the *individual* approach to the past, Cała's
work figures very much as evidence that there might indeed be *no* limits to
critical inquiry. There are others like her: young Polish intellectuals willing
to explore some of the darkest sides of the collective past, a past, one
should add, they themselves are not responsible for. It is not a massive
trend by any means, but these investigations belie any claims about general
rules as to the examination of conscience. But from another point of view,
that of *collective* memory, the "no rule, no limit" picture no longer
applies. Even if today—and tomorrow—critical voices are being raised,
the odds are that their impact on public perceptions of the "Jewish
question" will not move much beyond the small circle of people ready to
hear them. It is one thing to conduct a study of village anti-Semitism in
the 1940s; it is quite another to "inject" the results into collective memory,
even after they have been made public. And there are few signs that the
realm of collective memory is receptive to ideas which go against the very
grain of collective self-definition. It may be possible for a Pole to tell Poles
that forty or fifty or sixty years ago they were not victims but *agents* of
oppression, but it is very difficult to make this image a legitimate part of
popular mythology, the very "stuff" of collective memory.

It is an image that simply does not fit: It does not fit the prevailing vision
of Polish history, and it does not fit any of the current ideas about the
present. It is an image which goes well beyond the ever-popular consideration of the "national faults," since even when Poles today debate the
virtues and vices of their "national character," the one thing which they
take as a given is their dependence on greater political and historical
forces.[32] The very structure of discourse, built on the premise that Poles
as a nation have always been on the defensive, allows scarcely any room
for taking the exact opposite premise as a basis for a critical examination
of the past.

Earlier, I argued that it was the Poles' perception of themselves as
victims of the Nazis—and only as victims—which made it so difficult for
self-criticism to emerge. Yet to understand the full implications of the
"victimological definition" of the Polish historical experience, we must
also consider a much less justifiable and a much more taken-for-granted
idea—the connecting of Jews with *Communism*.

It would be wrong, I think, to explain the murder of hundreds of Jews in
1945 and 1946 solely by the fact that, for so many Poles, Jews symbolized
the much despised new system. The Kielce pogrom followed an accusation
of ritual murder, individual killings in the villages were often for no reason

whatsoever, and greed played an ominous role as well. But it would be equally wrong to forget that, for the Church at least, anti-Jewish violence was perfectly understandable given the Jews' involvement with the regime. And, to go back further, we might recall that accusing Jews of treason for their participation in the Soviet occupation of Poland in 1939 and 1940 had a tremendous impact on popular attitudes at the time.

What we have here, then, is not an innocent idea. Today, this idea may have lost much of its potential to damage human lives. It has also lost much of its power to explain the present, especially as it is continuously under attack from people who oppose the Communists and who are wary of the dangers of "diversionary tactics." Where its hold appears the strongest, however, is within the still fresh memory of the past.

That "Poles as victims of Jewish Stalinists" would be a popular image should not surprise us, considering its fairly long history as well as its perfect fit with the "victimological" definition of the Polish experience. That it is so very popular, even among people who openly and strongly condemn anti-Semitism does raise a few questions, though. Cywiński (1984), in the lecture on contemporary Polish-Jewish relations discussed previously, states unhesitatingly that this is the only image truly a part of collective memory, besides of course, that of the Jew murdered by the Nazis. Niezabitowska, the journalist co-author of *Remnants* (1986), was equally frank in her conversations with me.Even people who could not possibly be suspected of anti-Jewish sentiments, people who, in the case of the older generation, had a record of active aid to the Jews during the war—when queried about the nationalistic trends within the opposition, would often concede that these trends should be given credit for making the public more aware of the crimes committed by Jewish Communists.[33]

In a debate surrounding *Shoah* within the Polish émigré community— where such matters can, after all, be discussed in the open—the whole question of "Jewish crimes" was to gain an added significance,[34] now serving as a kind of proper balance to the acccusations thrown at Poles for their stand during the "Final Solution." It would also be made perfectly clear that Jews had themselves to blame for the Poles' indifference to their fate—did the Jews not greet the Soviets with enthusiasm when Poland was being invaded from the East in September of 1939? In this morbid account-ing of *mutually* inflicted harm, both Jews-as-Communists and Jews-as-Communist-sympathizers provided good reasons for understanding, if not actually condoning, anti-Jewish sentiments and actions.

The reasoning itself is neither new nor original. The idea that it is the Jew himself who is responsible for anti-Semitism has been popular among anti-Semites and Jews alike for at least two centuries. It was, after all, the notion that only an "improved" Jew could fully enjoy social and political

equality which brought about the reforms of "Jewish Enlightenment."
Even under the most trying of circumstances—or perhaps especially
then—such as those in Germany in the 1930s or in France in the early
1940s, the "modern" Jews sought to disassociate themselves from the
"backward" Jews arriving from the East for fear of being subject to the
same anti-Semitic reaction (see: Rajsfus 1980; Aschheim, 1982). And even
today, in places as advanced in democracy as Canada, some Jews still fear
the effects of their behavior on popular attitudes.[35] Almost everyone has
heard down-to-earth remarks about one particularly obnoxious Jew being
enough to turn people into anti-Semites.

Yet if the idea appears to have enjoyed wide currency over the years, its
grip on the structure of discourse about things Jewish in Poland extends
beyond the realm of the generally expected. As I have been pointing out
throughout this study, the notion that Jews constitute a *problem* by their
very presence is one of the core premises of *any* analysis of the "Jewish
question," past and present.[36] For the young "return Jews" in Warsaw,
anti-Semitism was and remains something they interpret as a result of the
particular economic and socio-political situation of the Jews (see also:
Weschler, 1984: 21–24). They, together with Lipski, also see anti-Semitism
as a *tool* in the hands of forces hostile to an independent Poland. The
question of just what makes possible its being a tool is not raised.

Among all the different neutralizing mechanisms we have discussed
here, this one is at once the most pervasive and the most varied in
consequences. The very fact that the equation between Jews and problem
emerged not only unquestioned, but strengthened after the Holocaust
makes us realize that it can be a dangerous way of thinking indeed. The
fact that it persists, which could be understood as a result of part-
universalizing, part-Polonizing the memory of the Holocaust, makes us
realize that its hold on the Poles' awareness of the Jew may not be subject
to any radical change, all the clear condemnation of anti-Semitism notwithstanding. This line of reasoning is not seen as part-and-parcel of anti-
Semitism, nor is it seen as a morally questionable proposition; it simply
exists. And shared as it appears to be by many Jews and non-Jews in other
times and in other places, it has nearly perfect plausibility.

If we look at the work actually done on the "Jewish memory project,"
we too might decide it is of little consequence that the perception of Jewish
presence as problematic by definition. The idea that one should study the
condition of the Jews to illuminate the sources of anti-Semitism does leave
enough room for studies dealing with Jews and Jews, as well as for
presentations of Jewish tradition and culture. More importantly, perhaps,
this idea is *not* shared by a number of serious scholars (see esp. Eisenbach,
1983; Cała, 1984), who have looked beyond the Jewish experience and into

the area of Polish "definitions of the situation." Finally, whatever the underlying premises of the Poles' emphasis on Jewish martyrology,[37] the fact remains that since 1983, the Holocaust as a Jewish experience has been broadly publicized with source books, memoirs, films, poems, photographs. As we have seen, this renewed exposure to the Jew as victim does not in any way guarantee the displacement of an "Auschwitz without Jews." Nevertheless, it makes the gradual recognition of the uniqueness of the Holocaust more meaningful than editorial pronouncements alone.[38]

Only time can tell whether recognizing the Holocaust as a Jewish experience will lead to at least some *general* reflections on the sources of anti-Semitism. The problem here might be that Poles were such close witnesses that they automatically interpret any general question about the Holocaust as a challenge. But an even more serious problem, as I have argued here, is that, at least now, general questions about the Holocaust are *not* read as a challenge to Polish Catholicism. And it is precisely in this area that the view of anti-Semitism as a totally natural phenomenon, scientifically explainable by economics, social structure and psychology may function as effectively a foreclosure to critical inquiry. Polish Catholicism, taking the lead from the universal Church, may be admitting to a wrong interpretation of the life and death of Jesus (see: Polak, 1983, Salij, 1986) and to its past errors vis-á-vis the Jews. It is also working hard to improve its record. But beyond admissions, beyond condemnations of anti-Semitism, there is very little if any examination of the full significance of the religious dimensions of anti-Jewish phobias.[39] More generally—and this is equally important—there has been very little recognition of the *mythic* structure of anti-Semitism. There is a great deal of mention given to "stereotypes" and "prejudice;" there are now serious efforts both to study them and to make them disappear by enlightening the public. But the very optimistic tone of this endeavor echoes much too closely the idea that now, when the Jews are gone, education is the panacea.

Again, only time can tell whether the mythic-theological approach to Polish-Jewish relations can become a viable alternative to the preoccupation with rational explanations. Poles, after all, are very well versed in mythic discourse. At the same time, though, it is the very rational "naturalness" of anti-Semitism which performs a mythological function by effectively dissolving most of the questions of the Poles' own contribution to the "Jewish problem."[40] It is difficult, but not altogether impossible, to leave this rational myth behind. What it requires, though, is something which the "Jewish memory project" is not really designed for, namely leaving the territory of Polish-Jewish memory altogether. In other words, as long as questions about anti-Semitism are raised and answered by talking about *Poles* and Jews, their very emotional charge, together with the intellectual limitations of such parochialism of concerns is almost guaranteed to reproduce the established patterns of neutralizing memory.

These patterns are a complexity of experiential base and collectively shared presuppositions. They all work as well as they do because they offer comfort and protection to the collective self. At present, the *need* for such protection is undeniably great, considering just how difficult and hopeless life in Poland has become. And the memory invitation extended to the Jew is not really meant to disturb the all-too-problematic peace. The idea that Jewish heritage *enriches* Polish culture is not without competition on the current socio-political scene, but it is also a part of a very legitimate and very Polish vision of Poland's past, present and future.[41] It may be in conflict with other such visions, but it is *not* in conflict with the core elements of collective self-definition. Indeed, in the present context, it might well be that *pluralism,* in all its ramifications for different zones of Polish culture, cannot function successfully unless it provides room for the Jew.

Yet if the re-discovery of Poland's Jewish heritage remains an attractive proposition, it is also because the Jew can perform an ultimately very comforting role for his Polish hosts. His very presence, however symbolic, can be seen as a testimony to their good will and generosity, a testimony that Poland, the real Poland, is a democratic society.[42]

In countries where Jews live in considerable numbers, looking at their place within the social fabric is indeed one of the most reliable tests for the extent of democratic principles and practices. In the absence of Jews, though, the test loses most of its strength unless it is applied in the field of collective memory. Many young Germans understood this very well as they challenged their parents' pro-Jewish gestures and compensation policies (see: Rabinbach and Zipes, eds. 1986). Without mastering the past, the turn-abouts in the present remain self-congratulation. Poland's record towards the Jews is obviously of a radically different moral weight. But precisely because it is so much more ambiguous than what Germany has to come to terms with, precisely because it can so easily be read as a clean record, in short, because it has so much potential to be neutralized, it becomes both extremely difficult and absolutely necessary to examine it with the sharpest of critical eyes.

The task here does not belong to the Jews. (Indeed, if the response to *Shoah* is any indication, Jewish voices might best be left out of the discussion altogether.[43] The task belongs to the Poles themselves. As hosts to the "Jewish memory project," they have all the right to choose and select what interests them, enriches them, diverts them. But they also have an obligation *to themselves*—if this project is to be at all meaningful for their future—to reckon with the past in the most uncomfortable and uncomforting of ways.

We should not be surprised that this is not a popular proposition. But it exists, explicit in the voices of some Polish intellectuals we met on the "Jewish memory project" and still undefined for the many others who might join them. The hope lies with the younger generations, people for whom the future is a primary concern and for whom the past is so much less of a direct moral burden. There are no guarantees that they will take up the challenge; there are no guarantees that theirs will be a challenge which the collective self will not reject on principle. Yet there is a chance, both for those willing to ask the tough questions and for their listeners to come to this discussion much better prepared. The re-discovery of Poland's Jewish heritage, however fitted into Poland's sense of itself, has brought into their world a whole new set of resources. Their sense of the Jew, in one of history's cruelest ironies, may be finally that of an interesting Stranger, who is both worth knowing and worthy of respect.

## Notes

1. A brief comparative note might be of help here. In Poland, it is positively inconceivable to encounter the kind of "historical revisionism" practiced in France, the United States, Canada or Germany—the denial of the Holocaust. It is equally impossible to find the kind of fascination with Nazism which has entered cultural discourse in the West (see: Friedländer, 1984). The only type of symbolic transformation which is both widely practiced (by the regime) and appears to resonate with popular sentiments is the shift in vision from the "Jew = victim" to the "Jew = aggressor." [As I was told in Warsaw, there are now studies showing that the years of anti-Zionist propaganda have not been without effect on the young people in particular.] But even there, there is still enough anti-Soviet sentiment—and, by extension, anti-Arab sentiment—to mitigate this position.

2. Cracow's *Arka* has put this call into action in its recent discussion on nationalism (nos. 10 & 11, 1985). [Scharf (1984) made this point very explicitly—from a Jewish perspective—in his presentation at the Oxford conference on Polish-Jewish relations. *Arka* took up his challenge, see: *Redakcja "Arki"* (1987).]

3. In the official critique of Lipski, there was no mention of anti-Semitism, only of the unacceptable good will towards the Germans (those in West Germany, of course).

4. The special issue of *Znak* opened with just such a dedication to "those who died with dignity." The official coverage was rather uneven with its overall focus on "martyrdom" balancing the exaltation over the heroism of the Ghetto fighters. In all fairness, the equating of dignity in death with armed struggle is not a uniquely Polish problem, as witness the heated debate surrounding both Arendt's (1965) and Hilberg's (1961) claims about the Jews' passivity, or Bettelheim's (1960) studies of concentration camps (see: Donat, 1964). What does make it more pronounced is that the theme of the Jews' passively going

to their death is still dominant in the high school history manuals—as reported in *1987* by Drozdowski (*Tygodnik Powszechny,* May 17, 1987).

5. The emphasis on tolerance is historically correct in that Jews came to Poland in large numbers as they were fleeing persecution in fifteenth century Germany and France. It is a cornerstone of the Polish vision of the past; the fact that something else happened *after* the initial invitation is usually quietly ignored.

   The emphasis on *shared* struggles for independence speaks directly to the Poles' sense of history as a long struggle. It is also a way of "rehabilitating" Jews. Once again, the notion that the Jews must pay in blood to belong to a nation is *not* a Polish one. Both French and German Jews were very keen on military service.

6. The principle of "divide and conquer" has a long history; both the Russian partition authorities and the Soviet ones were indeed very skilled at turning Poles against Jews (and both were masters at anti-Semitism, see: Poliakov, 1981 & 1983). Once again, the mythic interpretation gains a lot of plausibility from reality.

7. At issue here was also the very "weight" of Lipski's voice; Sandauer's (1982) analysis was more critical, yet written, as it was, by a "court Jew", it would have been heard very differently.

   Majchrowski (1983), writing for the special "Jewish" issue of *Więź,* saw the calls for economic boycott in the 1920's and 1930's as a perfectly legitimate response to the Jews' dominance in trade and commerce. Turian (1983), reviewing a book about Maximilian Kolbe, praised the author's objectivity, in this case meaning that Kolbe's anti-Semitism was judged as a perfectly legitimate defense against the Jews' strangling of the Polish economy.

8. Woroszylski (1986) comments at some length on the importance of "really looking" at *Shoah,* that is, of watching the whole film without paying attention to the media debates. But he also notes how only a few people saw the whole film when it became available in the theaters, therefore reducing the potential for any serious reflection.

9. Again, this is not to say that all the articles carried by *Polityka* were along the unpopular lines. Krzemiński (May 11, 1985), for example, argued at some length that *Shoah* was offensive, while discussing the difficulty for Polish Jews in Germany to speak of Poland in ways which would not prove offensive to the Poles.

10. The two articles appeared side-by-side on August 3, 1985 *(Polityka).* Sandauer stressed how moving *Shoah* was, how important for understanding of what happened. Rem (a pen name of Jerzy Urban) was less impressed with the film itself, but more concerned with confronting Poles with their own statements, or what he called the presence of an "obscurantist minority."

11. The official media did their utmost to boost their credibility by giving exposure to views from abroad: those of Garliński, a respected émigré historian, protesting against the portrayal of Poles in *Shoah* in the London *Tygodnik Polski* (Oct. 19, 1985) and those of the Congress of Polish Americans.

12. It was reported, *inter alia,* by Skoczylas in *Przegląd Tygodniowy* (no. 11 (207), 1986). No figures are given to allow us to assess the statistical significance here, but it is likely that its accuracy is on a par with that of similar surveys in the West.

13. With respect to the general "universalization" of memory of the Holocaust, two considerations are worth signaling. First, it was *during* the Holocaust that

the Jewish victims were often defined as "victims" and not as Jews (see: Lipstadt, 1986), perhaps for the fear of lessening public sympathy in the West. Immediately *after* the Holocaust, Jewish survivors in France were defined as "deportées"—when the category also included those in forced labor in Germany—and not treated in any special way (see: Namer, 1983, Rioux, 1983). In Canada, it was "refugees" who came in 1947–48; much effort went into making their immigration as invisibly Jewish as possible (Abella & Troper, 1983).

14. In this section, I rely on Grynberg's (1984a:65–89) essay, which also brings into focus the whole issue of how neither Jews nor non-Jews can face the uniqueness of the Jewish fate during the Holocaust, Jews out of fear, and non-Jews—because of guilt.

15. On the Pope's most recent visit to Poland in June 1987, his itinerary included Majdanek, another camp where both Poles and Jews were victims. According to Canadian reports [*Tygodnik Powszechny,* which published many of the Pope's homilies as well as reports on his meetings with a variety of people and organizations, had *no* information, beyond the mention that the Pope visited the camp], the Pope again made no reference to the Jews who died as Jews.

16. The conference itself, while widely reported in the press, did not change this overall perception. There was very little coverage of presentations by Israeli scholars—who would likely offer a different perspective on the Holocaust; presentations by Polish contributors, reiterating the standard view, were quoted at length.

17. One must realize that Poles *were* the first prisoners in Auschwitz, before it became a killing center for the Jews; they were also the majority among the concentration camp inmates.

    Borowski, who was himself a prisoner in Auschwitz, wrote one of the earliest and most powerful stories (1948) in Polish "camp literature", where the experience of the Jews is only a marginal theme (see also: Grynberg, 1984b).

18. Krajewski's voice was in stark contrast to that of another Polish Jew, *Polityka's* columnist R. M. Groński, who argued—from a universalistic position—that *no* prayers should be said in Auschwitz, for none are appropriate in a place abandoned by God (May 3, 1986).

19. Within the Holocaust literature, Auschwitz occupies a special place, not only because of the magnitude of the destruction, but also because in Auschwitz, there *were* survivors (Elie Wiesel, Primo Levi, David Rousset are just the best known among them). Lanzmann's *Shoah* was a unique effort to make Treblinka comprehensible; for this alone, he deserves a great deal of praise.

20. The question should read: why the Jews *and the Gypsies?* It is only very recently that the fate of the Gypsies has become subject to some attention, among Holocaust scholars and the Gypsy organizations as well. I am grateful to Gabrielle Tyrnauer for sharing with me her extensive knowledge on the subject, as well as her concern with *that* silence (in 1985 she submitted a report to the United States Holocaust Memorial Council; one hopes that it will be effective).

    In the writing of the following discussion, I too have succumbed to the "exclusively Jewish" view of the Holocaust. If I decided to retain this emphasis on the Jews, it is in part because when talking about Poland, we are talking about *not* forgetting the Gypsies, but rather, using their rightful claims to be remembered as victims of genocide as a further justification for universalizing memory of the Holocaust. Furthermore, the Nazis appear to have been much more ambivalent towards the Gypsies, which would indicate that the "Final Solution" demands a *separate* analysis.

21. It is important to consider what happens when the Nazi obsession with the Jew is *not* acknowledged. A good point to start here is with Arendt's "banality of evil" (1965) and to compare her interpretation with Eichmann's own testimony (von Lang & Sybyll, eds., 1983).

22. This too is a *common* problem. There are now many studies documenting how the basic history books in particular assign a minor position to the Holocaust, if they mention it at all. Soviet Union (Fish, 1978) and Rumania (Lavi, 1974) may be the most extreme cases, but neither the American (Korman, 1970), nor the Canadian (Glickman & Bardikoff, 1982), nor the French books (Centre . . . , 1982) scored all that much better.

    The case of Germany is, obviously, a special one. Essays collected in the volume *Germans & Jews After the Holocaust* (Rabinbach & Zipes, eds., 1986) as well as a detailed analysis of the schoolbooks (Kolinsky & Kolinsky, 1974) make one acutely aware of the capacity to neutralize memory without resorting to silence.

23. Both of these were written during or immediately after the Holocaust; both have been made available to Poles today. One of the best illustrations that this is still an exceptional view comes in the form of a mini-debate in *Kultura*, between a Polish woman who prefers anonymity (she lives in Poland) and a respected Polish historian (who lives in London). For her, it is the memory of her Jewish husband and his family which makes it imperative to speak up: no, we Poles did not suffer the same fate. The response is anger. [See: Kozyr (1986); Garliński (1986).]

24. Lem (1984), in his series of "reviews of imaginary books" included an insightful essay on the Holocaust. Outside of Poland, Kolakowski included his *Genocide & Ideology* (1978) presentation to an American audience in a large collection of essays published in London (1982). The *first* widely publicized discussion on the meaning of the Holocaust (drawing on Steiner's work to some extent) is that in *Więź* (Między . . .", no. 7/8, 1986). [I do not consider the debate around *Shoah* as qualifying for the status of "reflection".] Rymkiewicz's *Umschlagplatz* (1988) is the most recent effort at understanding; it focuses on the deportations from Warsaw.

25. The contrast with the strong impact of 1968 we have discussed in chapter 3 is most illuminating here. In 1968, the expulsion of Jews *did* fulfill the stated goals of Polish anti-Semitic ideologues. In 1968, too, the people under attack were considered *friends* by those who would be most disturbed by the success of the anti-Semitic campaign. Indeed, the campaign itself was often defined as anti-Polish, and the losses it brought were seen as losses to Polish culture. Jews, in short, were then very much members in the common universe of concern.

26. "Self-critical" here means that one paragraph is devoted explicitly to the Church's responsibility for harboring anti-Semitism, but nowhere does Turowicz accept a share of the Poles' responsibility for the ultimate fate of the Jews. But if Turowicz disagrees with Błoński, he is also less emphatic about the absolute absence of any connection between Polish anti-Semitism and the events during the Holocaust, than he was when discussing *Shoah*.

27. Prekerowa's analysis satisfies even the most critical standards. Instead of providing numbers, Gilbert, for example, in his massive work on the Holocaust (1985), which includes several eye-witness accounts, concludes at one point

that "the historian is overwhelmed by the conflicting currents of human nature" (p. 493) when studying rescue and denunciation. Fein, in *Accounting for Genocide* (1984), which is the most extensive *comparative* analysis, discusses the situation in Poland only in terms of "high degree" of anti-Semitism.

28. In 1987, Jerzy Urban publicly raised this point, to a predictable fury of protest from the Church officials and laymen alike.

29. Kersten's book on the formation of the Communist power (published in Paris in 1986), does include a section dealing with Polish-Jewish relations at the time. Focus is on *understanding* the conflict, not on its moral implications for the Poles.

30. Cała began in ethnography, earning a master's degree with the study we discuss here; she then did a doctoral dissertation in history (1984) on the problems of assimilation. She went on to work at the Warsaw's National Library sorting out and cataloguing the library's vast collection of Judaica (she taught herself Hebrew and Yiddish). Her work is exemplary. She too is very much a member of the " '68 generation" of Poles forced to confront their attitudes towards the Jew.

31. When we met in Warsaw, she told me about the study itself, stressing that she did not want to publicize it in the West for fear of misinterpretation. [My reporting it here is due to the fact that a much more comprehensive account of the events has since been published in France (Hillel, 1985).]

32. Once again, this vision of dependence and continuous victimization would not have as strong a hold were it not for its factual plausibility. After the shock of the Martial Law in particular, it is next to impossible for a Pole not to feel like a victim.

33. Strictly speaking, Torańska's collection (1985) of interviews with the Communist leaders is not a part of the "Jewish memory project." The fact remains that among the seven unrepentant Communists, *five* are Jewish. That the book was an immediate hit makes it even more significant here.

    Polish Jewish writers *in* Poland are not without blame here either. Stryjkowski's novel (1982) very much perpetuates the established views on Jews and Communism. Krall's work (1985), where this theme is marginal to the overall contrast between (Polish) "light" and (Jewish) "darkness," can also be read as a confirmation of the centrality of Communism in thinking about Jews.

34. Émigré publications are literally filled with the images of "Jewish crimes." What is troubling is not their presence in writings of the nationalistic Right, but their prominent position within what appear as perfectly objective historical studies—see, for example, Micewski (1978)—or in the context of fiction aiming to present historical truth (see: Guzy, 1983).

35. Two recent and widely publicized trials brought this concern into the public sphere.

    In both cases, the accused were people denying the existence of the gas chambers and believing the world is ruled by a "Jewish conspiracy." In both cases, many within the Canadian Jewish community expressed worries about the negative impact of their speaking up in protest.

36. To take another example: Kieniewicz (*Polityka,* Dec. 15, 1984), a prominent Polish historian, when presenting Polish-Jewish relations in the 19th century first calls for *objectivity* in approaching the subject. To him, the virtual absence of non-Jews among students of Polish Jewish history makes for a very *partial* view on the subject. It is then up to Polish historians to redress the imbalance,

or to move away from focusing on discrimination against Jews and on their contributions towards a broader study of social change in all segments of Polish society. A number of Jewish scholars could not agree more; a recent sociological study of Jews and modernization, for example (Goldscheider & Zuckerman, 1984), denies any uniqueness to the Jews' situation in all of Europe. As one reads Kieniewicz' analysis (see also 1986), though, it becomes clear that "balance" and "objectivity" refer to pointing out those aspects of Jewish attitudes and behavior which could explain anti-Semitic reactions. We are thus back to the idea that the problem lies with Jews. Memory work switches from the critical to the instrumental mode.

37. The interest in Jewish martyrology may not spring from interest in Jews; it could still stem from a more universalistic concern with human behavior in *extreme* situations. [This point was made in respect to Polish films' increased exposure of Jewish martyrology by Pietrasik (*Polityka*, Sept. 29. 1984).]

38. Of those, the statement by Turowicz in *Tygodnik Powszechny* (April 5, 1987) is by far the most important.

    Back in November 1980, Moczar (the man behind the 1968 anti-Semitic campaign) and then a president of the war veterans' association, made a point of emphasizing *Jewish* victims among the Polish losses; his speech, though widely reported, was at least in one case cut to exclude this particular passage (see: Walden, *Polityka*, Nov. 22, 1980).

39. Just how much work is needed here may best be illustrated by what the Polish bishops say when they *do* reflect on the religious significance of the Holocaust (see: Musiał, *Tygodnik Powszechny*, May 17, 1987). When Edith Stein (a Jewish-born nun and a Catholic philosopher) was recently honored with a mass in Birkenau, her death and the death of all Jews was described in terms of "sacrifice", very much like that Jesus had made, for the peace of mankind. Edith Stein's own reflections (quoted by Grygiel, *Tygodnik Powszechny*, May 3, 1987) confused things even further; she saw her death as atonement for the Jews' refusal to accept Jesus.

40. Tazbir's study of the traditional image of the Jew (*Polityka*, Dec. 21–27, 1985) is one of the best examples of the "absolving" function of rational analysis; there, attitudes to Jews become exactly the same as those towards any foreigner.

41. Both positive and negative memories are working to support the "multicultural" vision of Poland. On the positive side, Poland was strongest when it did in fact welcome other cultures; among the country's greatest artists and scientists, there are many of mixed ancestry (to take Chopin as one example). On the negative side, Poland's inability, as an independent state (in 1918–1939), to accommodate national minorities was one of the key factors in determining its tragic fate during the Second World War (especially in the East).

42. When this mechanism operates on a collective level, it suffers from serious plausibility problems. Neither the regime, nor the opposition, nor the Church can completely cover up for manifestations of anti-Semitism within their ranks by pro-Jewish actions. On an individual level, though, it is much easier to convince oneself that being a friend of the Jew (or a friend of a Jew) excludes the very possibility of anti-Semitism.

43. The main problem with *Shoah*, I believe, is that its voice, when critical of the Poles, is so strident that it almost has to be neutralized. And the fact that Lanzmann relies on only one interpretation of history, Hilberg's view of the

"cyclical progression" from anti-Jewish (Christians') sentiments to extermination, runs counter to the core beliefs of most Poles. [Hilberg himself proposed this interpretation very much on the margin of his work on the machinery of destruction (1961:1–14); in the film, it is placed very much in the center, though.]

# Conclusions

People discussing things Jewish in Poland today often say that their country no longer has a "Jewish problem." It is precisely this absence of a real problem which is then credited with opening a way to a Polish-Jewish dialogue, just as it becomes a basis for hope that anti-Semitism, this "remnant of the past", will soon disappear altogether. On these terms, the "Jewish memory project" would have certainly been inconceivable some twenty-five years ago, when the Jews were active in Polish politics and culture. But on these terms, the project's public prominence today carries little potential for significant change. As long as Poles take for granted that the Jews' physical presence constitutes a problem, the Jew's symbolic presence does not challenge Polish conscience. As long as anti-Semitism is considered understood in all its "sociological inevitability," the issue of moral responsibility does not arise. And as long as a condemnation of anti-Semitism replaces efforts to delve into its mythic structure, as long as the admission of sin closes the records of the Catholic Church, the past can remain comfortable enough to be remembered.

Neutralizing memory of the Jew to fit Poland's sense of a decent and honorable history is not something which began with the "Jewish memory project." Indeed, what began with that re-discovery of Poland's Jewish heritage has been a gradual recognition that not all of the country's history is decent and honorable. This recognition of morally problematic chapters in history, if given a chance, may sometime translate into a full confrontation with the past. But to be given a chance, it must acquire as much popular appeal as the traditional urge to turn to the past for solace and hope. Considering Poland's dire present situation, a shift in public attitude is not very likely.

Mastering a difficult past is hard under any circumstances; doing it when the country is plagued with mutual distrust, apathy and daily hardships

175

takes a very special effort. That such an effort is undertaken at all today is therefore important. We should not ignore the possibility that this effort will continue and grow, as increasing numbers of people, especially the younger generation, learn more and more about the Jew. To encounter the Other, to listen to the Other's views on a shared past requires empathy, a certain ability to see things from the Jew's perspective. Learning about the Other, without the tint of "the problem," is the first step.

For this reason, we should not dismiss the often naive and elementary, exoticized and sentimentalized approach to the Jew, here termed the "nostalgic" mode of memory work. (Analytically speaking, we cannot dismiss it, as it accounts for the bulk of the "Jewish memory project" and for its continuing popularity.) As much as this general interest in or even fascination with Jewish culture can neutralize the past, it also has a normalizing effect on discourse about the Jew. It makes empathy possible. Watching "Fiddler on the Roof" may be a poor substitute for delving into the riches of Yiddish storytelling, but shedding some tears at the plight of Tevye does bring one closer to seeing the world through his eyes.

Here, Art (or art) is the prime vehicle for nostalgia. Music and poetry, film and drama, fiction and the beauty of objects—all these transform the Jew into an Other once interesting and complex. Whatever their "truth value," they speak warmly and emotionally of a world forever lost. They become appealing both to people who wish to remember that world in just such a warm glow and to people who have never known it. They are appealing in a way that only art can be. If the "Jewish memory project" is to continue, it must draw on that appeal. Is it remembrance? It may not be, if we insist that to remember Poland's Jews means remembering their anguish and suffering. But it is a beginning, a "memory bridge," as it were, to a people long unknown.

What we are discussing now are the potential consequences of wide exposure to the culture of the Jewish Jews. Perhaps the current fascination will pass before such an empathy effect takes significant hold. Perhaps the knowing of that culture will be framed exclusively in the theological terms of the Catholics' rediscovery of their "older brother" and thus much of that potential will be lost. But perhaps also the growing opening towards Israel, with practical aspects of travel and exchange, will provide a necessary infusion of the Jewish present to strengthen the idea of the "normality" of Jewishness and transform at least some of the symbolic empathy into feelings of friendship.

I do not think this last point too optimistic. Despite the two decades of anti-Zionist propaganda, which, as we have seen, has not been totally ineffective, the Poles' sympathy for Israel has some rather solid basis both in the past and in the present. To appreciate the prewar appeal of a Zionist solution to Poland's "Jewish question," one does not have to agree with the reasoning behind it. Nor does one have to share the "soldier ethos" to appreciate that, for many Poles, the Israeli warrior redeems the Jew. The difficulties of living among hostile neighbours are not unknown to Poles. And we must not forget that Poles have great respect for those resisting the Soviet might. Finally, it is in Israel that Polish culture has retained its strongest appeal for Polish Jews, a fact not lost on Polish artists and policy-makers and one that makes an especially good impression on Poles accustomed to hearing about the disdain of Western Jews for Poland.

The gradual opening to Israel is not a symbolic exercise: it is a political act with international implications. As such, it is outside the jurisdiction of the "Jewish memory project". There is no question, though, that Poland's rediscovery of its Jewish heritage both helps and is helped by the improvement of relations. It remains to be seen what impact the closening of ties with Israeli scholars in particular will have on the views of the Polish students of Polish-Jewish history. But, again, the potential exists for some necessary correctives to many an axiom.

Academic and artistic exchanges with Israel matter a great deal, both for and beyond their immediate returns. Contacts with Jewish scholars and artists from the Diaspora matter too. To put it bluntly, all offer a rare opportunity for at least some Poles to encounter, talk to, listen to and see real Jews, Jews for whom Jewishness is not a problem.

Despite the significant contribution of the young "return Jews" to the "Jewish memory project", responsibility for normalizing the human side of Polish-Jewish relations cannot be carried by them alone. They are too few, too freshly different and still not secure enough about the relative merits of being Polish and being Jewish. Their sense of the "Jewish problem" is still too close to that of many Poles to challenge this way of thinking. And it is precisely this way of thinking, the persistent identifica-tion of "Jewishness" with "problem," that most endangers the translating of the normality of the present into a critical understanding of the past.

It is no accident that the best critical work so far comes from a student of assimilation, Alina Cała, who could evaluate the debates in the nine-teenth century without the typical admiration for progress inherent in leaving the ghetto. Thus, she could expose the prevailing assumptions that Polonization spelled "advancement," an assumption shared by both Polish and Jewish advocates of assimilation.

The problematics of assimilation, however small its part in Polish-Jewish history, must nevertheless be questioned if one is to leave the confines of the "Jewish problem" to understand anti-Semitism and its Polish forms. Why? Precisely because, for most Poles today, not being an anti-Semite means feeling that Jewishness does not matter.

Among the topics which the "Jewish memory project" brought to public attention, assimilation remains a marginal concern, though. We may attribute its position to the continuing presence of assimilated Jews among Polish intelligentsia, a presence which both sides might prefer not to question. We should also keep in mind just how strong of a lesson was derived from the Holocaust, or how much the very mention of someone's Jewishness came to be identified with anti-Semitism. The additional factor here is of more recent origin: it was during the 1968 campaign that thousands of Poles were indeed reminded of their Jewishness. For people thus introduced to the "Jewish question"—including, as we have seen, many core memory workers, this was and is the meaning of anti-Semitism.

Of course, to single the Jews out for being Jews is anti-Semitism. What happens, though, when the lines are drawn by the Jews themselves in struggling to retain their identity as a people? When being Jewish is considered both positive and important to preserve? Here is one of the central dilemmas of modern Jewish history. One may talk meaningfully about the elimination of anti-Semitism only once Jews are respected as Jews, and not despite the fact.

In this regard, the work done on the "Jewish memory project" represents a modest beginning. Memory workers are contributing to a shift in perceptions of Jewishness despite their not confronting the issue directly or not discussing the givens of assimilation. Here again, it is the nostalgic mode which is the key, if only because it brings forth, piece by piece, the richness of Jewish tradition. Exposure to the precepts of Judaism or to modern Jewish philosophy, to Hassidic tales or to works by I. B. Singer, does not automatically produce respect for the Jews. But since this is the first time that Poles are entering the Jew's territory on terms close to his own, such exposure matters. Once again, we are talking about a potential effect, not a realized one. And once again, it is among the younger generations that the "Jewish memory project" may make the most difference.

What would matter even more, though, is something that the memory workers appear not ready to provide—a general recognition of the Polish Jewry's contribution to Poland's development. Individual Jews, be they printers in the nineteenth century or poets in the twentieth, are now being praised for their contribution to Polish culture. Individual Jews, as scholars or teachers, may be praised for their role in Poland's intellectual life. Individual Jews are slowly gaining recognition for their part in the country's economic development. As Poles of Jewish origin, proponents of liberal and democratic politics may enter the honor rolls. But the Jewish community, in its social and especially economic functions, is still considered a "problem".

It could be argued that it is simply too early for a collectively framed recognition of the Jews' role in Poland's history. It has been, after all, only a few years since the country's Jewish heritage gained a memory status. Calls are indeed being issued for a thorough inquiry into the shared Polish-Jewish history. Work is in progress, in other words. Just as it takes time and resources to commemorate the presence of Jewish communities in so many Polish towns and cities, it takes time to examine and make public the roles of these communities at different points in the past. (For example, historians of Łódź, that important industrial city, are finally mentioning its Jewish inhabitants.)

The argument is partly correct. It will take time and a great deal more research to define, in any detail, the part played by Jews in Poland's social, economic, political and cultural life. Yet it takes more than time to dislodge the premise for examining the past, the idea that Jews as Jews are a problem.

Few Poles today would agree that it was mainly thanks to the efforts of Jewish industrialists and traders that Poland started its modernization. Observations made by Aleksander Hertz, in his 1961 analysis of "Jews in Polish culture", regarding the crucial role of the Jewish middleman in transmitting information before the advent of modern communications, would likely meet with astonishment, if they were published in Poland. It is not that popular history has nothing to say on the subject. It is just that what it does say about the Jew in modern times or the Jew as middleman is mainly a basis for explaining anti-Semitism. The principle of the "sociological inevitability" of conflict and hostility demands attention to the Jews' economic and social position, whatever they did, though, is then seen only as a source of anti-Jewish sentiments and actions.

This view of anti-Semitism, solidly founded on scientific interpretation, performs a very important neutralizing function. Because it has all the trappings of science and objectivity, it can remain unquestioned even by people strongly critical of both Polish nationalism and anti-Semitism. They may grant, of course, that nationalist ideologues and practitioners made too much of Jewish economic domination, or that it was wrong to see Jewishness as corrupting the polish soul. But they also appreciate that, given the realities of Polish and Jewish existence, and the Jew was a problem.

For a sociologist to argue against a sociological interpretation of history may seem strange. It should be remembered, though, that the particular sociology involved here reduces the complexity of feelings and perceptions to direct results of experience. Ideas that people had about the Jew are not irrelevant in this scheme of things; they are, however, deprived of their creative power. The hard facts of the matter are what explain attitudes.

The notion that these facts might be themselves a social construction lies outside this frame of reference. That the Jew had to be defined as an intruder for his economic activity to be perceived as threatening to the Poles—to take but one example—cannot be considered, let alone analyzed by tracing such definition to its ideological and religious sources.

Because the "sociological inevitability" principle is prominent in discussions of anti-Semitism by non-professionals, we must seek its roots outside the realm of academic disputes. What I have suggested here indeed applies to people before they become investigators, or even begin reflecting on anti-Semitism at all. Part experience, part definition, it is the "Auschwitz without Jews" which makes anti-Jewish feelings so situationally understandable. The experience of having been a victim of the Nazis, together with Jews, and the idea that Poles too were destined for extermination do not deny the reality of the Holocaust. If anything, they make the Holocaust appear even larger, because it is shared. Such a shared Holocaust speaks harshly of Nazi racism, including anti-Semitism. It does not speak of the Nazi obsession with the Jew. And it does not speak of the European history of anti-Semitism or Christianity.

Many Westerners accept that everyone bears some responsibility for what happened to European Jewry, for everyone is a member of the civilization which made the "Final Solution" possible. We have also come to accept that reflection on the Holocaust is not just something we owe to the victims, but something we owe to ourselves. We may never be able to comprehend what happened, but we must try to understand why. And an important step towards understanding the why is a realization that anti-Semitism, both the vicious one and the benign, is *not* "sociologically inevitable."

That Poland belongs to the Western and Christian civilization is something that Poles believe very strongly. Yet the serious reflection on the meaning of the Holocaust, practiced in the West, is only beginning to emerge in Poland. It is as if in this one important respect, the country's culture and history were outside Europe. Yet Poland was the very closest of witnesses to the Holocaust; it is there that one would expect to find the most direct, the most experientially grounded response to the trauma. Why is it absent?

We might need a psychoanalyst to provide a full answer here. My own reading of the records of the past suggests that what was happening to the Jews was not directly relevant for most Poles. Before, during and after the Holocaust, the Jew remained outside the common universe of concern. His fate at the hands of the Nazis, as horrible as it was, did not change—for most—the basic terms of Polish-Jewish relations. The Jew was never a member of the same family; caring or not caring about him had none of the same moral implications as feelings for fellow Poles. His disappearance was not mourned in a way one would mourn the death of a brother. He was *not* a brother; he was a problem.

There is a second part to the answer, the intellectually and emotionally larger issue of responsibility. As victims of the Nazis and as people who, even at their worst, never ascribed to the idea of mass extermination in solving the "Jewish question," Poles felt and feel that only the Nazis themselves bear responsibility for the "Final Solution". As people continuously challenged in that view by critics from outside, Poles have come to define this matter even further in terms of direct responsibility. Because they were so close, the idea of moral responsibility speaks to them only of their action or inaction; the much larger terrain of feelings, perceptions and attitudes towards the Jew is no consideration.

When defined solely in terms of facts and figures, the question of the Polish role in the destruction of the Jews may never be settled, just as we may never be able to apportion, with certainty, the blame for the "Final Solution" among the other historical actors: the Allies, the Churches, and the Jews in the free world. Understanding what made the Holocaust possible is not reducible to a search for people bearing direct responsibility. Indeed, thinking only in terms of direct responsibility may preclude any understanding.

The general Polish view on the matter—that the "Final Solution" was the work of the Nazis, that they alone should be blamed, and that, under the circumstances, only the criminal margins of Polish society could be held co-responsible for the fate of the Jews—closes the questions about history with a plausible list of facts. It is argued Polish anti-Semitism was not implicated in the Holocaust because the indifference of the majority had little impact on the ultimate survival rates, and because the sheer size of the Jewish community made the rescue of millions impossible. Once absolved of responsibility, Polish anti-Semitism loses any theoretical connection with the Nazis' anti-Jewish phobia as well. Thus Polish anti-Semitism can remain comprehensible in terms of the Polish Jews' own historical condition.

This severing of all connection between Polish anti-Semitism and the Nazi anti-Jewish obsession has a dual role in the neutralization of memory. It directly contains difficult questions about Polish-Jewish relations during the Holocaust to a very narrow sphere of concrete and individual actions. It also indirectly strengthens the plausibility of an objective interpretation of local developments, an interpretation perfectly within the frame of "the Jew as a problem" vision of the past. An "Auschwitz without Jews" then renders such an interpretation ever more plausible, for now, even the Nazi anti-Semitism as such loses its obsessive qualities. It becomes subsumed in the general category of racism, with Poles as prime victims. Thus its capacity to force the question "why the Jews?" is lost as well.

In Poland, though, neither the separation between local anti-Semitism and the Nazi solution nor disregard for the uniqueness of the Holocaust is solely a memory operation performed on the past. Both are deeply rooted in the historical experience. As we have seen, Poles could, in the midst of deportations, discuss their "Jewish question" and debate possible solutions. They could also feel that theirs was to be the same fate as the Jews', that they were next in line for extermination centers. Finally, we know from what happened after the Holocaust that local anti-Jewish sentiments and actions were not shakes by the "Final Solution," that, if anything, the Nazis' murdering of the Jews made Jewishness even more of a problem.

The "Jewish memory project" is a memory operation. It has the capacity to redefine the past, the capacity to uproot many a long-held view of the Jew and the capacity to transform Polish-Jewish history into a moral challenge. By the same token, though, it also has the capacity to neutralize the past even further, now that the Jew is to have a permanent place in Poland's memory household. The odds here are not even. For a critical understanding of the past to emerge, let alone to be absorbed into collective memory, each one of the neutralizing strategies has to be countered on its own. The very process of neutralizing memory must, therefore, become subject to an inquiry. It is not enough merely to draw a different picture of Polish-Jewish relations or to proffer a different image of the Jew. One must also try to understand what made the old ones viable. It is not enough to call for remembrance, one must also learn about forgetting. It is not enough to break the silence surrounding things Jewish; one must also ask about its hold in the past. It is not enough to declare that there is no more "Jewish problem" in Poland; one must also make the notion itself problematic.

The need for an effort on many simultaneous fronts is clarified when we look at the current ways of dealing with the period immediately following the Holocaust. For example, since 1981, first the opposition, then the regime as well as the Catholic Church have come publicly to acknowledge, discuss and commemorate the July 1946 pogrom in Kielce. In and by itself, this recognition could lead to a confrontation with the darkest chapter of Polish-Jewish history. But it does not, precisely because "Kielce" stands by itself. Focusing on Kielce keeps other killings invisible behind a politically charged screen. Condemning Kielce, while claiming that such condemnation had been the policy and the sentiment in 1946, isolates the pogrom even further. Talking about Kielce, with suitable self-critical gestures, allows everyone in the end the comforts of absolution. (When a researcher like Cała challenges this comfort with her data on the post-war naturalness of Jewish death, the structures of remembrance already in place make it easy to cry in protest and disbelief.)

The key historical actor cleared by this reading of the past is the Catholic Church. Indeed, with respect to the "Jewish memory project" overall, the one force behind Polish anti-Semitism remaining largely beyond critical scrutiny is Catholicism. And if the need to bring together the new attitude towards the Jew with questions about the old attitudes applies throughout, it is especially acute in the sphere of Catholic-Jewish relations. What makes it so is not just the importance of the Church in Polish life, but rather the already fixed terms of the Catholic rapprochement with the Jews.

When talking about this rapprochement in Poland, we must distinguish between the policies and actions of the Church hierarchy and the direct involvement on the "Jewish memory project" of many Catholic intellectuals. While they both promote a dialogue with Jews, it is the laity that actively encourages an interest in Jewish culture and history beyond that in Judaism. The Church hierarchy—and one must include Pope John Paul II here—still has tremendous difficulties accepting the uniqueness of the Holocaust. The debate around prayers in Auschwitz and the prayers already said there on various occasions shows that, even when the Jewishness of the victims is restored, reflection on the Holocaust can remain cast in such universalized theological terms that it precludes a self-critical examination. The need for delving into the records of Catholicism is further obscured by the insistence, so common in Poland, on facts and figures. That the Church can claim credit for saving Jewish lives becomes a key argument in the discussions of the Holocaust and responsibility. The Church can also claim credit for its present policies towards Jews, as it has indeed done on many occasions. The positive attitudes expressed today do have a way of making the past seem much less important and much less questionable.

For the Polish Church as an institution, a new dialogue with the Jews is only one of many concerns. For Poland's Catholic intellectuals, on the other hand, recovering the country's Jewish heritage has assumed much higher priority, if one is to judge from the amount of attention devoted to things Jewish in the lay Catholic journals and other public activities. The apparent pride taken in openly discussing Polish-Jewish relations or in calling for remembering the Jew has a very solid basis in fact. But, like the present goodwill of the Church, it also provides a fair amount of self-reassurance, not to say self-congratulation. In the case of the Kielce pogrom, such self-reassurance translates into forestalling any further inquiry. In more general terms, the work done today on the "Jewish memory project", or all the rather sudden "noise" surrounding things Jewish, can have a potentially deafening effect on other difficult aspects of the Polish-Jewish past.

When cast in religious language, this effect becomes especially powerful. To discuss Polish-Jewish relations during the Holocaust, to discuss them openly and honestly, and to discuss them without the outside stimulus of a Western critique is a valuable development. The editors of the lay Catholic weekly *Tygodnik Powszechny,* which undertook the task in early 1987, can be justifiably proud. Yet to frame the self-criticism in terms of "sin" and "repentance" is not to open an inquiry, but to close it. The very act of talking, as in a confessional, becomes a way to secure spiritual comfort, not a basis for self-examination.

Besides the direct implications of self-reassurance on furthering critical understanding, there is a more subtle dynamics here. Now that anti-Semitism is loudly condemned, now that the Jew is talked about with warmth and concern, now that the whole subject of Polish-Jewish relations is declared open to scrutiny, it is easy to forget that things once looked quite different. For the older generation of memory workers, the current shift of perspectives may be a source of satisfaction; it is their decent and pluralistic tradition which has finally won. Quite naturally, that tradition begins to look better and larger than it otherwise would; quite naturally, it is now beyond criticism. The decades of silence, blamed on the regime in general and its censorship in particular, fail to speak of that very tradition's significant contribution to the deconstruction of Jewish memory. Acting to preserve that memory in the present makes it easy to claim—and to believe—that one was always equally concerned.

For the younger generation, memory workers and their audiences alike, the Jew is becoming increasingly "normal". Their attitude signals that, in the future, Poles may well approach the Jew with empathy, respect and interest, a positive development, of course. But in the present, "normalizing" the discussion of things Jewish, unless accompanied by tough critical questions about the past, creates too unproblematic an impression of shared history. Normalizing memory by according the Jew full status as a member of the Polish community, without probing into his never having had that status before, neutralizes that history. Ultimately, the very act of remembering, in all its new naturalness, may become a way to forget.

For the time being, though, remembering the Jew is still very far from natural. Memory workers justify their efforts in a variety of ways. Poland's moral obligation to remember its Jews is cited side-by-side with the more pragmatic advantages of improved foreign relations. The need for self-understanding competes here with the potential benefits of an improved image abroad; the call to fill in the blank spaces in the historical record joins the calls to draw more tourists. With memory work in progress, the very meaning of remembrance is something that is not settled. Even when there does appear to be an agreement, as in evoking pluralism, the role assigned to the Jew varies with the definition, from a counter-force to Catholicism to a much needed spice in a bland, because now so homogeneous, culture.

As we were taking stock of the "Jewish memory project", I argued that results count far more than intentions, that whatever the reasons behind inviting the Jew, it is the effect of his presence that must be considered first. Noone in Poland today makes remembering the Jew appealing for its capacity to ease forgetting. There are no calls to disarm the Jew by making him a welcome guest. The "Jewish memory project" is not a sophisticated scheme finally to neutralize the past. That it can do it is something we learn only from observing the memory practice, not from listening to practitioners.

By the same token, it is through looking at the results of memory work, rather than the reasons behind it, that we may point to the potential for countering the force of neutralization. Cautiously, since this could also work in the opposite direction, one must begin with the empathy and respect for the Jew that can derive from the wide exposure to Jewish tradition. Cautiously, since we are now talking about the earliest stages of a long process, the gradual recognition of the uniqueness of the Holocaust could bring the question "why the Jews?" into the center of inquiry. The 1983 commemoration of the Warsaw Ghetto Uprising, for all its political strife and all its internal contradictions did make available, often for the first time, many resources for viewing the Holocaust from the Jewish perspective. The 1985 screening of *Shoah,* for all its political ramifications and the Poles' loud cries of slander, did make a few more people reflect on the "Final Solution". The 1987 discussion of Polish-Jewish relations during the Nazi occupation, for all the protests and all the comforts of confessing to a sin, did bring to the public forum some very important statements on the difference between Polish and Jewish victimization.

The continuing stream of publications devoted to the Holocaust, like the continuing exposure to Jewish Jews, does not automatically displace the old patterns. But it does make such a displacement possible. Reflection on the meaning of the Holocaust does not necessarily lead to a critique of Catholic teachings, but it may lead to questions about the mythic structure of anti-Semitism. And the question "why the Jews?", once on the agenda, may lead to a critical re-evaluation of the axiom that the very presence of Jews is problematic.

In short, the "Jewish memory project", without directly challenging the Poles' sense of themselves, does challenge their sense of the Jew. In doing so, in rendering the Jews interesting and in offering some resources for viewing the past from a Jewish perspective, current memory work is gradually laying the foundation for a future reckoning with the moral dimensions of Polish-Jewish experience as well.

The schoolchildren who come to visit the Warsaw synagogue might still be hearing from their parents about the crimes of Jewish Stalinists. In their history books, they might still be reading how Jews could not be saved from their fate during the Nazi occupation because of their own lack of resistance. In the local church, these children might still be told that a people who rejected Christ cannot be saved. But now, if and when they decide that their country's Jewish heritage is worth exploring, they do have a growing storehouse of resources to rely on. They also have social and institutional support. Many of these young people may have problems understanding what made talking about things Jewish so difficult in the past. Some may come to feel, based on their own experience, that Poland's stand towards the Jews has always been fair. There is a chance, though, that more than a few will begin questioning their elders, questioning the lack of response to the Holocaust and questioning the ease of reclaiming the memory of the Jew. There is a chance that once remembering the Jew is taken as a given, the hard work of confronting the past can properly begin.

# References

Abella, Irving and Harold Troper. 1983. *None Is Too Many. Canada and the Jews of Europe 1933–1948*. Toronto: Lester & Orpen Dennys.

Abramsky, Chimen, Maciej Jachimczyk and Antony Polonsky, eds. 1986. *The Jews in Poland*. Oxford: Basil Blackwell.

(a.g.). 1983. Review of *Zydzi Polscy*. *Polityka* (January 8).

Alaton, Salem. 1986. "A powerful and grim portrait of death." *Globe and Mail* (June 13).

Anonymous. 1971. "USSR and the Politics of Polish Antisemitism 1956–1968." *Soviet Jewish Affairs* 1 (no. 1): 19–40.

Anonymous. 1984. Varsovie: Juif et opposant au régime (interview). In *Combat pour la diaspora*, no. 14. Paris: Syros.

Arendt, Hannah. 1965. *Eichmann in Jerusalem. A Report on the Banality of Evil*. (rev. ed.) Penguin Books.

———. 1973. *The Origins of Totalitarianism*. (new ed.). New York: Harcourt Brace Jovanovich.

Aschheim, Steven E. 1982. *Brothers and Strangers (The East European Jew in German and German Jewish Consciousness, 1800–1923)*. Madison: University of Wisconsin Press.

Ash, Timothy Garton. 1985. *The Polish Revolution: Solidarity*. London: Coronet Books, Hodder & Stoughton.

———. 1986. "Shoah and Poland" (reply to Turowicz' letter). *The New York Review of Books* (May 8).

*Austeria*. 1982. Kawalerowicz, Jerzy, director. Screenplay by T. Konwicki, J. Stryjkowski, and J. Kawalerowicz. Warszawa: Film Polski.

Baczko, Bronislaw. 1984. *Les imaginaires sociaux. Mémoires et espoirs collectifs*. Paris: Payot.

Bałaban, Maier. 1983. *Historia Żydów*. Warszawa: Państwowe Wydawnictwo Naukowe.

Banas, Josef. 1979. *The Scapegoats. The Exodus of the Remnants of Polish Jewry*. Trans. from the Polish by Tadeusz Szafar. London: Weidenfeld & Nicholson.

Bartoszewski, Wladyslaw. 1986. "Polish-Jewish Relations in Occupied Poland, 1939–1945." *The Jews in Poland.* Abramsky et al., eds. Oxford: Basil Blackwell.

Bartoszewski, Władysław & Zofia Lewinówna, eds. 1969. *Ten jest z ojczyzny mojej. Polacy z pomocą Żydom 1939–1945.* 2nd enlarged ed. Kraków: Wydawnictwo Znak.

Bass, David. 1973. "Bibliographical List of Memorial Books Published in the Years 1943–1972." *Yad Vashem Studies* IX: 273–323.

Bauer, Yẹhuda. 1970. *Flight and Rescue: BRICHAH.* New York: Random House.

Bauman, Zygmunt. 1969. "The End of Polish Jewry: A Sociological Review," *Bulletin on Soviet and East European Jewish Affairs,* no. 3 (Jan.):3–9.

Bednarczyk, Tadeusz. 1983. "Prawda o pomocy Żydom." *Rzeczywistość* (April 10 & 17).

Bentley, Eric, ed. 1964. *The Storm Over "The Deputy."* New York: Grove Press.

Berberyusz, Ewa. 1987. "Wina przez zaniechanie." *Tygodnik Powszechny* (Feb. 22).

———. 1987. "Czarna dziura." Interview with Stanisław Krajewski. *Tygodnik Powszechny* (April 5).

Berger, Bennett M. 1981. *The Survival of a Counterculture. Ideological Work and Everyday Life Among Rural Communards.* Berkeley: University of California Press.

Berger, Peter & Thomas Luckmann. 1967. *The Social Construction of Reality.* New York: Anchor Books.

Bettelheim, Bruno. 1960. *The Informed Heart.* New York: Free Press.

Bielecki, Czeslaw. 1986. "Kochani moi synkowie . . ." *Kultura,* no. 7/466-8/467: 33–70.

Bieńkowski, Władysław. 1971. *Socjologia klęski. Dramat gomułkowskiego czternastolecia.* Paris: Instytut Literacki.

Blit, Lucjan, ed. 1968. "The Anti-Jewish Campaign in Present-Day Poland; Facts, Documents, Press Reports." London: Institute of Jewish Affairs.

Blumsztajn, Seweryn. 1985. *Polonais, juif, membre du KOR et de Solidarité. Je rentre au pays.* Paris: Calmann-Lévy.

Błoński, Jan. 1987. "Biedni Polacy patrzą na getto." *Tygodnik Powszechny* (Jan. 11).

Bogusławski, Andrzej. 1981. "Gucia ciemnogrodzka." *Polityka* (September 12).

Borowski, Tadeusz. 1948. *Pożegnanie z Marią.* Warszawa: Spółdzielnia Wydawnicza "Wiedza."

Borsten, Joan. 1981. "Il y a encore des Juifs en Pologne." in: *Notre Communauté,* Belfast, June.

Borwicz, Michał M. 1947. *Pieśń ujdzie cało . . . Antologia wierszy o Żydach pod okupacją niemiecką.* Warszawa: Centralna Żydowska Komisja Historyczna w Polsce.

Borwicz, Michal. 1969. *Vies interdites*. Paris: Casterman.

Borwicz, Michał. 1980. *Spod szubienicy w teren*. Paris: Księgarnia Polska.

Borwicz, Michal. 1986. "Polish Jewish Relations, 1944–1947. In *The Jews in Poland*, edited by Abramsky et al. Oxford: Basil Blackwell. (Also in Polish, in *Puls*, no. 24 [1984/85]: 58–66).

Boukhobza, Chochana. 1987. "Périple: Retour à Tolède." *l'Arche*, no. 352 (May).

Bourdieu, Pierre & L. Boltanski, R. Castel, J.-C. Chamboredon. 1965. *Un art moyen; essai sur les usages sociaux de la photographie*. Paris: les Editions de Minuit.

Brandys, Kazimierz. 1981. "Miesiące 1978–1979." Paris: Instytut Literacki.

———. 1983. "Miesiące." *Kultura*, no. 6/429: 19–41.

Breton, Raymond & G. Caldwell, G. Houle, E. Mokrzycki & E. Wnuk-Lipinski, eds. 1986. National Survival in Dependent Societies: the Cases of Canada and Poland. Publication pending.

Bromke, Adam. 1967. *Poland's Politics: Idealism vs. Realism*. Cambridge, Mass.: Harvard University Press.

Bujak, Zbiqniew. 1983. "Robotnicy 1968." *Zeszyty Edukacji Narodowej*, no. 1 (presentation at the 1981 session at Warsaw University).

Cała, Alina. 1984. Kwestia asymilacji Żydów w Królewstwie Polskim (1864–1897). Pozycje, konflikty, stereotypy. Warszawa: Instytut Historii PAN (Ph.D. dissertation).

Centre de documentation juive contemporaine. 1982. *L'enseignement de la Choa. Comment les manuels d'histoire présent-ils l'extermination des Juifs au cours de la deuxième querre mondiale?* Paris.

Checinski, Michael. 1982. *Poland: Communism, Nationalism, Anti-Semitism*. Trans. in part by Tadeusz Szafar. New York: Karz-Cohl Publishing.

Chłopecki, Jerzy. 1985. "Uwagi na marginesie." *Prawo i Życie* (November 16).

Cohen, Phyllis Albert. 1977. *The Modernization of French Jewry: Consistory and Community in the Nineteenth Century*. Hanover, N.H.: Brandeis University Press.

Cohn, Norman. 1967. *Warrant for Genocide: The Myth of the Jewish World-Conspiracy and the Protocols of the Elders of Zion*. New York: Harper & Row.

Craig, Gordon A. 1987. "The War of the German Historians." *The New York Review of Books* (Jan. 15).

Curry, Jane Leftwich, ed. & trans. 1984. *The Black Book of Polish Censorship*. New York: Vintage Books

Cywiński, Bohdan. 1984. "Zagadnienie stosunków polsko-żydowskich w opozycji lat siedemdziesiątych." *Puls*, no. 24/85: 66–71.

———. 1985. *Rodowody niepokornych*. 3rd ed. Paris: Éditions Spotkania. (Original———1970, "Więź," Warszawa)

*Czarna księga cenzury PRL*. 1977. London: Aneks.
Czubakówna, Genowefa. 1967. *W habicie*. Warszawa: Ludowa Spółdzielnia Wydawnicza.
Davies, Norman. 1982. *God's Playground: A History of Poland*. 2 vols. New York: Columbia University Press.
———. 1984. *Heart of Europe: A Short History of Poland*. Oxford: Clarendon University Press.
Dawidowicz, Lucy S. 1976. *The War Against the Jews 1933–1945*. New York: Bantam Books.
———. 1981. *The Holocaust and the Historians*. Cambridge, Mass.: Harvard University Press.
Dejmek, Kazimiesz. 1983. "Casus 'Dziady' " in: *Zeszyty Edukacji Narodowej*, no. 1 (presentation at the 1981 session at Warsaw University.)
"Deklaracja." 1987. *Tygodnik Powszechny (March 15)*.
Dobroszycki, Lucjan. 1973. "Restoring Jewish Life in Post-War Poland" *Soviet Jewish Affairs*, no. 2: 58–72.
Donat, Alexander. 1964. *Jewish Resistance*. New York: Waldon Press.
Dossier Janusz Korczak. At Centre de documentation juive contemporaine (no. 16708).
Drozdowski, Marian Marek. 1987. "Dzieje najnowsze w maturalnych klasach." *Tygodnik Powszechny* (May 17).
Eisenbach, Artur. 1983. *Z dziejów ludności żydowskiej w Polsce w XVIII i XIX wieku*. Warszawa: Państwowy Instytut Wydawniczy.
Engel, David. 1983. "An Early Account of Polish Jewry Under Nazi and Soviet Occupation Presented to the Polish Government-in-Exile, February 1940." *Jewish Social Studies* 45 no. 1 (winter): 1–17.
———. 1987. *In the Shadow of Auschwitz: The Polish Government-in-exile and the Jews*. Chapel Hill: University of North Carolina Press.
Epstein, Helen. 1980. *Children of the Holocaust; Conversations with Sons and Daughters of Survivors*. New York: Bantam Books.
Ertel, Rachel. 1982. *Le Shtetl. La bourgade juive de Pologne; de la tradition à la modernité*. Paris: Payot.
Eytan, Edwin. 1982. "J'ai passé le séder à Varsovie." *Tribune Juive*, no. 719 (April 23–29).
Fein, Helen. 1984. *Accounting for Genocide: National Responses and Jewish Victimization During the Holocaust*. Chicago: The University of Chicago Press.
Finkielkraut, Alain. 1980. *Le Juif imaginaire*. Paris: Seuil.
———. 1982. "Réflexions sur l'ignorance." In *Colloque des intellectuels juifs. La Bible au présent. Données et débats*. Paris: Gallimard.
———. 1983. *La réprobation d'Israël*. Paris: Denoël/Gonthier.
Fish, Daniel. 1978. "The Jews in Syllabuses of World and Russian History: What Soviet School Children Read about Jewish History." *Soviet Jewish Affairs* 8 (no. 1): 3–26.
Friedländer, Saul. 1984. *Reflections of Nazism. An Essay on Kitsch and*

*Death*. Trans. from the French by Thomas Weyr. New York: Harper & Row.

Friedman, Philip. 1972. "The Lublin Reservation and the Madagascar Plan." In *Studies in Modern Jewish Social History,* edited by Joshua A. Fishman, 354–380. New York: Ktav Publishing House.

Fuks, Marian, ed. 1983. *Adama Czerniakowa dziennik getta warszawskiego 6.IX.1939–23.VII.1942.* Warszawa: Państwowe Wydawnictwo Naukowe.

Fuks, Marian and Zygmunt Hoffman, Maurycy Horn and Jerzy Tomaszewski. 1982. *The Polish Jewry, History and Culture.* Warsaw: Interpress Publishers. (also in Polish, German)

Garliński, Józef. 1985. "Bardzo bolesne sprawy" *Tydzien Polski* (October 19), London. (reprinted in *Życie Warszawy*)

———. 1986. Letter to the editor. *Kultura,* no. 4/463: 156.

Gershon, Karen, ed. and trans. 1969. *Postscript. A Collective Account of the Lives of Jews in West Germany Since the Second World War.* London: Victor Gollancz.

Gieysztor, Aleksander. 1986. "The Beginnings of Jewish Settlement in the Polish Lands." In *The Jews in Poland,* edited by Abramsky et al. Oxford: Basil Blackwell.

Gieysztor, Aleksander, Stefan Kieniewicz, Emanuel Rostworowski, Janusz Tazbir, Henryk Wereszycki. 1968. *Historia Polski.* (2nd ed., 1974). Warszawa: Panstwowe Wydawnictwo Naukowe. (also in English)

Gilbert, Martin. 1985. *The Holocaust. A History of the Jews of Europe During the Second World War.* New York: Holt, Rinehart & Winston.

Gilman, Stephen. 1972. *The Spain of Fernando de Rojas.* Princeton: Princeton University Press.

Glickman, Yaacov and Alan Bardikoff. 1982. *The Treatment of the Holocaust in Canadian History and Social Science Textbooks.* Canada: League for Human Rights of B'nai B'rith.

Goldscheider, Calvin and Alvin S. Zuckerman. 1984. *The Transformation of the Jews.* Chicago: The University of Chicago Press.

Groński, Ryszard Marek. 1983. "Idzie jeż," *Polityka* (February 26).

———. 1986. "Strefa." *Polityka* (May 3).

———. 1987. "Dni ciemnoty." *Polityka* (May 23).

Gross, Jan Tomasz. 1979. *Polish Society Under German Occupation. The Generalgovernement, 1939–1944.* Princeton: Princeton University Press.

———. 1986. "Ten jest z ojczyzny mojej . . . ale go nie lubię" *Aneks,* no. 41–42:13–36.

Gross, Jan Tomasz and Irena Grudzińska-Gross. 1983. *"W czterdziestym nas matko na Sybir zesłali . . ." Polska a Rosja 1939–1942.* London: Aneks. [*War Through Children's Eyes. The Soviet Occupation of Poland and the Deportations, 1939–1941.* Trans. from the Polish by Ronald Strom and Dan Rivers. Stanford: Hoover Institution Press, 1981.]

Grygiel, Ludmiła. 1987. "Świadek prawdy i miłości" (Błogosławiona Siostra Teresa Benedykta od Krzyża 1891–1942) *Tygodnik Powszechny* (May 3).

Grynberg, Henryk. 1984. *Prawda nieartystyczna*. West Berlin: Biblioteka Archipelagu.

————. 1984. "Holocaust w literaturze polskiej." *Archipelag* (West Berlin), no. 1(6) and 2(7).

Grzegorczyk, Andrzej. 1985. "Kwestia żydowska." *Polityka* (November 16).

————. 1985. "Może się dogadamy?" *Polityka* (December 21–27).

Gutman, Yisrael. 1982. *The Jews of Warsaw, 1939–1943. Ghetto, Underground, Revolt*. Trans. from the Hebrew by Ina Friedman. Bloomington: Indiana University Press.

————. 1986. "Polish and Jewish Historiography on the Question of Polish-Jewish Relations During World War II." In *The Jews in Poland*, edited by Abramsky et al. Oxford: Basil Blackwell.

Guzy, Piotr. 1983. "Wielkie nieszczęście." *Kultura*, no. 1/424–2/425:66–104.

Halbwachs, Maurice. 1968. *La mémoire collective*. Paris: Presses Universitaires de France.

Halecki, O. 1961. *A History of Poland*. New York: Roy Publishers.

Halimi, André. 1983. *La délation sous l'occupation*. Paris: éditions Alain Moreau.

Harris, André and Alain de Sédouy. 1979. *Juifs & Français*. Paris: Grasset.

Heller, Celia S. 1980. *On the Edge of Destruction. Jews of Poland Between the Two World Wars*. New York: Schocken Books.

Hemmendinger, Judith. 1986. *Survivors. Children of the Holocaust*. Bethesda, Md.: National Press.

Hertz, Aleksander. 1961. *Żydzi w kulturze polskiej*. Paris: Instytut Literacki.

————. 1979. *Wyznania starego człowieka*. London: Oficyna Poetów i Malarzy.

Hilberg, Raul. 1961. *The Destruction of the European Jews*. Chicago: Quadrangle Books.

Hillel, Marc. 1985. *Le massacre des survivants. En Pologne après l'holocauste (1945–1947)*. Paris: Plon.

Hirszowicz, Lukasz. 1981. "Jewish Themes in Polish Crisis." *Research Report* (Aug.). London: Institute of Jewish Affairs.

————. 1982. "Poland's Jewish Policies under Martial Law." *Research Report* (May). London: Institute of Jewish Affairs.

Hirszowicz, Lukasz. 1986. "The Jewish Issue in Post-War Polish Communist Politics." In *The Jews in Poland*, edited by Abramsky et al. Oxford: Basil Blackwell.

Hirszowicz, Lukasz, ed. 1981. "Antisemitism in Today's Poland—Documents." *Soviet Jewish Affairs* 12, no. 1 (Feb).

Hobsbawn, Eric and Terence Ranger, eds. 1984. *The Invention of Tradition*. Cambridge: Cambridge University Press.

Hochberg-Mariańska, Maria and Noe Grüss. 1947. *Dzieci oskarżają*. Centralna Żydowska Komisja Historyczna w Polsce.

Hughes, H. Stuart. 1983. *Prisoners of Hope. The Silver Age of the Italian Jews, 1924–1974*. Cambridge, Mass.: Harvard University Press.

*Information Please Almanac*. 1987. (Atlas and Yearbook 1987). Boston: Houghton & Mifflin.

Jagielski, Jan and Monika Krajewska. 1983. "Polskie bóżnice: odbudowa pamięci." *Znak*, no. 339–340(2–3) (Feb./March):412–423.

Jastrzębowski, Jerzy. "Na róznych plaszczyznach." *Tygodnik Powszechny*, April 5, 1987.

Jedlicki, Witold. 1962. "Chamy i Żydy." *Kultura*, no. 12.

Jelen, Christian. 1972. *La purge: Chasse au Juif en Pologne populaire*. Paris: Fayard.

Kainer, Abel. 1983. "Żydzi a komunizm." *Krytyka*, no. 15 (spring 178–206).

Kałużyński, Zygmunt. 1982. "Pół dnia w Chicago." *Polityka* (November 27).

———. 1985. "Odmawiam przebaczenia." *Polityka* (December 7)).

Karpinski, Jakub. 1982. *Count-Down: The Polish Upheavals of 1956, 1968, 1970, 1976, 1980*. New York: Karz-Cohl Publishers.

Karski, Jan. 1944. *Story of a Secret State*. Boston: Houghton Mifflin Company.

———. 1987. "Niespełniona misja." In conversation with Maciej Kozłowski. In *Tygodnik Powszechny* (March 15).

Karsov, Nina and Szymon Szechter. 1970. *Monuments Are Not Loved*. Trans. from the Polish by Paul Stevenson. London: Hodder & Stoughton.

Kersten, Krystyna. 1981. "Kielce—4 lipca 1946 roku." *Tygodnik Solidarność* (Dec. 4).

———. 1986. *Narodziny Systema Study. Polska 1943–1948*. Paris: Libella.

Kieniewicz, Stefan. 1984. "Polacy i Żydzi w XIX wieku." *Polityka* (December 15).

———. 1986. "Polish Society and the Jewish Problem in the Nineteenth Century." In *The Jews in Poland*, edited by Abramsky et al. Oxford: Basil Blackwell.

Kirshner, Sheldon. 1983. "Outlook for Jewish Community of Poland Bleak." *The Canadian Jewish News* (June 16).

Kolinsky, Martin and Eva Kolinsky. 1974. "The Treatment of the Holocaust in West German Textbooks." *Yad Vashem Studies on the European Jewish Catastrophe and Resistance* X:149–217.

Kołakowski, Leszek. 1982. "Ludobójstwo i ideologia" (1978). In: *Czy diabeł może być zbawiony i 27 innych kazań*. London: Aneks.

Korbonski, Stefan. 1978. *The Polish Underground State. A Guide to the*

*Underground, 1939–1945*. Trans. from the Polish original by Marta Erdman. Boulder: East European Quarterly.

Korboński, Stefan. 1983. Letter to the editor. *Kultura*, no. 9/432:156–158.

Korman, Gerd. 1970. "Silence in the American Textbooks." *Yad Vashem Studies* VIII: 183–203.

Korzec, Pawel. 1980. *Juifs en Pologne. La question juive pendant l'entre-deux-querres*. Paris: Presses de la Fondation Nationale des Sciences Politiques.

Kozłowski, Józef. 1986. "Chyba się nie dogadamy." Letter to the editor. *Polityka* (January 18).

———. 1986. "Korczak z daleka." Letter to the editor. *Polityka*, (March 22).

Kozyr, Stanisława. 1986. Letter to the editor. *Kultura*, no. 3/462: 161.

Krajewska, Monika. 1983. *Czas kamieni*. Warszawa: Interpress (also available in German).

———. 1983. "Cmentarze żydowskie—mowa kamieni." *Znak*, no. 339–340(2–3) (Feb./March): 397–411.

Krajewski, Stanisław. 1986. "Auschwitz, klasztor i Żydzi." *Tygodnik Powszechny*.

Krakowski, Shmuel. 1984. *The War of the Doomed. Jewish Armed Resistance in Poland, 1942–1944*. Trans. from the Hebrew by Orah Blaustein. New York: Holmes & Meier Publishers, Inc.

Krall, Hanna. 1985. *Sublokatorka*. Paris: Libella (one chapter previously appeared in *Pismo* (Wrocław), May–June 1983, no. 5/6.)

———. 1986. *Shielding the Flame. An Intimate Conversation with Dr. Marek Edelman, the Last Surviving Leader of the Warsaw Ghetto Uprising*. Trans. from the Polish by Joanna Stasinska and Lawrence Weschler. New York: Henry Holt and Company (Polish original: *Zdążyć przed Panem Bogiem*, Warszawa, 1977).

Kridl Valkenier, Elizabeth. 1985. "The Rise and Decline of Official Marxist Historiography in Poland, 1945–1983." *Slavic Review* 44, no. 4 (winter): 663–681.

Krzemiński, Adam. 1985. "Kadisz w Polsce." *Polityka* (May 11).

Krzemiński, Ireneusz. 1986. "Swiat zakorzeniony." *Aneks*, no. 43: 91–120.

Kugelmass, Jack and Jonathan Boyarin, eds. & trans. 1983. *From a Ruined Garden: The Memorial Books of Polish Jewry*. New York: Schocken Books.

Kuroń, Jacek. 1983. "Między październikiem 56 a marcem 68." *Zeszyty Edukacji Narodowej*, no. 1. (Edited paper presented at the 1981 session at Warsaw University.)

———. 1986. "Zośka." *Aneks*, no. 41–42: 77–89.

Kwiatkowski, Stanisław. 1987. "Na ręcznym hamulcu. Co jest najważniejsze dla Polaków." *Polityka* (March 21).

Lang, Jochen von and Claus Sybyll, eds. 1983. *Eichmann Interrogated*.

*Transcripts from the Archives of the Israeli Police.* Trans. from the German by Ralph Manheim. Toronto: Lester & Orpen Dennys.

Lanzmann, Claude. 1985. *Shoah.* Paris: Fayard (also in English; New York: Pantheon).

Laqueur, Walter. 1980. *The Terrible Secret: An Investigation into the Suppression of Information about Hitler's 'Final Solution.'* London: Weidenfeld & Nicholson.

Lasota, Grzegorz. 1986. "Producent czy pajac." *Polityka* (December 20).

Lavi, Theodor. 1974. "Jews in Rumanian Historiography." Trans. from the Hebrew by George Mandel. *Soviet Jewish Affairs* 4, no. 1: 45–53.

Lem, Stanislaw. 1984. *Prowokacja.* Kraków-Wrocław: Wydawnictwo Literackie.

Lendvai, Paul. 1972. *Anti-Semitism in Eastern Europe.* London: Macdonald & Co.

Lichten, Józef. 1983. "Kościół a judaizm w dialogu." *Znak,* no. 339–340(2–3) (Feb./March): 238–249.

———. 1983. "Janusz Korczak—Żyd polski." *Więź,* no. 4(294) (April): 11–19.

Lichten, Joseph. 1986. "Notes on the Assimilation and Acculturation of Jews in Poland, 1863–1943." *The Jews in Poland,* edited by Abramsky et al., eds. Oxford: Basil Blackwell.

Lifton, Robert Jay. 1986. *The Nazi Doctors. Medical Killing and the Psychology of Genocide.* New York: Basic Books.

Lipski, Jan Józef. 1982. "Two Fatherlands—Two Patriotisms." *Survey* 26, no. 4(117) (autumn). (Original: NOWA, Warszawa, 1981.)

———. 1983. "Polscy Żydzi." *Kultura,* no. 6/429: 3–9.

———. 1983. "Kwestia żydowska." *Zeszyty Edukacji Narodowej,* no. 1. (Presented at the 1981 session at Warsaw University.)

———. 1983. *KOR. Komitet Obrony Robotników. Komitet Samoobrony Społecznej.* London: Aneks. (Also available in English.)

Lipstadt, Deborah E. 1986. *Beyond Belief. The American Press and the Coming of the Holocaust 1933–1945.* New York: The Free Press.

"List do Sekretariatu Ks. Prymasa Polski (March 11, 1987)." 1987. *Kultura,* no. 6/477: 52.

Łastik, Salomon. 1961. *Z dziejów Oświecenia żydowskiego. Ludzie i fakty.* Warszawa: Państwowy Instytut Wydawniczy.

Łastik, Salomon, comp. Arnold Słucki, ed. & intro. 1983. *Antologia poezji żydowskiej.* 2nd ed. in 1986. Warszawa: Państwowy Instytut Wydawniczy.

Ł. J. 1983. "List z kraju." *Kultura,* no. 9/432: 135–139.

Łukaszewicz, Łucja. 1983. "Stereotyp Żyda u studentów." *Znak,* no. 339–340(2–3) (Feb./March): 453–463.

Majchrowski, Jacek. 1983. "Problem żydowski w programach głównych obozów politycznych 1918–1939." *Znak,* no. 339–340(2–3) (Feb./March): 388–395.

Marcus, Joseph. 1983. *Social and Political History of the Jews in Poland 1919–1939*. Berlin: Mouton Publishers.

Marrus, Michael R. and Robert O. Paxton. 1981. *Vichy France and the Jews*. New York: Basic Books.

Matywiecki, Piotr. 1983. "Fotografie pamięci." *Więź*, no. 4(294) (April): 52–58.

Mendelsohn, Ezra. 1969. "Jewish Assimilation in Lvov: The Case of Wilhelm Feldman." *Slavic Review* 28, no. 4 (Dec.): 577–590.

———. 1981. *Zionism in Poland: The Formative Years, 1915–1926*. New Haven and London: Yale University Press.

———. 1983. *The Jews of East Central Europe Between the World Wars*. Bloomington: Indiana University Press.

———. 1986. "Interwar Poland: Good for the Jews or Bad for the Jews?" In *The Jews in Poland*, edited by Abramsky et al. Oxford: Basil Blackwell.

Micewski, Andrzej. 1978. *Współrządzić czy nie kłamać? PAX i Znak w Polsce 1945–1967*. Paris: Libella.

Michnik, Adam. 1979. *L'Eglise and la gauche. le dialogue polonais*. Trans. Agnes Slonimski et Constantin Jelenski. Paris: Seuil. (*Kościół, Lewica, Dialog;* Paris: Instytut Literacki, 1977).

———. 1985. *Letters from Prison and Other Essays*. Trans. from the Polish by Maya Latynski. Berkeley: University of California Press.

"Między antysemityzmem a holocaustem" (Dyskusja redakcyjna). 1986. *Więź*, no. 7–8(333–334) (July–August): 14–48.

Milosz, Czeslaw. 1981. *The Captive Mind*. (1951) Trans. from the Polish by Jane Zielonko. New York: Vintage Books.

Morawski, Jerzy and Piotr Pytlakowski. 1986. "Mroczne stany." *Przeglad Tygodniowy* (August 10).

Morga, Paweł. 1986. "Notatki o ćwiczeniu w antysemityźmie." *Kultura*, no. 9/468: 35–47.

Morse, Arthur D. 1983. *While Six Million Died. A Chronicle of American Apathy*. Woodstock, N.Y.: The Overlook Press.

Mrożek, Sławomir. 1984. "Nos." *Kultura*, no. 7/442–8/443: 37–45.

———. 1985. "Podejrzenie." *Kultura*, no. 11/458: 42–44.

"Msza Św. w rocznicę zbrodni kieleckiej," in Kronika religijna. *Tygodnik Powszechny*, August 20, 1986.

Musiał, SJ, Stanisław. 1987. "II Spotkanie w Genewie." *Tygodnik Powszechny* (March 15).

———. 1987. "Dziękczynienie w Brzezince." *Tygodnik Powszechny* (May 17).

Nałkowska, Zofia. 1956. *Medaliony*. Warszawa: Czytelnik.

Namer, Gérard. 1983. *Batailles pour la mémoire. La commémoration en France de 1945 à nos jours*. Paris: Papyrus.

Neusner, Jacob. 1981. *Stranger at Home. "The Holocaust", Zionism and American Judaism*. Chicago: The University of Chicago Press.

Niedzielski, Henry. 1986. "Objectivity in Sociological Reports: The Case of Gentile-Jewish Relationship in Poland." Paper presented at the World Congress of Sociology, New Delhi.

Niezabitowska, Małgorzata. 1983. "Przymiarka do tematu." *Więź*, no. 4(294) (April): 28–40.

———. 1983. "Polak który próbuje być Żydem." *Tygodnik Powszenchy* (April 24).

———. 1986. *Remnants: The Last Jews of Poland*. New York: Friendly Press. (Excerpts in *National Geographic*, Sept. 1986)

Nowakowska, Irena. 1983. "Zagadnienie ojczyzny." (1950). *Więź*, no. 4(294) (April): 102–112.

Nurenberger, M. J. 1985. *The Scared and the Doomed. The Jewish Establishment vs. The Six Million*. Oakville, Ont.: Mosaic Press.

Olszewska, Barbara W. 1986. "Za pan brat czy na bakier?" *Polityka* (October 25).

Orlicki, Józef. 1983. *Szkice z dziejów stosunków polsko-żydowskich*. Szczecin: Krajowa Agencja Wydawnicza.

Ostow, Robin. 1986. *The Children of Moses in the Land of Marx: Interviews with Jews in the German Democratic Republic*. Publication pending.

Pankiewicz, Tadeusz. 1982. *Apteka w getcie krakowskim*. (2nd ed.—1st in 1947). Kraków: Wydawnictwo Literackie.

Passent, Daniel. 1983. "Z Olimpu do sutereny." *Polityka* April 23.

Philippe, Béatrice. 1979. *Être juif dans la société française*. Paris: Editions Montalba.

Pietkiewicz, Barbara. 1983. "Wszyscy chcą, gościć Helę" *Polityka* (May 28).

Pietrasik, Zdzisław. 1984. "Kino bez sumienia." *Polityka* (September 29).

Pilichowski,Czesław, intro. & ed. 1979. *Obozy hitlerowskie na ziemiach polskich 1939–1945. Informator encyklopedyczny*. (Główna Komisja Badania Zbrodni Hitlerowskich w Polsce.) Warszawa: Państowe Wydawnictwo Naukowe.

Płużański, Marek. 1984. "Orzeł i lwy." *Polityka* (March 10).

Podemski, Stanisław. 1987. "Do szuflady. Cztery lata ustawy przeciw pasożytom." *Polityka* (February 28).

Polak, Grzegorz. 1983. "Jezus był Żydem." *Więź*, no. 4(294): 79–84.

"Polemiki." 1985. *Kultura*, no. 3/450: 160–165.

Poleski, Maciej. 1985. "Monolog." *Kultura*, no. 12/459: 51–61.

Poliakov, Léon. 1981. *Histoire de L'antisémitisme*. New ed. Paris: Calmann-Lévy.

———. 1983. *De Moscou à Beyrouth. Essai sur la désinformation*. Paris: Calmann-Lévy.

Polonsky, Antony, ed. 1980. "Jews in Eastern Europe After World War II: Documents from the British Foreign Office." *Soviet Jewish Affairs* 10, no. 1 (Feb.)

Polonsky, Antony and Boleslaw Drukier. 1980. *The Beginnings of Communist Rule in Poland*. London: Routledge & Kegan Paul.
"Pomnik Janusza Korczaka." 1983. *Polityka,* March 5 and January 15.
Porter, Jack Nusan and Peter Dreier, eds. 1973. *Jewish Radicalism, A Selected Anthology*. New York: Grove Press.
Prekerowa, Teresa. 1982. *Konspiracyjna Rada Pomocy Żydom w Warszawie 1942–1945*. Warszawa: Państwowy Instytut Wydawniczy.
———. 1987. " 'Sprawiedliwi' i 'bierni'." *Tygodnik Powszechny* (March 29).
Rabinbach, Anson and Jack Zipes, eds. 1986. *Germans and Jews Since the Holocaust. The Changing Situation in West Germany*. New York: Holmes & Meier.
Raczek, Tomasz. 1983. "Poskromienie szmoncesu." *Polityka* (July 17).
———. 1986. "Marsz po okruchach zwierciadła." *Przegląd Tygodniowy* no. 25(221).
Rajsfus, Maurice. 1980. *Des Juifs dans la Collaboration: L'UGIF (1941–1944)*. Paris: Études et Documentation Internationales.
Raczka, Jan Władysław. 1982. *Krakowski kazimierz*. Kraków: Wydawnictwo Literackie.
Redakcja "Arki." 1987. "Filolodzy kontra komunizm." *Kultura,* no. 1/472–2/473: 173–191.
Rem, Jan. 1985. "Szpetni i dzicy." *Polityka* (August 3).
Ringelblum, Emanuel. 1974. *Polish-Jewish Relations During the Second World War*. Edited by Joseph Kermish & Shmuel Krakowski. Translated from the Polish by Dafna Allon, Danuta Dabrowska, Dana Keren. Jerusalem: Yad Vashem.
———. 1983. *Kronika getta warszawskiego wrzesień 1939—styczeń 1943*. Intro. by A. Eisenbach; trans. from the Yiddish by Adam Rutkowski. Warszawa: Czytelnik.
Rioux, Jean-Pierre. 1983. "Rétour des deportés et prisoniers en France." Presentation at the Sorbonne, Dec. 16.
Rothenberg, Joshua. 1984. "Contradictions and Incongruities." *Soviet Jewish Affairs* 14, no. 1 (Feb.): 61–71.
Rosenzweig, Luc, ed. 1979. "Catalogue pour des juifs de maintenant." *Recherches,* no. 38 (Sept.)
Rudnicki, Adolf. 1987. *Teatr zawsze grany*. Warszawa: Czytelnik.
Rymkiewicz, Jarosław, Marek. 1988. *Umschlagplatz*. Paris: Instytut Literacki.
Ryszka, Franciszek, 1983. "Antysemityzm." *Polityka* (April 16).
Sachar, Howard M. 1986. *Diaspora. An Inquiry Into the Contemporary Jewish World*. New York: Harper & Row.
Sakowska, Ruta, ed. 1980. *Archiwum Ringelbluma. Getto Warszawskie lipiec 1942—styczeń 1943*. Warszawa: Państwowe Wydawnictwo Naukowe [ZIH].
Salij, Jacek OP. 1986. "Czy Żydzi ukrzyżowali Pana Jezusa?" *Więź,* no. 7–8(333–334) (July–Aug.): 52–58.

"Samotność." 1983. *Tygodnik Powszechny* (April 23) (discussion: Marek Edelman, Stanisław Broniewski, Jerzy Jedlicki, Roman Zimand, Hanna Krall, Marcin Król).

Sandauer, Artur. 1982. "O sytuacji pisarza polskiego pochodzenia żydowskiego w XX wieku." Warszawa: Czytelnik. (Sections in *Polityka*, June 12, 1982; June 19, 1982; June 26, 1982).

———. 1985. " 'Shoah' a sprawa polska." *Polityka* (August 3).

Scharf, Rafael F. 1984. "Cum ira et studio." *Puls*, no. 24: 72–78. (Longer and edited version of 1984 Oxford presentation).

Scherr, Lilly. 1980. "Juif à la mode." *Les Nouveaux Cahiers*, no. 60.

Schnapper, Dominique. 1980. *Juifs et israélites*. Paris: Gallimard.

Shahak, Israel. 1986. "Normalność w nieludzkim świecie." *Aneks*, no. 41–42: 52–67. (In "The Life of Death: An Exchange," *The New York Review of Books*, Jan. 29, 1987.)

Shatzky, Jacob. 1972. "Warsaw Jews in the Polish Cultural Life of the Early 19th Century." *Studies in Modern Jewish Social History*, edited by Joshua A. Fishman. pp. 44–57. New York: Ktav Publishing House.

Singer, Isaac Bashevis and Richard Burgin. 1985. *Conversations with Isaac Bashevis Singer*. Garden City, N.Y.: Doubleday.

Skoczylas, Joanna, 1986. "Telewizyjne hity." *Przegląd Tygodniowy*, no. 11(207).

Smolar, Aleksander. 1986. "Tabu i niewinność." *Aneks*, no. 41–42: 89–134.

Smólski, Władysław, ed. 1981. *Za to groziła śmierć. Polacy z pomocą Żydom w czasie okupacji*. Warszawa: Instytut Wydawniczy PAX.

Steiner, George. 1971. *In Bluebeard's Castle. Some Notes Toward the Redefinition of Culture*. London: Faber & Faber.

———. 1987. "The Long Life of Metaphor. An Approach to 'the Shoah.' " *Encounter* (Feb.): 55–62.

Steinsbergerowa, Aniela. 1983. "Protokoły Mędrców Syjonu." *Krytyka*, no. 15 (spring).

Sternhell, Zeev. 1983. *Ni droite ni gauche. L'idéologie fasciste en France*. Paris: Seuil.

Stryjkowski, Julian. 1982. *Wielki Strach*. London: Index on Censorship. (*Zapis* 14, April 1980).

Suchodolski, Bogdan. 1980. *Dzieje kultury polskiej*. Warszawa: Wydawnictwo Interpress (also in French, English, German).

Sulzbach, C. A. 1987. "Genèse d'un dialogue . . ." *l'Arche*, no. 361 (April).

Symmons-Symonolewicz, Konstantin. 1983. *National Consciousness in Poland: Origin and Evolution*. Meadville, PA: Maplewood Press.

Szafar, Tadeusz. 1983. "Anti-Semitism: A Trusty Weapon." In *Poland: Genesis of a Revolution*, edited by Abraham Brumberg. New York: Vintage Books.

Szulczyński, Andrzej. 1985. "Strażnik nieistniejących cmentarzy." *Kultura*, no. 1/448-2/449:185–192.

"Szum wokół 'Shoah', czyli jak skłócić Polaków na tle rasowym." 1985. *Wolny Głos Ursusa,* Dec. 18, 1985.

Śpiewak, Paweł. 1986. "Szoah, drugi upadek." *Więź,* no. 7–8(333–334) (July–August): 3–14.

Tannen, Deborah and Muriel Saville-Troike, eds. 1985. *Perspectives on Silence.* Norwood, N.J.: Ablex Publishing Corporation.

Tazbir, Janusz. 1985. "Staropolski obraz Żyda." *Polityka* (December 21–27).

Tec, Nechama. 1984. *Dry Tears. The Story of a Lost Childhood.* New York: Oxford University Press.

———. 1986. *When Light Pierced the Darkness. Christian Rescue of Jews in Nazi-Occupied Poland.* New York: Oxford University Press.

Thomas, W. I. and Florian Znaniecki. 1954. *The Polish Peasant in Europe and America.* Chicago: University of Chicago Press.

Teoplitz, Krzysztof Teodor (KTT). 1983. "Zagadka własnego losu." *Polityka* (May 7).

——— 1985. "To jest kwestia ideologiczna." Polityka (November 30).

Tomaszewski, Jerzy. 1984. "Kwestia sumienia." *Polityka* (January 7).

———. 1985. "Pamięci zgładzonego narodu." (letter to the editor) *Polityka* (November 16).

Tomaszewski, Tomasz. 1985. *Współcześni Żydzi polscy. Ostatni.* Exhibition at gallery of Związek Polskich Artystów Fotografików, opened Nov. 6.

Torańska, Teresa. 1985. *Oni.* London: Aneks. (also Warszawa: Przedświt, 1985).

Toruńczyk, Barbara, ed. 1983. *Narodowa Demokracja. Antologia myśli politycznej "Przeglądu Wszechpolskiego".* London: Aneks.

Touraine, Alain, François Dubet, Michel Wieviorka, Jan Strzelecki. 1982. *Solidarité. Analyse d'un movement social. Pologne 1980–81.* Paris: Fayard.

Trachtenberg, Joshua. 1983. *The Devil and the Jews. The Medieval Conception of the Jew and Its Relation to Modern Anti-Semitism.* First ed., 1943, Yale U. Press. Philadelphia: The Jewish Publication Society of America.

Trunk, Isaiah. 1982. *Jewish Responses to Nazi Persecution. Collective and Individual Behavior.* New York: Stein and Day.

Trzeciakowski, Wiesław. 1984. "Na granicy dwóch światów." *Polityka* (July 21).

Turian. 1983. "Zdaniem laika: Zydek." *Więź,* no. 4(294)(April): 45–48.

———. 1983. "Zdaniem laika: Kolbe żywy." *Więź,* no. 5(295) (May): 57–61.

Turowicz, Jerzy. 1973. "The Changing Catholicism in Poland." *Gierek's Poland,* edited by A. Bromke and J.W. Strong. New York: Praeger Publishers.

———. 1985. " 'Shoah' w polskich oczach." *Tygodnik Powszechny* (Nov. 10).

———. 1986. " 'Shoah' and Poland" (letter). *The New York Review of Books* (May 8).

———. 1987. "Racje polskie i racje żydowskie." *Tygodnik Powszechny* (April 5).

Tyrnauer, Gabrielle. 1985. "The Fate of the Gypsies During the Holocaust." Report to the United States Holocaust Memorial Council.

Urban, Jerzy, ed. 1986. "Potwór w smokingu." *Polityka* (March 29).

Vidal-Naquet, Pierre. 1981. *Les Juifs, la mémoire et le présent.* Paris: Maspero.

Vincenz, Stanisław. 1977. *Tematy żydowskie.* London: Oficyna Poetów i Malarzy.

Vinecour, Earl. 1977. *Jews: The Final Chapter.* (photos by Chuck Fishman). New York: New York University Press.

Walc, Jan. 1983. "Ruszamy z posad bryłą świata." *Zeszyty Edukacji Narodowej,* no. 1. (Presented at the 1981 session at Warsaw University.)

Walden, Jerzy. 1980. "Przeoczenie" (letter to the editor). *Polityka* (November 22).

Wein, Abraham. 1970. "The Jewish Historical Institute in Warsaw." *Yad Vashem Studies* VIII: 203–215.

———. 1973. " 'Memorial Books' as a Source for Research Into the History of Jewish Communities in Europe." *Yad Vashem Studies* XI: 255–273.

Weinryb, Bernard D. 1973. *The Jews of Poland. A Social and Economic History of the Jewish Community in Poland from 1100–1800.* Philadelphia: The Jewish Publication Society of America.

Weschler, Lawrence. 1984. *The Passion of Poland. From Solidarity Through the State of War.* (The complete *New Yorker* reports on Poland.) New York: Pantheon Books.

Wiesel, Elie. 1968. *Legends of Our Time.* New York: Holt, Rinehart & Winston.

Wieviorka, Annette and Itzhok Niborski. 1983. *Les livres du souvenir. Memoriaux juifs de Pologne.* Paris: Éditions Gallimard/Julliard.

Wieviorka, Michel. 1984. *Les Juifs, la Pologne et Solidarność.* Paris: Éd. Denoël.

Wilkanowicz, Stefan. 1983. "Antysemityzm, patriotyzm, chrześcijaństwo." *Znak,* no. 339–340(2–3) (Feb./March): 171–177.

Wilson, Stephen. 1982. *Ideology and Experience. Antisemitism in France at the Time of the Dreyfus Affair.* East Brunswick, N.J.: Associated University Presses.

Wisse, Ruth R. 1978. "Poland Without Jews." *Commentary* 66, no. 2 (Aug.): 64–68.

———. 1987. "Poland's Jewish Ghosts." *Commentary* 83, no. 1 (Feb.): 25–34.

Wolowski, Alexandre. 1977. *La vie quotidienne à Varsovie sous l'occupation nazie 1939–1945.* Paris: Hachette.

Woroszylski, Wiktor. 1986. "Mechanizm." *Więź,* no. 4(330) (April): 156–160.

Wóycicki, Kazimierz. 1983. "Jankiel i Reuchlin." *Więź,* no. 4(294) (April): 62–67.

———. 1983. "Inny i Bóg. Nad książkami Emmanuela Lewinasa." *Więź,* no. 5(295) (May): 18–29.

Wróblewska, Dorota. 1986. "Młodzież i seks (Prawie wszyscy zaczynają przed ślubem).'"*Polityka* (October 25).

Wyman, David S. 1984. *The Abandonment of the Jews. America and the Holocaust 1941–1945.* New York: Pantheon Books.

Zagórski, Wacław. 1971. *Wolność w niewoli.* London: Oficyna Poetów i Malarzy.

"Zbrodnia Kielecka." Editorial. 1986. *Tygodnik Powszechny (July 6).*

*Zimand, Roman. 1982. "W nocy od 12 do 5 rano nie spałem" Dziennik Adama Czerniakowa—próba lektury.* Warszawa: Państwowy Instytut Wydawniczy.

Zipes, Jack. 1986. "The Vicissitudes of Being Jewish in West Germany." *Germans and Jews Since the Holocaust. The Changing Situation in West Germany,* edited by A. Rabinbach and J. Zipes. New York: Holmes & Meier.

# Index